The **Orthodox Churches** in a **Pluralistic World**

The **Orthodox Churches** in a **Pluralistic World**

An Ecumenical Conversation

Edited by Emmanuel Clapsis

WCC Publications, Geneva

Holy Cross Orthodox Press
Brookline, Massachusetts

Cover design: Rob Lucas

© 2004 WCC Publications
World Council of Churches
150 route de Ferney, P.O.Box 2100
1211 Geneva 2, Switzerland
ISBN 2-8254-1397-6

Holy Cross Orthodox Press
50 Goddard Avenue
Brookline, MA 02445, USA
ISBN 1-885652-71-2

Printed in Switzerland

Contents

Foreword

It is a joy to have available the present, single-volume publication of the final papers presented at the international conference entitled "Orthodox Churches in a Pluralistic World: An Ecumenical Conversation", which was held at the Holy Cross Greek Orthodox School of Theology, 3-5 October 2002. The convening of this conference was heaven-sent, as it yielded significant insights from scholars throughout the United States and abroad on the contemporary issues of pluralism and globalization. These issues characterize the challenges and opportunities faced today by Orthodox churches in their offering of a Christian witness that promotes healing and reconciliation among diverse communities, and which is engaged in dialogues within the public domain.

The organization of this timely conference was the result of a collaborative endeavour, sponsored jointly by the faculty of the Holy Cross School of Theology, in cooperation with the World Council of Churches, the Boston Theological Institute, and the Initiatives in Religion and Public Life of Harvard Divinity School. Their direct and substantive contributions, as well as the valuable insights presented by others, enriched not only the conference participants, but also the Holy Cross community – faculty, students and guests alike – with an infusion of fresh ideas and perspectives on a subject with tremendous, practical implications for ministry.

The papers that follow, and the many discussions which took place during the conference, reveal aspects of pluralism and globalization that surely must be taken into account in any further study of these two major contemporary issues. Several of the conference participants in their papers revealed striking insights into many complexities of pluralism and globalization which have been overlooked until now. These complexities, while typically not at the centre of relevant discussions on the theme, are nonetheless of considerable importance for Orthodox churches as they contemplate their sacred call by God to fulfil creatively their role in civil society and the public square.

As president of the Board of Trustees of Hellenic College and Holy Cross, I would like to express my thanks to the president of Hellenic College and Holy Cross, the Rev. Fr Nicholas Triantafilou; to the dean of the Holy Cross School of Theology, the Rev. Fr Emmanuel Clapsis; and to the Holy Cross faculty for their initiative in organizing this important conference and hosting it on the beautiful Holy Cross campus. I should also like to express my thanks to Dr Konrad Raiser of the World Council of Churches, to Dr Rodney Petersen of the Boston Theological Institute, and to Prof. David Little of Harvard Divinity School for their important contributions to the realization of this conference. It is not accidental that this gathering has been called a "conversation" on pluralism and globalization, for this term characterizes the spirit of true cordiality, honesty and human warmth which pervaded this gathering. It is my hope that further "conversations" of this kind may be held in other locales throughout the United States and abroad, so that a diverse array of communities may also experience the growth and dynamism which can only result from a deliberate listening to and learning from one another.

I close this foreword by expressing my gratitude to the Holy Cross Press and to the World Council of Churches, for their kindness in jointly publishing these papers. It is my heartfelt prayer that this volume will constitute a substantive contribution to an ongoing conversation on the important issues of pluralism and globalization, and the manner in which these issues inform, influence and enhance the contemporary witness and ministry of the churches.

> Archbishop Demetrios
> Primate of the
> Greek Orthodox Archdiocese of America

Preface

I welcome the opportunity, as general secretary of the World Council of Churches, to offer a preface to this remarkable volume which makes available the addresses and papers contributed to an international conference on the Orthodox church in a pluralistic world by the Holy Cross Greek Orthodox School of Theology at Brookline/Boston in October 2002. While the World Council of Churches, together with the Boston Theological Institute and the Initiatives in Religion and Public Life at Harvard Divinity School, was invited to co-sponsor the conference, its planning and evident success was entirely due to the efforts and the courage of the leadership of the Holy Cross Greek Orthodox School of Theology, and in particular to its dean, the Rev. Fr Dr Emmanuel Clapsis. Together with his colleagues he deserves congratulations and thanks for having undertaken this initiative.

Globalization and pluralism have become dominant features of contemporary social life. While pluralism has been an emerging reality for some time already, opening up hitherto homogeneous communities, its dynamic has increased under the impact of globalization which has given rise to new conflicts around cultural identity while at the same time apparently leading to a levelling out of cultural differences. The interaction between globalization and pluralism calls for deeper reflection and the initiative of this international conference is a timely and welcome contribution to this task.

The Christian churches, as well as all other religious communities, are exposed to the challenges of globalization and pluralism. They are sources of communal identity while at the same time trustees of a message of universal salvation. The Orthodox churches have entered into a particularly close relationship with the cultural identity of the people and therefore feel more acutely the impact of growing plurality in societies that have traditionally been predominantly Orthodox. In the United States of America the Orthodox Church has had to adjust to a pluralistic context and to enter into an ecumenical conversation with Christians from other traditions and with people of different faiths. As a diaspora community the Orthodox Church in the USA was thus obliged to struggle with issues that have meanwhile become a challenge to other Orthodox churches as well.

In taking the initiative to organize this conference, the Holy Cross Greek Orthodox School of Theology has rendered a service to all of

Orthodoxy and demonstrated once again that it has become one of the leading institutions of Orthodox theological reflection and scholarship. This is evidenced by the fact that it was possible to invite a wide cross section of Orthodox church leaders and theologians to offer contributions to this conversation, in addition to competent experts from other Christian traditions. The table of contents of this volume is an indication of the sensitive preparatory analysis of the issues to be addressed as well as of the careful selection of speakers to deliver addresses and participate in panel discussions.

Five keynote addresses present the main issues of pluralism and globalization; the Orthodox perspectives are developed by Archbishop Demetrios, Dr Elizabeth Prodromou and Dr Emmanuel Clapsis and are complemented by the reflections of such eminent scholars as Dr Diana Eck and Prof. Richard Falk. The character of an "ecumenical conversation" is captured in the four round-table discussions which explore specific dimensions of the overall theme: human rights; violence, forgiveness and reconciliation; ethnicity and nationalism; and the understanding of mission in a pluralistic world. A listeners' report summarizes the insights gained during the two days of the conference.

The conference opened a very rich dialogue which is of significance for the Orthodox churches in their effort to consider their place in a pluralistic world, and offers very important insights for the wider ecumenical discussion. There are plans on the part of the Holy Cross Greek Orthodox School of Theology to organize further international conferences on similar issues of ecumenical concern. The present volume is indeed a very promising beginning which demonstrates that the Orthodox churches have a vital contribution to make to the ecumenical conversation.

Geneva, November 2003   Konrad Raiser
                                        General Secretary
                                        World Council of Churches

Greetings

Welcome to our campus which we lovingly call *Ieros Lofos*, Holy Hill! The entire community of Hellenic College and Holy Cross Greek Orthodox School of Theology is delighted and appreciative of your participation in this important international conference and especially for your presence on our campus.

From its establishment in 1937, Holy Cross Greek Orthodox School of Theology has served the mission and witness of the Orthodox Church, particularly here in the USA. Its purpose is to educate and train priests and laity who will participate in God's mission for the salvation of the world. Holy Cross is the space of creative and bold theological thinking that empowers those who serve the Church to respond to its pastoral challenges in our complex, fast-changing and pluralistic world. This twofold aspect of the School's mission cannot be separated without impairing the mission and the very existence of this institution.

The Orthodox ethos that we desire to instill in our students is best expressed in the lives, witness and theology of the Cappadocian fathers. The Cappadocian fathers were faithful to God's revelation, rooted in the liturgical and philanthropic life of the Church, and in conversation with the scientific and philosophical world of their times. It is our goal as an Orthodox theological school to embody and communicate this ethos as a faithful and responsible expression of Orthodoxy in the modern world.

The fact that this international conference is jointly sponsored by Holy Cross and the World Council of Churches in cooperation with the Boston Theological Institute and with the Initiatives in Religion and Public Life of Harvard Divinity School is a sign of continuity with the dialogical ethos of the Orthodox Church and its ecumenical spirit. In this conversational setting we will explore together the complexities and the challenges of the modern world, for the purpose not of compromising the truth of the Christian gospel but of finding ways to connect the modern world with its salvific truth. We are deeply grateful to all the participants for their contributions.

Finally, I wish to acknowledge the presence in our midst of the chairman of Archbishop Iakovos Leadership 100 Endowment, Mr Arthur C. Anton, who has been a generous supporter of our School and its mission for many years: this conference is generously funded by Leadership 100 and we are indebted to all members for their continued support that enables us to meet the expectations of our Church. To the Rev. Dr Emmanuel Clapsis I express deepest appreciation for his tireless effort in the planning, organizing and execution of this conference. He has creatively and insightfully crafted a most engaging, timely and significant gathering.

Nicholas C. Triantafilou
President, Hellenic College
and Holy Cross

The Orthodox Churches in a Pluralistic World

An Ecumenical Conversation

ARCHBISHOP DEMETRIOS OF AMERICA

We are calling this conference a "conversation". But in the spirit of this gathering on pluralism, we should not be too ready to take at face value our own description of it. This conference is more than a conversation; it is more than just an exchange of words.

We recall from the field of linguistics the idea of "performative speech acts". These are sentences which not only convey information, but also accomplish some action just in the process of being spoken. For example, the statement "I apologize" not only conveys information about the speaker's mental state, but also performs the work of creating an apology; just as the use of the phrase "I promise" can bring about the existence of a promise, or the words "I thank you" effect an expression of gratitude.

What we do here in holding this ecumenical conversation on Orthodoxy and pluralism is not simply the conveyance of information between one another. This conversation is itself a performative speech act, whereby we create the very thing we are talking about. We are living out, albeit in a small way, Orthodox values and priorities in a pluralistic world through this conversation with members of the wider American and international theological community. We are not merely talking theologically; to borrow a modern expression, we are truly "producing theology" by the words that we exchange here in a spirit of mutual respect, interest and love.

But we are going to have more than a performative speech act. The Polish poet Czeslaw Milosz, a Nobel prize winner in 1980, wrote a remarkable poem under the title *Readings*. The text begins with the following five lines:

You asked me what is the good of reading the gospels in Greek.
I answer that it is proper that we move our finger

> Along the letters more enduring than those carved in stone,
> And that, slowly pronouncing each syllable,
> We discover the true dignity of speech.

We discover the true dignity of speech. This conversation on pluralism is also a marvellous opportunity to discover and to promote the true dignity of speech, in addition to producing a performative speech act.

Let us then proceed with a few thoughts on the challenge of pluralism for Orthodoxy, grouped around three themes: (1) the challenge of pluralism for Orthodoxy, (2) the context of our conversation, and (3) suggestions for responding to the pluralistic challenge.

The challenge of pluralism for Orthodoxy

From the outset, we must be clear about the issues before us. Pluralism and globalization are intimately related to one another and are questions of profound interest, not only for Orthodox Christians in America but in every place in the world. The effects of globalization are felt everywhere, especially through the means of the internet, e-mail, cellular telephone technology, and the different forms of electronic media. Even in communities around the world which do not have the cultural or racial heterogeneity of the United States, there is nonetheless a sort of "pluralism by proxy", due to the power of modern technologies of communication to represent the wealth of human diversity across vast distances, almost instantaneously.

What this means, then, is that a given society can be a cultural island no more. The market-place of ideas is open to all, and geographic isolation is no longer an issue in the dissemination of ideology. No society is "immune", so to speak, from the possibility of influences from outside. The Orthodox Church in Greece, for instance, must take into account the same ideas and societal trends that are faced by the Orthodox churches in America or in other places. With the advent of globalization, every community is a pluralistic community, even those societies which try to be closed to outside influences. Let us then deal more specifically with the dimensions of our pluralistic reality that, through globalization, are common to all civilized societies, and therefore common to all Orthodox churches across the world.

In a period of rapid globalization, in a world community that is increasingly conscious of its pluralistic character, the Orthodox churches face a great challenge. The word "challenge", however, is not to be understood as having negative connotations, but rather in the most positive and optimistic sense. The pluralistic world is not an obstacle to Orthodoxy; it is rather an opportunity. In a pluralistic global society, the

Orthodox Church is challenged to match her incarnational Christology with an equally incarnational ecclesiology.

At this point, it is important to bring to our conversation a truly programmatic passage from St Paul's First Epistle to the Corinthians. In chapter 9, he speaks of his labours as a true apostle of Christ, defining his apostleship not in terms of rank or privilege, but in terms of servanthood and sacrifice. He says:

> For though I am free with respect to all, I have made myself a slave to all, so that I might win more of them. To the Jews I became as a Jew, in order to win Jews. To those under the law I became as one under the law (though I myself am not under the law) so that I might win those under the law. To those outside the law I became as one outside the law (though I am not free from God's law but am under Christ's law) so that I might win those outside the law. To the weak I became weak, so that I might win the weak. I have become all things to all people, that I might by all means save some. I do it all for the sake of the gospel, so that I may share in its blessings. (9:19-23)

Ἐλεύθερος γὰρ ὢν ἐκ πάντων πᾶσιν ἐμαυτὸν ἐδούλωσα, ἵνα τοὺς πλείονας κερδήσω· καὶ ἐγενόμην τοῖς Ἰουδαίοις ὡς Ἰουδαῖος ἵνα Ἰουδαίους κερδήσω· τοῖς ὑπὸ νόμον ὡς ὑπὸ νόμον, μὴ ὢν αὐτὸς ὑπὸ νόμον, ἵνα τοὺς ὑπὸ νόμον κερδήσω· τοῖς ἀνόμοις ὡς ἄνομος, μὴ ὢν ἄνομος θεοῦ ἀλλ ἔννομος Χριστοῦ ἵνα κερδάνω τοὺς ἀνόμους· ἐγενόμην τοῖς ἀσθενέσιν ἀσθενής, ἵνα τοὺς ἀσθενεῖς κερδήσω· τοῖς πᾶσιν γέγονα πάντα, ἵνα πάντως τινάς σώσω. πάντα δὲ ποιῶ διὰ τὸ εὐαγγέλιον, ἵνα συγκοινωνὸς αὐτοῦ γένωμαι.

If we were to attach a label to St Paul's approach to evangelism, we might call it "personal pluralism". The apostle takes a positive approach to the pluralism that he finds in the Roman world of the 1st century AD, by seeking to express, in the microcosm of his own personhood, the full panoply of human diversity: Jewish, Gentile, under the law, outside the law, strong or weak.

And why does he exhibit this "personal pluralism?" The apostle tells us, "I do it all for the sake of the gospel, so that I may share in its blessings" [πάντα δὲ ποιῶ διὰ τὸ εὐαγγέλιον, ἵνα συγκοινωνὸς αὐτοῦ γένωμαι] (1 Cor. 9:23). We are not to understand by this statement that St Paul expects to earn the blessings of the gospel through his pluralistic labours: such a sentiment would be completely incongruous with St Paul's experience and theology of salvation by grace. Rather, by this statement we understand the apostle to mean that he enjoys the blessings of the gospel in and through his work of being "all things to all people". The blessing is the pluralistic labours, directly related to the salvation of the people.

The reason for this statement is transparent if we understand correctly the Christology of St Paul. Becoming all things to all people requires an act of personal *kenosis*, a self-emptying, accomplished in order to accommodate the needs of the other, followed by a journey into the depths of one's humanity to discover the fullness and variety of our extraordinary nature as creatures who bear the image of an infinite God. And having found within himself the potential to become all things for all people, and having the true apostolic freedom to become all things for all people, the apostle shows himself an "imitator of Christ" *[μιμητής Χριστοῦ]* (cf. 1 Cor. 11:1), who "took the form of a slave" *[μορφὴν δούλου λαβών]* (Phil. 2:7) in order to redeem our enslaved race, who condescended to come even "in the likeness of sinful flesh" *[ἐν ὁμοιώματι σαρκὸς ἁμαρτίας]* (Rom. 8:3) in order to save sinners. For St Paul, therefore, the pluralistic encounters of his apostolic ministry become a means for greater Christ-likeness within his own person. His work is a most existential and experiential way of living in union with Christ so that he might declare, "It is no longer I who live, but it is Christ who lives in me" *ζῶ δὲ οὐκέτι ἐγώ, ζῆ δὲ ἐν ἐμοὶ Χριστός* (Gal. 2:20).

This, then, is the challenge of a pluralistic society for our Orthodox Church: to encounter the contemporary world as St Paul did in imitation of Christ, the God who became a human being. The more pluralistic encounters we effect for the sake of the gospel, the more opportunities we have to become all things to all people, in the Pauline sense, sharing in the blessings of the gospel.

The context of our conversation

It would be wise for us, at the beginning of our conversation on pluralism, to take a moment to consider the context in which we find ourselves. This is a necessary exercise: to examine thoughtfully our present situation, the historical antecedents and the trends leading into the future for our global society.

There would seem to be a general consensus among Americans that we are living in an increasingly pluralistic society and in a world that is rapidly evolving towards greater and greater diversity. Objectively, however, quite the opposite might be true. If anything, the standard cultural markers point to the fact that the world is also rapidly growing more homogeneous. If we speak in terms of languages, for instance, we observe a rapid dying-off of indigenous languages around the world, and even of whole language groups in some places. Linguists predict that the number of distinct languages in the world will have shrunk from about 6000 to around 3000 by the end of this century – a loss of some thirty languages each year.

In conjunction with this trend is the increasing loss of bio-diversity in the ecological sphere, with a concomitant change in the life-style of indigenous peoples. Wetlands are being drained and paved. Desert communities are converted into lakeside resorts through the damming of rivers. Rain forests are rapidly being turned into grazing land for cattle. This trend goes hand in hand with the global spread of Western cultural expressions in terms of music, dress, cuisine, entertainment, and most recently electronic communications via the internet.

Sometimes, phenomena related to globalization and diversity might be misleading. Let me cite a pertinent example. In the USA, many Americans are able today to receive a Spanish-language television channel through their local cable system; twenty years ago this would not have been possible. Some would point to this as proof of a greater diversity in America in 2002 than in 1982. But the argument is weak. The United States has always been an ethnically diverse country, even from its very inception and up until the imposition of immigration quotas. Moreover, Spanish-speaking communities have been a significant part of many American cities for most of the nation's existence. The fact that they have their own television stations now is only proof that these communities are more visible to their neighbours than before, but not that they are part of a trend towards a more diverse society. In fact, in terms of content and appearance, the game shows, soap operas, movies and news programming of the Spanish channels on TV appear to borrow more from standard American network fare than to be an expression of authentic Hispanic-American culture. Therefore, in spite of appearances, the phenomenon of Spanish-language TV channels in America could be a pointer to homogenization rather than to diversity.

So while, on the one hand, it is certainly true that America is becoming more conscious of its pluralistic make-up, it is certainly not the case that America is necessarily becoming a more diverse society. America has always been home to a wide range of ethnic, linguistic, cultural and religious communities. If anything, one might argue rather that America is losing its diversity as the grandchildren of immigrants become more "Americanized", as the traditional ethnic neighbourhoods of towns and cities are transformed, as the Greek-towns and Chinatowns of our major cities shrink and change, and as electronic media promulgate the Hollywood standards for dress, behaviour and speech habits.

It is paradoxical, then, that in this period of increasing homogenization, America and many countries in the world find within themselves a growing conflict of cultural polarization. By cultural, we mean here a large spectrum of components including religion. But this perhaps is the main area of diversification. The so-called "culture wars" have been escalating year after year, and the battlefields are the school board meetings, the radio call-in shows, the sidewalks around women's health clinics, the jury rooms and the voting booths. From the vast relevant literature let me mention as an example the book *Culture Wars: The Struggle to Define America* by James Davidson Hunter.[1] In this book the author describes the combatants most actively engaged in the struggle: the advocates from both sides are deeply patriotic, committed to the founding values of America, profoundly moralistic, fully engaged in their religion (or philosophy of life), well-read and well-spoken, and open to forming non-traditional alliances to further their cause.

Hunter also documents the fact that the lines of today's cultural struggle do not fall along any of the old societal boundaries like race or creed, but rather cut across them. Catholics oppose Catholics at the abortion clinic picket lines, Jews vilify Jews in the media, and Protestants lambaste Protestants at the town meeting. In this sense, the pluralism of contemporary America and several modern countries is quite different from the diversity of the past. Increasingly, America is becoming a neighbourhood of "houses divided", so to speak. The new diversity of America is not in the variety of languages spoken in the market-place, but in the use of a common vocabulary of words, symbols, myths and meanings to express radically different visions of national life. And this has a tremendous importance for our conversation.

This, in fact, is the chief battleground of the culture wars: a semantic tug-of-war to impose a particular set of definitions and a particular narrative and interpretation of national history on the population as a whole. As specialists say: "The battle will be nearly over when the linguistic preferences of one side of the cultural divide become the conventions of society as a whole."[2]

What this means for our conversation here is that we must be sensitive to the fact that pluralism is often obscured by common speech habits. In former times, the pluralism of American society was a visible and audible property, observed in differences in skin colour and language. Today, however, the most authentic pluralism seems to be ideological rather than racial, and this pluralism is often invisible and inaudible, unless one knows how to decode the shared keywords of the various parties on the ideological spectrum. This challenges us as Orthodox Christians, therefore, to be extremely careful and sensitive in our use of language. It forces us to reassess what we truly intend to mean by our theological speech, to examine how it is likely to be understood by other citizens in this society. It is not enough to say the right thing, objectively. In many cases, we will need to discover fresh metaphors and narratives to articulate our beliefs in this pluralistic society of ours. This task is facilitated by our classical cultural Hellenic heritage, which is in essence transcultural and favours creative usage of language and expression of ideas and beliefs. To use the gospel metaphor, we need new wineskins, in terms of communication and language, for the new wine of our Orthodox faith in America (cf. Matt. 9:17).

This, in short, is an oversimplified overview of the context in which we conduct our conversation. We are mistaken, however, if we think ourselves to be inhabiting an entirely novel cultural milieu, unlike any seen before. A quick look at the cultural setting of 1st-century Palestine will reveal to us several affinities with our own time. Jesus Christ was born into a society that was struggling with the frictions of an uncomfortable pluralism. In the mix were a Jewish ruling class with accommodationist attitudes towards the regime of Caesar, Hellenized Jews, conservative Sadducees, progressivist Pharisees, isolationist Essenes, along with Samaritans, Gentiles and Roman overlords. One could not have predicted that from within this cultural chaos and ideological diversity would emerge a way of life that would unite men and women of every social class, nation, tribe and tongue, and ultimately even the fractured Roman empire itself. And yet this was precisely the power of the gospel in that ancient reflection of our own times. And by the grace of God, it can have this same power again in our own times as well.

Responding to the pluralistic challenge: three suggestions

Within this cultural-ideological diversification, within this pluralistic context, what can we as Orthodox churches offer to contemporary society? Allow me to submit three suggestions, which I imagine are well known and which it might be useful to remember in our discussions.

1. The first is a suggestion related to the story of Pentecost and to the practice of the early Church. The central event in Pentecost was the fact that the apostles were empowered by the Holy Spirit to speak the good news in all the languages of the multitude gathered that day in Jerusalem.

It is noteworthy that the miracle of Pentecost was not that the assembled crowd was made to understand the speech of a single man in a single language, regardless of the native tongue of the hearers. Rather, the miracle was that the one gospel was expressed equally in a variety of languages. Anyone who recognizes the intimate link of language to culture must also recognize the bold statement that Pentecost makes: the truth of Christ can be embodied in more than one or two cultural-linguistic systems. The work of the Church is not to construct a single universal culture; instead, the kingdom of God created by the one Holy Spirit contains many languages, many cultures. In the words of Fr Emmanuel Clapsis, Pentecost tells us about "the active presence of God in all cultures".[3] This is a strong Orthodox view of the kingdom, and for it we can lay claim to a long-standing tradition of insisting that "the Christian faith must become incarnated (or indigenized) in order to produce authentic fruits of dynamic human cooperation with God".[4] In this instance, let us consider the practice of the early Church. How did it treat the holy scriptures? The Greek language was still the *lingua franca* of the Roman world even into the era of the Church fathers. And for most Greek speakers of the time who employed the variety known as *koinē*, around the Mediterranean Sea, the language of most of the New Testament would have been accessible and understandable in the original.

And yet, very early on in the life of the Church, we find a significant commitment to the work of translating the scriptures into the various local vernaculars: Syriac, Ethiopic, Georgian, Armenian, the Vulgate of St Jerome, Coptic in both the Sahidic and Bohairic dialects, and Gothic. What does this multiplicity of Bible versions demonstrate, if not a strong sense among the early Christian fathers that the faith of Christ must be indigenized, so to say, to the greatest extent possible?

We all know that translation is an inexact science, that the difficulty of finding equivalent renderings can introduce unintended meanings to a text, or conversely limit the range of purposeful ambiguities. We know also that in the face of the Gnostic movements, early Christianity was deeply concerned about "the standard of sound teaching" (2 Tim. 1:13), about vocabulary and nuances of meaning. Nevertheless, despite the risks inherent in the translator's art, the early Church responded to its mission in a pluralistic world by deliberately advancing its own linguistic pluralism in the core expression of the faith, the holy scriptures. This diversity was matched as well by a diversity of liturgical expressions, and an openness to variety in other facets of life for the Christian communities of the Eastern empire, so that even in the "globalized" environment of the ancient Roman world, the Church never neglected the particular and specific cultural elements of local parishes, never overlooked the socio-cultural or ethnic pluralism.

2. The second suggestion refers to our Orthodox notion of personhood, and the importance of this idea in our dealing with the challenge of the pluralistic world of today. With the theological term "person" we express a complex of ideas and values. Among persons there is a fundamental commonality of essence, while at the same time an indelible distinction of uniqueness. Personhood at one and the same time implies the existence of the other through the shared nature, and yet also upholds the primacy of the individual, as significant and precious in his or her own right.

Modern society has a tendency to reduce persons to the description of their external characteristics. How often, for example, do we see reports in the media that present demographic information solely in terms of the categories of race, gender or social class? How much of our political rhetoric is shaped by the notion that the nation is simply a collection of constituencies: blacks, whites, senior citizens or blue-collar workers? This sort of reductionism is offensive to the anthropological sensibilities of Orthodox theology, and as loyal citizens of our society we should resist it. By no means should the pressures of modern globalization be allowed to define the emerging global community simply in terms of focus groups and market targets.

As Metropolitan John Zizioulas of Pergamon has written in his book *Being as Communion*:

> Uniqueness is something absolute for the person. The person is so absolute in its uniqueness that it does not permit itself to be regarded as an arithmetical concept, to be set alongside other beings, to be combined with other objects, or to be used as a means, even for the most sacred goals. The goal is the person itself.[5]

Our Orthodox insistence on the uniqueness of personhood is strongly evident even in our liturgical practice. To give an example, every sacrament is personalized by the recitation of the name of the Christian who has been given a renewed personhood and a new name in Christ.

And yet our Orthodox notion of personhood is altogether distinct from the American idea of "individualism". For personhood is fulfilled only in community, only in the relationship of love and openness to the other, as different as the other might be. Thus, no matter how advanced is the state of globalization, no matter what forms pluralism will take in the near or distant future, our Orthodox notion of personhood will be of paramount importance and has to be constantly emphasized in any and every pluralistic context.

3. The third and final suggestion connects the pluralistic challenge to the eucharistic community of the Orthodox parish. Whereas the apostle Paul practised a kind of personal pluralism, our parishes should be the proponents of a parish pluralism, being all things to all people, by their make-up and their outlook and above all by their communal mode of life, instantiating constructively a "unity in diversity" that could be a model for our whole society. This idea has been articulated by Christos Yannaras, among others, in his book *The Freedom of Morality*,[6] where he identified the eucharistic community – the local parish – as the starting-point for an Orthodox programme of a more comprehensive social engagement, an emphasis on personal relationships within the eucharistic community and a fostering of strong communal and eucharistic life among our people. The spiritual reconstruction of the local parish into an

authentic community is, then, not simply one of the priorities for Orthodoxy in this era, but the "priority programme". As we conduct our conversation on pluralism, let us be mindful about how our ideas and proposals can be translated into the concrete actions of community church life, leading our parishes into offering some sort of a parish pluralism. Such a parish pluralism, saving the uniqueness and integrity of the person and the unity and vitality of the community, could serve as a superb model for our globalized and pluralistic society.

Conclusion

At the beginning of this presentation, we quoted, as a guiding text, the declaration of St Paul in 1 Corinthians 9:22: " I have become all things to all people, that I might by all means save some." We end with the same phrase: "I have become all things to all people, that I might by all means save some." An adequate theology of pluralism is not simply a philosophical nicety for our Orthodox churches of the 21st century. It is the necessary tool for our accomplishment of the work set before us by the Lord in his Great Commission to go forth into all the world to preach the gospel. Unless we understand how we, as a Church and as local parishes and as theologians and clergy and laity, can become "all things to all people" in an appropriate, authentic and Orthodox way; unless we understand how to live our pluralism while still holding fast to the one truth of the one Lord Jesus Christ, and one Church; we will by no means save any. And we will by no means respond to the sublime mandate of the same Lord telling us, "As the Father has sent me, so I send you" (John 20:21).

NOTES

[1] J.D. Hunter, *Culture Wars: The Struggle to Define America*, New York, Basic Books, 1991.
[2] *Ibid.*, p.184.
[3] E. Clapsis, "Gospel and Cultures: An Eastern Orthodox Perspective", in Ioan Sauca ed., *Orthodoxy and Cultures*, WCC, 1996, p.21.
[4] *Ibid.*, p.8.
[5] John Zizioulas, *Being as Communion*, Crestwood NY, St Vladimir's Seminary Press, 1985, p.47.
[6] Christos Yannaras, *The Freedom of Morality*, Crestwood NY, St Vladimir's Seminary Press, 1984, see esp. chapter 11.

The Christian Churches and the Plurality of Religious Communities

DIANA L. ECK

There can be no more important question in our world today than the question of how we negotiate our religious differences in a world in which all of us now live together in greater proximity than ever before. We all have new responsibilities now – as theologians, as church leaders, as educators, and as participants in multi-religious societies throughout the world.

As we think about the movements that have reshaped the world in which we live in the past half-century, even in the past decade, there are many key words that come to mind. Among them is the term "globalization" which has many meanings, both positive and negative. Globalization has made all of us more acutely aware of the ways in which our currencies, our economies, our political fortunes, our attempts at waging war and our attempts at building peace are all inter-linked, although the policies of our governments and the vision of our churches may be slow to recognize this fact.

Along with the globalization of world systems has come the movement of people as refugees and as economic and political migrants. The demography of our world has changed, and our way of looking at a world of religious, cultural and ethnic difference must now begin to catch up with those changes. One of my colleagues at Harvard has described the post-cold war world as one that will be marked by rigid adherence to civilizational identities, and ultimately a "clash of civilizations". Some people believe that his dire predictions of a clash of Islam and the West has been borne out in the events of 11 September 2001 and their global aftermath. Perhaps one could make a persuasive case for this analysis, but it is missing any critical perspective on the changing demography of our world. It is missing any critical analysis of the global currents of culture and religion that have come with this new reality.

Just where, we must ask, are the so-called Confucian, Islamic and Hindu worlds that will be the forces with which the West must reckon?

They are everywhere, today. It is precisely the interpenetration and proximity of great civilizations and cultures that is the hallmark of the 21st
century. The map of the world in which we live cannot be colour-coded
as to its Christian, Muslim or Hindu identity, but each part of the world
is marbled with the colours and textures of the whole. This is a fact with
which we are grappling anew in the United States, for America has
become, over the past forty years, a truly multireligious society. New
immigrants have come to American shores from all over the world and
have become citizens. They have brought with them not only their lug-
gage and economic aspirations, but their Qurans and Bhagavad Gitas,
their images of Krishna and Murugan, their incense to light before the
Bodhisattvas on their Buddhist altars.

Religion in America

As an American today, I would like to make clear that the "Islamic
world" is not somewhere else other than America. No indeed, the United
States is part of the Muslim world. Chicago with its seventy mosques
and 500,000 Muslims is part of the Muslim world. Washington DC,
where the Islamic Society of North America gathered 30,000 strong for
their annual convention in September 2002, is part of the Muslim world.
Los Angeles with its multitude of Buddhist communities spanning the
whole of Asia – its Chinese temples, its Korean and Japanese temples,
its Vietnamese, Cambodian, and Lao temples, its Euro-American Buddhist communities – partakes of the cultures and religious ways of all of
Asia. Cities like Pittsburgh, Nashville, Atlanta, Boston and Houston
have splendid Hindu temples and have seen the magnificence of temple
consecration rites most of these new immigrants had never witnessed in
India. They are part of whatever one might mean by the "Hindu world"
in which new American immigrants move back and forth from India to
the Silicon Valley with a fluidity my own immigrant grandparents could
never have imagined. And there are Sikhs who have built gurdwaras
from coast to coast and litigated for their right to wear a turban on a hard-
hat job or on the Los Angeles police force. And there are Jains, too, who
have trained their children in a curriculum of nonviolence and insist that
school cafeterias have clearly marked vegetarian options.

I speak about the United States, not because America has the
answers, but because America has struggled with these issues of religious tolerance and democracy from the very beginning. The Pilgrims
and Puritans who sailed the seas to establish communities in a new world
wanted to be free to practise their religious faith. They were not thinking
about a wider ethic of religious freedom when they clung to the shores
of the Atlantic south of here in Plymouth, and when they created the

Massachusetts Bay Colony. History reminds us that they were concerned primarily with religious freedom for themselves and did not see religious freedom as a foundation for common life with people who differed from them. In 17th-century Puritan Boston, for example, Solomon Franco, a Sephardic Jewish merchant, was "warned out" of town. An anti-Catholic law was enacted stating "that no Jesuit or ecclesiastical person ordained by the authorities of the pope shall henceforth come within our jurisdiction..." The Puritan establishment of Boston put four Quakers to death on the gallows on Boston Common. Dissenters like Roger Williams and Anne Hutchison had to flee the Massachusetts Bay Colony because of their nonconformist religious beliefs, settling in what is now Rhode Island.

During the long argument that produced a nation out of 13 colonies, there were those who wanted to establish a state religion in the new world and those who urged tolerance and freedom for all religions. The principle of religious freedom eventually won the day and was written into the Bill of Rights: that there shall be no establishment of any given religion, no sect of Christianity, not even Christianity itself, and that there shall be no infringement of the free exercise of religion. The freedom we seek for ourselves, we must also cherish for everyone, even those with whom we disagree. Interestingly, they argued their case for a secular constitution on religious grounds: our freedom is grounded in the God-given freedom of the mind to think and to choose. Standing for religious freedom – even freedom from any form of religion – is grounded in the very freedom ordained by God. A state that would enforce uniformity of religion is against the very principles of God's sovereignty and ultimacy. God did not propagate truth by coercion, so why should we?

Such a vision of religious freedom was not part of the heritage of most European newcomers to America. In England and France there had been state-established and supported religion. And there had been a ghastly legacy of bloody wars in the name of religion. The new American democracy turned away from that legacy towards the separation of church and state, and the free exercise of religion.

Interestingly, religion in the new country became stronger precisely because the churches no longer had any support from public tax coffers; they had to compete with one another in the free market of Christian ideas in order to thrive, and one of the consequences of this unprecedented approach to religious freedom was the proliferation of churches. When the Frenchman Alexis de Toqueville travelled around America in the 1820s, he discovered, to his surprise, that severing the ties between church and state seemed to make religion stronger, rather than weaker.

Unlike France, where the spirit of religion and the spirit of freedom seemed to march in opposite directions, in America they seemed "intimately united" and "reigned in common over the same country".[1] Churches needed to win the support of parishioners in order to survive, and the spirit of voluntarism inspired a lively and intense competition in religion and the creation of a multitude of "denominations" that have become a distinctive feature of American religion. De Toqueville called religion the "first of political institutions", astutely discerning that while the churches were not supported by the government and were not directly involved in politics as such, they were nonetheless extremely influential in the political sphere.

Today's religious diversity

As we know, the history of making this unprecedented vision of religious tolerance and religious freedom into a firm foundation for a complex society is actually a very rocky one. If you want to know just how rocky it has been, look at 19th-century American history. Ask the Catholics and Jews, whose history here has included bitter periods of anti-Catholicism and anti-semitism. Ask how the Chinese were received, who built makeshift temples on the west coast and in the Rocky mountains in the 1850s and 1860s, or ask how it went for the first Sikhs who built their first places of worship in California in the 1910s. Ask the Japanese Buddhists who were imprisoned in America's own concentration camps during the second world war. Ask the Native peoples of America, who did not win the clear right to practise their religious lifeways until the passage of the Native American religious freedom act in 1968.

The transformation of America's religious landscape in the period since the 1965 immigration act was passed has been gradual. For many years, you still had to look for it. The Hindu temple might be in a former convenience store in Sunnyvale, California, or in a former church at the corner of Polk and Pine in Minneapolis. The mosque might be in a former U Haul office in Pawtucket, Rhode Island, or a gymnasium in Oklahoma City. A two-car garage in Claremont, California, became a Vietnamese Buddhist temple room. For the most part, we could drive right by and not notice anything new at all. But the distinctive visible presence has gradually become apparent over the last two decades, with dramatic architectural statements that enunciate that presence. The huge white dome of a mosque flanked by its minarets rises from the cornfields just off the interstate outside Toledo. A great Hindu temple with elephants carved in relief at the doorway stands on a hillside in the western suburbs of Nashville. A Cambodian Buddhist temple and monastery with just a hint of a South East Asian roofline is set in the farmlands south of Minneapolis and on a suburban road outside Washington DC. In suburban Fremont, California, flags fly from the golden domes of a new Sikh gurdwara on a street renamed Gurdwara Terrace. These are the architectural signals of a new religious America.

Over the past few years, speaking across America with students, civic leaders, religious congregations, I discovered how surprised many of us were to find that there are more Muslim Americans today than Episcopalians, more Muslims than members of the Presbyterian Church USA, probably as many Muslims as Jews. We are astonished to be told that Los Angeles is the most complex Buddhist city in the world, with a Buddhist population spanning the whole range of the Asian Buddhist world and with a multitude of native-born American Buddhists. We know that many of our internists, surgeons and nurses are of Indian origin, but we have not stopped to consider that they too have a religious life, that they might pause in the morning for few minutes' prayer at an altar in the family room of their home, that they might bring fruits and flowers to the Shiva-Vishnu Temple on the weekend.

Many people, perhaps some of us, are still surprised to learn about America's new religious diversity and reluctantly challenged to think about what this diversity means for the American pluralist experiment. Muslim voter registration drives? Hindu temples being built in the suburbs? Turbaned Sikhs going to court over job discrimination? A faith-based initiative that might provide support for the Hare Krishna food programme along with others? At least until last autumn, these were relatively new considerations for most of us.

But on that brilliant blue September morning in 2001 when hijacked planes exploded into the towers of the World Trade Center and the Pentagon, a new era began for us all. Within hours an unprecedented rash of xenophobic incidents began – from low-level harassment, ethno slurs, broken windows and threatening calls, to arson, beatings and murders. While the roster of hate crimes was growing, so were prodigious efforts at local and national outreach across religious boundaries – interfaith services and interfaith education programmes. It is too soon to gauge the climate of the new religious America in which we all now live. One thing is certain. The challenge of relations between and among people of different religious and cultural traditions, both here in the United States and around the world, is moving to the top of the agenda.

Over the past ten years, the Pluralism Project has documented the ways in which today's minority religious communities have experienced the violence of attacks on their visible religious institutions. For example, in February 1983 vandals broke into the newly constructed Hindu-

Jain temple in Pittsburgh and smashed all the white marble images of the Hindu deities. The sacred scripture of the Sikhs, housed on a side altar, was torn to pieces. The word "Leave!" was written across the main altar. In 1993, the temple of a tiny Cambodian Buddhist community in Portland, Maine, was vandalized with an axe, its doorjambs hacked, its doors broken, its altars desecrated and the words "Dirty Asian Chink, Go Home!" written on the walls. In September 1994, a nearly-completed mosque in Yuba City, California, was burned to the ground in a fire that the sheriff deemed to be arson. There have been dozens of these incidents every year and they are now documented by such groups as the Council on American-Islamic Relations.

Violence has brought stronger inferfaith connection

The documentary register of acts of violence is easier to assemble than the register of new initiatives of cooperation and understanding. Yet assembling the evidence of new patterns of inter-religious encounter and relationship is also important in discerning how the "we" is being reconfigured in multireligious America. Looking back to the 1990s, we see that the 1993 ground-breaking for a new Islamic Centre in Sharon, Massachusetts, brought Jews, Christians and Muslims together from the greater Boston area. There, on a hillside overlooking the fields of a former horse-farm, rabbis and priests, imams and Muslim leaders each turned a shovel of earth for the Islamic Centre of New England. Two weeks later, across the country in Fremont, California, St Paul's United Methodist Church and the Islamic Society of the East Bay broke ground together for a new church and a new mosque, to be built side by side. They named their common access road "Peace Terrace", and they are now next-door neighbours. "We want to set an example for the world," said one of the Muslim leaders.

The past year has amplified the record of hostility to difference and outreach efforts to bring religious communities together for dialogue and common work.[2] On the side of hostility, we can see the record of violence and suspicion, not only against Muslims, but against anyone who has the look and feel of being different. On 13 September 2001, men entered the Colorado Springs mosque and threaten to burn it down; a crowd approached the Bridgeview mosque in Chicago shouting anti-Arab slogans; a man smashed his car through the front entrance of the mosque in Cleveland; a firebomb landed in a mosque in Denton, Texas; and rifle-fire pierced the dome of the mosque in Toledo, Ohio. A Sikh was shot and killed in Phoenix in his gas station and convenience store; a Coptic Christian grocery store owner originally from Egypt was shot and killed in his store in San Gabriel, California; a Pakistani Muslim grocer was shot and killed in Dallas. And there were a multitude of smaller incidents, many of them not reported: obscene graffiti on the walls of the mosque in Stirling, Virginia, or bricks wrapped with hate messages thrown through the windows of an Islamic bookstore in Alexandria, Virginia. And, of course, there have been the ongoing violations of the basic civil liberties of American Muslims, some of whom have been incarcerated for months, without due process of law.

The amplification and strengthening of interfaith connection has also been part of religious America in the past year. While one misguided would-be patriot shot and killed a Sikh in Arizona, thousands poured out to the gas station he had owned and to the civic arena where his memorial service took place to say, with one voice, "This is not who we are!" By January 2002, the family of this Sikh man had received more than 10,000 letters and messages of support. In Denton, Texas, a circle of interfaith leaders assembled immediately at the mosque for prayer and protection. The Palestinian bookstore owner in Alexandria, Virginia, stunned by the shattered glass and its message of hatred, soon discovered hundreds of supportive neighbours he did not know who sent him dozens of bouquets of flowers and hundreds of cards expressing their sorrow at what had happened. In Toledo, as Cherefe Kadri, the woman who is the president of the Islamic community, told it, "That small hole in the dome created such a huge outpouring of support for our Islamic community. A Christian radio station contacted me wanting to do something", she said. "They called out on the airwaves for people to come together at our centre to hold hands, to ring our mosque, to pray for our protection. We expected 300 people, and thought that would be enough to circle the mosque, but 2000 people showed up. I was amazed!"

Not surprisingly, the interfaith networks and councils that had grown in America during the 1990s sprung into action with immediate civic leadership, and cities that had never had an interfaith civic council formed one. Virtually all of the community services in cities and towns across America involved leaders from a wide spectrum of religious communities. At the National Cathedral in Washington, Muzamil Siddiqi, leader of the Islamic Society of North America, was among those offering prayers. The Episcopal Bishop Jane Holmes Dixon said, "Those of us who are gathered here – Muslim, Jew, Christian, Sikh, Buddhist, Hindu – say to this nation and to the world, that love is stronger than hate." At an interfaith service in the Bay Area, the governor of California, Gray Davis, put it clearly: "Our enemies have failed to divide us. We are one people. We are Americans. We don't care if you were born in the Mission District or the Middle East." The anniversary observances of 11 September likewise expressed this strengthening interfaith connection.

Getting to know each other

Education and outreach, fundamental to building relationships in a pluralist society, has been another positive prognostic of this period. As our huge bombers were leaving an air force base in Missouri to fly non-stop to Afghanistan, mosques all over America were holding open-house, inviting neighbours in to learn more about Islam in the face of a wave of Islamophobia. The Islamic Society of Boston in Cambridge, Massachusetts, for example, published an open letter to its neighbours, saying: "We utterly condemn the use of terror to further any political or religious cause. As Muslims, we abhor the killing of innocent civilians. Our holy book, the Quran, teaches: 'If anyone kills an innocent person, it is as if he has killed all of humanity. And if anyone saves a life, it is as if he has saved all of humanity' (ch. 5, v. 32)." The letter announced a community open-house to be held the following Sunday. It closed, "God willing, we can lend one another strength to find hope in these uncertain times." More than 700 people came to the open house, many of them visiting a mosque for the first time. The story was the same across the country. In Austin, Texas, for example, hundreds showed up for the Sunday afternoon open house. A woman interviewed by the *Austin American-Statesman* put the matter plainly and succinctly for all of us when she said, "The time of not getting to know each other is over."

Getting to know each other also has profound theological dimensions, and never have theological confusion and bigotry been expressed so openly and publicly. Following an interfaith memorial in Yankee Stadium in September 2002, the conservative Missouri Synod Lutheran Church suspended the leader of its Atlantic district for participating in the event and demanded that he apologize to the Lord and to all Christians for offering a prayer on the same platform with "pagans". Many people, including those in the national television audience, were clearly moved by the event, as was a participating Missouri Synod Lutheran pastor, the Rev. David Benke. As he looked out on 20,000 people holding the pictures of their lost loved ones, he referred to everyone there as "sisters and brothers". He said that "God is love" and asked them to take the hand of a neighbour and "join me in prayer on this field of dreams turned into God's house of prayer". He closed his prayer in the name of Jesus, which no doubt made some non-Christian participants uncomfortable, but from them there was no protest. The protest came from his own church. They charged him with "an offence both to God and to all Christians". The event wrongly signalled, they said, that "all religions pray to the same God". Equally offensive, however, was "to give the impression that there might be more than one God". The only satisfactory conclusion seemed to be that there is only one God, and that God is ours, perhaps a Missouri Synod Lutheran to boot. No one seemed to wonder if the one they call "God" just might be expansive enough to receive the prayers of all people.

This incident is instructive, for it gives us a sense of the need for theological leadership that this new era requires, including the leadership of Christians with long experience of relationship with Muslim neighbours. How do we understand the one we call "God" in the prayers, presence and faith of our non-Christian neighbours? Especially among those exclusivist Christians who have absolutized their "God" language, there has been an unprecedented burst of dissonant theological pronouncements. Prominent Southern Baptist clergy have averred that the God Muslims worship is not the same God known to Christians and Jews. A leader of the denomination insisted that "Allah is not Jehovah", while another insisted that Muslims worship a "different God than Christians", although he later said he had no time to learn anything about Islam. A prominent cabinet officer and member of the Assemblies of God Church insisted that "Islam is a religion where you send your son to die for God, but Christianity is a faith where God sends his son to die for you". And the *New York Times* has cited an interview with the Rev. Jerry Falwell, calling Muhammad "a man of war".

There are many things Christians must find disturbing about such statements, and they must leave many a Baptist worshipper yearning for a more adequate understanding of God in the universe of faiths. Today our religious neighbours, whether Hindu, Muslim or Buddhist, are closer than ever before. They are not around the world, but literally across the street. And yet our ignorance of one another has become sadly evident. Allah is, after all, Arabic for God and is the same term Arab Christians use in their prayers and praises. The rash of restrictive pronouncements about God's presence, person and names does no justice to anyone's understanding of God.

Pluralism – a dynamic process

Pluralism is not an ideology, not a new universal theology, and not a freeform relativism. Rather, pluralism is the dynamic process through which we engage with one another in and through our very deepest differences. Through this engagement, new theological understandings may well emerge, and I, for one, hope they do. In the meantime, let me close with three points on what I understand to be the nature of pluralism.

First, I would argue that "pluralism" is not just another word for diversity. It goes beyond mere plurality or diversity to active engagement with that plurality. Religious diversity is an observable fact of

American life today – from Flushing, New York, where Sikhs and Jews worship across the street from one another, to San Diego, California, where the Islamic centre and the Lutheran church are next door neighbours. On that stretch of New Hampshire Avenue in Silver Spring, Maryland, the Vietnamese Catholic church, the Ukrainian Orthodox church, the Muslim community centre, the Disciples of Christ church, the Cambodian Buddhist temple and the Gujarati Hindu temple lined up one after another vividly dramatize the possibility of a new pluralism. One can study this diversity, complain about there being too much diversity, or even celebrate diversity. But the diversity alone is not pluralism. Pluralism is not a given, but must be created. Pluralism requires participation, and attunement to the life and energies of one another.

Second, I would propose that pluralism goes beyond mere tolerance to the active attempt to understand the other, like the step taken by Milwaukee's Christians and Muslims last year when they signed that covenant pledging themselves to the process of mutual understanding. Although tolerance is no doubt a step forward from intolerance, it does not require new neighbours to know anything about one another. Tolerance comes from a position of strength. I can tolerate many minorities if I am in power, but if I myself am a member of a small minority, what does tolerance mean? Tolerance can create a climate of restraint, but not a climate of understanding. Tolerance alone does little to bridge the chasms of stereotype and fear that may, in fact, dominate the mutual image of the other. It is far too fragile a foundation for a society that is becoming as religiously complex as the USA's.

We ourselves may be very religious, yet we may have a very low level of religious literacy beyond our own tradition. Beginning to root out the stereotypes and prejudice that bear false witness against our neighbours and form the fault-lines of fracture is critical for a society that has absorbed so much difference, with so little understanding of our differences. Yet few theological schools training leaders for churches require basic literacy in the world religions as part of that training.

Third, I would insist that pluralism is not simply relativism. It does not displace or eliminate deep religious commitments. It is, rather, the encounter of commitments. Some critics have persisted in linking pluralism with a kind of valueless relativism, in which all cats are grey, all perspectives equally viable and, as a result, equally uncompelling. Pluralism, they would contend, undermines commitment to one's own particular faith with its own particular language, watering down particularity in the interests of universality. I consider that view a distortion of the process of pluralism. I would argue that pluralism is the engagement, not the abdication, of differences and particularities.

As Archbishop Demetrios has said so eloquently, it is this very process of engagement, mutual learning and dialogue that will begin to produce a theology of pluralism. The power and dignity of speaking and listening are themselves creative and illumining. Orthodox theologians consistently remind us all that the realm of the Spirit has no frontiers. We cannot place limits upon the freedom of the Holy Spirit, which blows where it wills and burns in the hearts of many. Today, may the freedom and fire, the creativity and guidance of the Holy Spirit enable us to meet the challenges of life and leadership in a world of many faiths.

NOTES

[1] Alexis de Toqueville, *Democracy in America*, New York, Vintage, 1990, vol. 1, p.308.
[2] See the "In the News" section of the Pluralism Project, website: http://www.pluralism.org.

Orthodox Christianity and Pluralism
Moving beyond Ambivalence?[1]

ELIZABETH H. PRODROMOU

The parameters of inquiry into Orthodoxy and pluralism

The project of exploring the public presence of the Orthodox churches in a pluralistic world is an undertaking with important theoretical and empirical dimensions, as well as one whose time is long overdue in view of recent history. The last half-century has offered rich empirical evidence of a trend of desecularization, thereby calling into question long-standing assumptions equating secularity with modernity;[2] religion has played an active role in local, regional and global events as diverse as the demise of communist regimes in Eastern Europe, cycles of communal violence in East Africa, and economic development in Asia and Latin America. Meanwhile, the events of 11 September 2001 in the United States have added urgency to discussions about the extent and implications of religious activity in the contemporary international system;[3] claims about the incompatibilities between non-Western religions and democracy[4] have been augmented with questions about the propensity of some religions for violence,[5] with associated arguments about the meaning of religious human rights and competing definitions of citizenship.[6] In short, Orthodox churches at the start of the 21st century must engage with pluralism at multiple levels, in the form of a pluralization of the faiths and denominations active around the world, as well as a pluralization in the possibilities for religious engagement in the world.

There are several indicators that help to situate and to characterize the engagement of Orthodox Christianity – whether in terms of ideas or practice – in the pluralism of the current historical moment. A review of the literatures on public religion and world affairs over the past decade alone reveals that Orthodox thinkers have been notable for their relative absence from[7] the renaissance of scholarship dealing with the causes and consequences of public religion in a world where modernity is still defined in Westphalian terms.[8] More specifically, these literatures also show that Orthodoxy has belatedly engaged the global phenomenon of pluralism,[9] where pluralism means institutions and ideas informed by and supportive of political and cultural difference, diversity and choice.

Of course, it is important to acknowledge the theological creativity and ecumenical dimensions of what Vassilios Makrides has character-ized as a "regeneration of Orthodoxy theology"[10] over the last several decades, centred on debates in Greece and Russia, but gradually incor-porating voices from Orthodox populations in South-eastern Europe and the United States. It is notable, however, that this scholarship has not managed to generate a systematic, interdisciplinary inquiry into the pub-lic role of Orthodoxy under conditions of social, political and cultural pluralism,[11] most plausibly because of the disciplinary restrictions to the domains of theology and philosophy[12] and, perhaps secondarily, because a preponderant proportion of the work has not been translated beyond the Russian and South-east European originals. Therefore, while Ortho-dox thinkers like Emmanuel Clapsis have argued that "the challenge of reconfiguring the public role of religion... reflects some continuity with the Orthodox ethos",[13] the extent of Orthodox churches' public conver-sation with pluralism has been comparatively limited.[14] Furthermore, despite the expanding diversity of subjects that have preoccupied schol-ars whose work might be considered part of an interdisciplinary field of "Orthodox studies", these scholars have not yet articulated a coherent research agenda expressly dedicated to developing a systematic social and political theory of pluralism rooted in Orthodox theology. Taken as a whole, the above limitations have had crucial implications for the role of Orthodox institutions and ideas in the myriad dynamics of pluralism associated with the global wave of democratization under way since the late 20th century.[15]

Interestingly enough, the annual assessment made by Freedom House, in *Freedom in the World (2001-2002)*,[16] places Orthodoxy within a comparative global context that offers intriguing data for considering Orthodox churches' engagement with pluralism in diverse social, politi-cal and cultural conditions. A comprehensive, cross-national ranking of indicators of political freedom and civil liberties, the Freedom House survey ranks Orthodox countries[17] well within the range of countries defined as democracies.[18]

This data suggests that Orthodox churches and, more specifically, Orthodox ideas and institutions, can exist and, possibly, thrive in the kinds of pluralist conditions encouraged by democratic regimes. Even so, country-specific and comparative studies of church-state relations in Orthodox countries (understood in terms of the Freedom House criteria), as well as works on the internal transformation of Orthodox churches, present significant evidence that the nature of Orthodoxy's engagement with pluralism is one of discernible ambivalence.[19] In short, the public presence of Orthodox churches in the contemporary international system indicates ambivalence by those churches, concerning the origins of pluralism, the implications of pluralism for Orthodoxy, and possible Orthodox responses to pluralism.

It is Orthodoxy's demonstrated ambivalence towards pluralism that constitutes the focus of this presentation. The general goal is to contribute to nascent efforts at systematic inquiry into the nature and implications of Orthodoxy's ambivalent encounter with the ideas and practices of pluralism in the public sphere in the 21st century. More specifically, this presentation aims to explore Orthodoxy's ambivalence towards pluralism within the context of democracy. After all, Orthodoxy faces a more direct and lively encounter with pluralism in democratic regimes, since democracy forces a direct engagement of Orthodox ideas (theology), institutions (the individuals and organizations that constitute churches), and practices (discourse and behaviours) with the principles of freedom and equality that generate contests over the delineation and protection of diversity and difference.[20]

The methodological linchpin of the inquiry into Orthodoxy's ambivalence towards pluralism is a case study of Greece, an Orthodox country according to the criteria of the Freedom House survey noted above, and a democracy according to the standard social-science template used in the democratization literature.[21] The utility of a case-study approach rests in the specific data that can be garnered to help construct a general portrait of Orthodoxy's approach to pluralism.

More specifically, the Greek case helps to elucidate general claims about Orthodoxy's encounter with pluralism in two ways. First, it helps to specify the nature of Orthodoxy's ambivalence towards pluralism, in the form of a gap between support for the legal-constitutional, or formal(ist) rights of freedom of religion and conscience, on the one hand, versus contradictions in the interpretation and application of those rights in a substantively expansive manner, on the other. Second, the Greek case helps to specify the multiple sources – local, regional and global – for change and stasis that inform Orthodoxy's ambivalent encounter with pluralism.

The arguments presented here contribute to studies of religion and international relations in two respects. First, the Greek case shows that the ambivalence in Orthodoxy's encounter with pluralism originates not only within the religious sphere but, equally important, is rooted in what Stephanos Stavros has aptly characterized as the "reluctance of the Greek state to trade its role as the protector of the Orthodox faith for that of impartial guarantor of the peaceful coexistence of various religious groups".[22] The reluctance of the Greek state points to a broader European phenomenon worthy of comparative study, namely, the demonstrated tendency of European Union (EU) states to consider reinforcing the legal and institutional bonds between states and a dominant national identity, as response to the noticeable religious pluralization of the EU since the end of the cold war.[23] Second, the investigation of the Greek cases within the EU and international contexts offers fecund data for reconsidering the meanings of secularity and modernity. Rather than a condition defined by the three markers specified in the conventional sociological theory of secularization,[24] secularity may be more fruitfully conceived in terms of elasticity, based on changes in the aforementioned three markers. Furthermore, the reconceptualization of secularity as an elastic condition allows for a methodological move in favour of modernity understood in plural terms. By accepting modernity as a condition of multiple possibilities with regard to secularity, social scientists, theologians and public policy-makers may begin to engage more effectively in identifying, and possibly supporting, the affinities between religion and democracy.

The presentation proceeds as follows. Part 1 offers a highly stylized summary of the Greek case, in order to characterize the nature of Orthodoxy's ambivalence towards pluralism. Part 2 provides a synoptic treatment of the historical legacy that informs and shapes Orthodoxy's ambivalence towards the ideas and practices of pluralism. Part 3 points to indications of a pluralist dynamic and affinities for pluralism already at work within the Orthodox world,[25] both of which suggest possibilities for a revolutionary shift towards a creative and active contribution by Orthodoxy in a pluralist world.

1. The Greek case: nesting pluralisms and Orthodox exceptionalism

Orthodoxy's encounter with pluralism in Greece has been played out in an environment of nesting pluralisms, on three analytical and operational levels. At the domestic level, democratization since 1974 has meant an expansion and reinforcement of a free, competitive public sphere in Greece.[26] At the regional level, Greece's geographical locus, the Balkans, has produced accelerated – and, importantly, relatively new – tendencies towards ethnic, religious, and generally demographic heterogeneity since the end of the cold war. Simultaneously, Greece's membership in the expanding EU, with the types of pluralization noted earlier, implicates the country in the EU's activities in the globalizing system of world affairs.[27] In short, Orthodoxy's conversation with pluralism in Greece can only be understood within the nested context of the country's position in local, regional and global dynamics of change.[28]

Within the context of nesting pluralisms, the constitutional arrangement regulating relations between the state and religion is the most useful point of departure for analyzing Orthodoxy's engagement with pluralism in Greece. The constitution, after all, establishes the minimum threshold for protecting what Alfred Stepan calls the twin tolerations for religion in a sustainable democracy – that is, religious freedom vis-a-vis the state and religious freedom within the public sphere of civil society.[29] Likewise, the constitution establishes the rules of the game for Orthodoxy's conversation with diverse political, social, economic and cultural currents in Greece. Furthermore, the constitution provides a superb mechanism for evaluating the parameters for religious pluralism that allow for a meaningful analysis of Orthodox Christianity and Greece in broad comparative terms.[30]

Indeed, consideration of Greece's position within the comparative framework of the EU is interesting. A review of the EU landscape reveals an impressive degree of diversity in the constitutional arrangements that regulate the relationship between religion and state.[31] For example, a sampling of EU member-states shows that, as of 1990, Greece, Denmark, Finland, Sweden and the United Kingdom (in England and Scotland, but not in Wales) had either fully or partially established churches.[32] Meanwhile, Germany is a case of a country without an established or prevailing church, but where both Protestantism and Catholicism are recognized as official religions, a status of considerable relevance for citizens' access to social services and, especially, for the provision of public and private education.[33] Finally, the Netherlands is a case of full dis-establishment of religion; according to the legal construct of equal treatment,[34] secular beliefs enjoy equal legal protection as religious beliefs,[35] so that the Dutch constitution allows for public funding for educational, cultural and social-service activities.[36]

Church-state relations

Against the above backdrop, it is evident that Greece is not an outlier vis-a-vis the range of EU constitutional options for regulating relations between state and religion.[37] Similar to many other EU member-states with established churches,[38] Greece has a prevailing religion model of church-state relations according to article 3 of the constitution, which states that the "prevailing religion in Greece is that of the Orthodox Church of Christ".[39] Freedom of religious conscience and practice are protected in article 13 of the constitution, which (identifying "freedom of religious conscience as inviolable") specifies that civil and individual rights are not dependent on an individual's religious conscience, prohibits proselytism and allows for freedom of worship.[40] Based on the prevailing-religion formula, religious instruction in public schools (which are non-denominational and secular) is mandatory for Greek Orthodox students and non-compulsory for non-Orthodox students.

If a synoptic review of the constitutional regulation of religion and state in Greece suggests that the country is not exceptional vis-a-vis a putative EU norm, what accounts for widespread charges of Greek exceptionalism on matters of church-state relations, and more broadly, religious freedom? Scholars such as George Mavrogordatos argue that "contemporary Greece appears oddly anachronistic with respect to [dominant standards for] religious freedom [in the EU]",[41] and Samuel Huntington and William Wallace reiterate the view of Greece as an outlier in terms of Euro-American models of religion and democracy, based on an argumentation that posits intrinsic incompatibility between Orthodox Christianity and pluralist democracy.[42] Meanwhile, journalists such as Helena Smith have noted that "the fracas over [eliminating the religious designation on] the identity cards... proves that liberty and equality, the values that drive democracy, are still in short supply in [Greece]", while Takis Michas has charged that the response of "the immensely popular Archbishop Christodoulos of the Greek Orthodox Church [to the 11 September 2001 terrorist attacks on the USA] underscores that Greece... simply does not share Western values and perceptions".[43] In short, there is an identifiable body of scholarship, journalism and popular writing that posits Orthodoxy as problematic for pluralism and democracy in Greece, and this collective argumentation has made its way into policy discussions about the cultural implications of EU enlargement.[44]

Arguments about Greek and, by extension, Orthodox exceptionalism on issues of democracy and modernity warrant critique, on the basis of theoretical and methodological weaknesses, not to mention empirical oversights.[45] While an extensive discussion of the relevant critical literature is beyond the scope of this presentation, the specifics of those arguments about Orthodoxy's incompatibility with democracy and modernity require careful consideration, as they are useful in problematizing Orthodoxy's encounter with pluralism.

Such consideration necessarily returns to those constitutional articles informed by the concept of the twin tolerations, as these articles have established the framework for freedom of religion and conscience as part of Greece's democratization trajectory.[46] Especially important is article 3, whose provisions deal with the inter-related issues of the legal personality of religions, proselytism and freedom of worship.

Article 3, section 2 of the Greek constitution states:

Every *known* religion (*sic*) is free and the forms of worship thereof shall be practised without any hindrance by the state and under protection of the law. The exercise of worship shall not contravene public order or offend morals. Proselytizing is prohibited.[47]

The 1975 constitution, consistent with all its predecessors, identified only Orthodox Christianity, Islam and Judaism as known religions, or legal persons of public law.[48] It was not until parliament passed legislation in July 1999 that the Catholic Church was extended the recognition under the same legal personality.[49] All other religions are considered legal persons of private law. Regarding proselytism, the constitution imposes criteria of intentionality and method to the general prohibition against proselytism.

Legal issues

The issue of the legal personality of a religion (in particular, the distinction between public and private types of legal personality), as well as the stipulations on public order,[50] have a host of financial and administrative implications for the various religions that operate in Greece, including access to titles to build places of worship, issues of property ownership and inheritance, and taxation,[51] as well as access to legal representation and due process in the judicial system.[52] Meanwhile, the issue of proselytism directly affects the degree of diversity and freedom that defines the operational parameters for religion in the public sphere in Greece.

In short, it is in what Nicos Alivizatos has called "the legal and factual consequences"[53] of the above constitutional provision that it is possible to specify the nature of the ambivalence towards religious pluralism (and associated forms of social, political and cultural difference) that exists in Greece as an Orthodox country.[54] The legal and factual consequences have been played out in the record of litigation, both in Greece's domestic judicial system and at the European Court of Human Rights (ECHR) at Strasbourg, whose jurisdiction Greece has accepted since becoming a signatory nearly two decades ago to the European Convention for the Protection of Human Rights and Fundamental Freedoms.

The body of cases filed at the ECHR by plaintiffs against Greece deals overwhelmingly with charges of human-rights violations and/or discrimination against religious minorities, including minorities located on the spectrum of legal personality noted above, as well as other minorities such as Protestants and Jehovah's Witnesses.[55] In many instances, the appeal to Strasbourg has followed decisions taken in the domestic judicial system in Greece.[56]

The legal and factual consequences of the aforementioned body of case law clearly reflect the gap between a commitment to the formal rubrics of pluralism, on the one hand, and a position of flexibility and expansiveness in the substantive application of those rubrics. This specific type of ambivalence – what can be understood as reliance on the letter of the law, at the expense of interpretation and implementation consistent with the spirit of the law – has been reflected in the predilection of the national courts in Greece towards a particularly narrow interpretation of constitutional rights of religious freedom for minorities.

Also suggestive of the gap between formalism and implementation are the deficiencies in the Greek court system in providing timely access to due process by plaintiffs charging violations of religious human rights, as well as the frequently "excessive length of proceedings [on religious human-rights issues] before its [Greece's] courts".[57] The particularities of the historical relationship between the Orthodox Church and the Greek state both reinforce and reflect the qualitative deficiencies in Orthodoxy's commitment to pluralism in Greece. This church-state relationship enables easy access by church officials to policy-makers in the state bureaucracy and legal system, thereby comparatively privileging Orthodoxy over other religions in Greece. In some instances, ease of access blends into participation by church actors in putatively civil processes, as in the legislative provision that requires the approval by the local Orthodox bishop of building permits for houses of worship for any religion in his territorial jurisdiction; while part of a legal regime formulated to regulate religion according to Greece's national security exigencies during the interwar period, the failure to abrogate the "Metaxas laws"[58] on religion underscores the ambivalence of both the Orthodox Church and the Greek state when it comes to matters of religious pluralism in Greece.

The overweening emphasis on formalism and legalism is, arguably, most pronounced in the domestic interpretation of the prohibition against proselytism, which also has its origins in the Metaxas regime of the 1930s. The large volume of cases dealing with proselytism in Greece brought to the ECHR are driven by plaintiffs' charges that, in practical terms, the Orthodox Church is exempt from the restriction on proselytism.[59] Strasbourg case law has not ruled categorically that the Metaxas laws are incompatible with the European Convention on Human Rights, but the Court has made many rulings that found evidence of the Greek state and the Orthodox Church having used the proselytism prohibition to limit freedom of religion and conscience.

In sum, over-stated claims about Greek and Orthodox exceptionalism vis-a-vis putative EU norms are, nonetheless, instructive in helping to clarify the nature of Orthodoxy's ambivalence towards pluralism in the Greek case: a legalistic and formalistic commitment to religious freedom, at the expense of support for bold legislative and judicial changes designed to expand the content and boundaries of tolerance for religious diversity. Perhaps most striking in the Greek case is the clear evidence that the ambivalence and conflictedness towards pluralism moves well beyond the boundaries of the Orthodox Church and extends to the domain of the state. In this respect, the Freedom House approach of defining countries in terms of dominant religious tradition – or, more specifically, in terms of religious traditions that have exerted a dominant influence on national identity and culture – is especially useful in thinking about Orthodoxy and pluralism in terms of the discrete, but related, components of state, church and national identity.

2. Confining conditions in Orthodoxy's ambivalence towards pluralism

The origins of Orthodoxy's ambivalent, and sometimes defensive, encounter with theories and practices of pluralism can be fruitfully explored in terms of Otto Kirchheimer's concept of confining conditions.[60] Kirchheimer developed his formulation in order to consider the prospects for successful regime change, whereby he posited confining conditions as "the particular social and intellectual conditions present at the birth of these [new] regimes".[61] If one understands Kirchheimer's proposition in terms of those antecedent conditions that have most powerfully determined the particular nature of Orthodoxy's ambivalence towards pluralism, confining conditions must also be recognized as "the conditions that have to be overcome"[62] in order to allow Orthodoxy to move beyond its current ambivalence towards a world whose defining feature is pluralism.

There are three crucial historical legacies, or discernible "traditions or profound collective experiences",[63] that have defined Orthodoxy's ambivalence towards pluralism. It is necessary, although not automatically sufficient, that these three confining conditions be overcome in order to facilitate Orthodoxy's move beyond its ambivalent stance towards pluralism. These three conditions, distinct from, yet related to, one another, are as follows: first, a historical long *duree* in which Orthodox churches, peoples or countries existed in contexts marked by the absence of democracy; second, institutional patterns of dysfunctional ecclesiastical behaviour related to the formal and informal interpenetration of institutions of church and state; and third, conceptions of national (and collective) identity that have been permeated and shaped over centuries by Orthodoxy.[64] A detailed analysis of each of these factors is well beyond the limitations of this presentation, but even a synoptic treatment underscores the powerful, iterative impact of this historical legacy on Orthodoxy's engagement with pluralism.

The absence of democracy

Orthodoxy's historical trajectory has been played out in political contexts that have been, for the most part, either pre-democratic, non-democratic or proto-democratic.[65] The pre-nation-state history of Orthodoxy was marked by experiences of empire that, extending over nearly two millennia, established the foundational perceptions of pluralism. Under the Byzantine empire, the church-state model of *symphonia* involved the (Orthodox) Church in a political project wherein religious pluralism implied the threat of imperial dissolution; under the Ottoman empire, religious pluralism and captivity were interpreted as synonymous by the (Orthodox) Church.[66]

The nation-state experience in the European heartland of Orthodoxy was mainly defined – with the exception of Greece, with its peripatetic and protracted democratization pathway – by the fight to survive under either authoritarian or totalitarian regimes.[67] Since the end of the cold war, Orthodox churches in Europe have evolved largely within the contexts of the still-unfinished democratization experiments of post-communist countries and the well consolidated, democratic regime in Greece. Outside of Europe, the nation-state era for Orthodox churches has been defined in terms of official or unofficial minority status in zones of semi-authoritarianism, such as that stretching from Turkey to the Middle East and the Transcaucasus, or in conflict regions, such as East Africa;[68] in all of the aforementioned spaces, religious and political pluralism have meant either experiences of oppression or threats to survival for Orthodoxy. Indeed, Orthodoxy's only experience in fully consolidated democratic contexts has been restricted, until the 21st century, to Western European, North American and Oceanic countries, in almost all of which Orthodox populations are a minority. Against this broad backdrop, then, the temporal parameters and geographic boundaries of Orthodoxy's participation in democratic regimes have been strikingly circumscribed. In this respect, the long *duree* of history helps to explain Orthodoxy's defensiveness vis-a-vis, and at times pessimism about, the implications of pluralism.

Institutional dysfunctionalities

The second confining condition follows logically from the historical endurance test of Orthodoxy in non-democratic contexts, in the form of important institutional dysfunctionalities in Orthodox ecclesiastical life. These institutional dysfunctionalities can best be characterized as demonstrated tendencies towards hierarchical hegemony, clerical apathy and lay passivity. There is ample evidence that these institutional dysfunctionalities have been significantly shaped by the efforts of the various ecclesiastical strata to adapt to acute operational exigencies whose hallmarks were the Ottoman and communist historical conjunctures.[69] Because the practical consequences of institutional cleavages within Orthodox churches were frequently interpreted within the context of political regimes hostile to Orthodoxy, ecclesiastical survival was privileged over ecclesiastical power struggles. Consequently, power and voice tended to accrue to those ecclesiastical actors – the hierarchy – whose symbolic and material resources were identified with Orthodoxy's survival in non-democratic environments. Furthermore, practical accretions and imbalances of power developed in tandem with an ecclesiastical culture that placed a premium on unity, rather than on the diversity of pluralism.

Interestingly enough, the institutional dysfunctionalities that have been so pronounced in Orthodox churches in non-democratic and newly democratic contexts are also discernible, albeit to a lesser degree and with differing manifestations, in the aforementioned democratic countries with Orthodox minority populations. A plausible explanation for the transnational perpetuation of such institutional tendencies lies in the fact that Orthodox churches established outside the historical heartlands of the Byzantine lands and Russia were founded by populations that migrated from these homelands. As Alexei D. Krindatch has pointed out,

> The patterns of development of Orthodox jurisdictions [and, therefore, institutions] in North America are closely connected with the history of ethnically diverse communities of Orthodox immigrants who came... for various reasons, at different times, and from many countries of Central and Eastern Europe and from the Middle East. Because of this and due to the linkage to the mother churches overseas, the Orthodox jurisdictions in the United States were always affected by the political, social, and religious transformations in the Old World.[70]

Immigration, therefore, helps to account for the initial reiteration, in transnational terms, of the historically rooted institutional dysfunctionalities that inform Orthodoxy's encounter with pluralism in democratic contexts. However, the intense competitiveness that defines religious pluralism in the long-consolidated democracies in North America has produced particularities in the institutional dysfunctionalities of Orthodox churches, given what appears as the admixture of what Mark Stokoe points out as the competing tendencies of Roman Catholic corporate structures, Protestant administrative practices and the immigrant self-signifier of diaspora.[71] The perpetuation of institutional dysfunctionalities at the transnational level bears emphasis not only because of the stickiness of this confining condition but, as will be examined in the concluding section, because of the dynamics for transformation and, therefore, potential resolution of this and other confining conditions on Orthodoxy's ambivalence vis-a-vis pluralism.

The interpenetration of church and state

Finally, related to the long *duree* of history and the above institutional dysfunctionalities is the third confining condition in Orthodoxy's encounter with pluralism, namely, the interpenetration of church and state in both pre-democratic and democratic political contexts. The historical origins of the interpenetration of Orthodox churches and the institutional structures of state lie in the Byzantine *symphonic* model, but were reiterated in the Ottoman *millet* model and, again, in the process of nation-state formation in Europe.[72] Regardless of the diversity of the aforementioned historical conditions and cross-national differences in the legal-constitutional arrangement of relations between Orthodox churches and states, the cause of the interpenetration of church and state was the latter's efforts to instrumentalize Orthodoxy for political purposes of collective-identity construction.

The coupling of church and state for the project of nationalism underscores the logic of the Freedom House construct of Orthodox countries,[73] because the ambivalence towards pluralism is reflected not only in the posture of Orthodox churches, but in the actions of states dealing with changes in their relationship to Orthodox churches under conditions of democracy. For their part, Orthodox churches utilized their political prerogatives to try to monopolize the interpretation and content of the religious dimensions of nationalism. The politicization of Orthodox theology and structures has conditionalized the legitimacy of Orthodox churches, thereby aggravating their ambivalence towards forms of religious, cultural and social pluralism that are the hallmarks of the competitive dynamics of democratization and globalization. The Greek case, again, is instructive in this regard. The continuing, highly contested reconfiguration of church-state relations underway since Greece's transition to democracy in 1974 has shown that legal-constitutional changes imply shifts in the political prerogatives and economic privileges of the Orthodox Church in Greece, vis-a-vis the state, within civil society, and within the three strata of the institutional church itself. Such shifts in the stock of resources of power have been multiplied by

Greece's membership within the EU and associated global networks and structures.

Furthermore, the various strata that constitute the Orthodox Church in Greece have come to understand democratic pluralism as a phenomenon that is intrinsically about competition at the domestic, regional and global levels. In so far as ecclesiastical leaders have come to understand the legitimacy of Orthodoxy as a function of the competitive capacity of the Church of Greece,[74] the reformulation of church-state relations – in Greece since 1974, and in Orthodox countries throughout Europe since the end of the cold war – has forced Orthodox church actors, and particularly the church hierarchy, to re-evaluate their competitive assets. The ambivalence towards pluralism is a reflection of anxiety about the vitality of Orthodoxy's competitive assets, including theological ideas, financial resources, institutional networks and human capital.[75]

By the same token, the policies of the post-1974 Greek state and post-cold war European states in Orthodox countries demonstrate that ambivalence towards pluralism is deeply rooted in state conceptions of legitimacy, as these relate to nationalism and associated domestic and external security issues. Democracy demands that the state meet standards of accountability vis-a-vis and expectations of behaviour by all citizenry. Given their poor record in meeting such standards and expectations in those Orthodox countries that had been part of the state-socialist bloc during the cold war, these states have been slow to give up the legitimating resources (both material and symbolic) accessible through Orthodoxy.[76] Similarly, in Greece, Stavrakakis correctly points out that "most attempts to intervene into issues related to religion, during the 1980s and 1990s, have ended in compromise for fear of alienating practising Orthodox voters",[77] a fact that underscores the recognition by state elites that Orthodoxy has provided legitimation benefits to the state. The willingness of Greek state elites to move fully beyond a religio-cultural conception of nationalism, towards a citizenship-based conception of national identity that grounds state legitimacy firmly in the principles of liberal democracy, has been tested repeatedly in terms of the issue of church-state reconfiguration. Indeed, the state's willingness and capacity to redefine the legal parameters of church-state relations has occurred within the context of a marked shift in the demographic content of the Greek nation, towards diversity and heterogeneity, largely on account of immigration flows from failed states on Greece's borders since the end of the cold war and partly due to the impacts of EU immigration patterns under the Schengen convention.[78] The intersection of the problematic of democracy-building with the challenges of responding to changes in Greece's security environment help to explain the "reluctant and clumsy"[79] efforts of the Greek state in reshaping church-state relations, as well as the continuing effects of the confining condition of church-state interpenetration.

The three confining conditions above are not meant to provide an exhaustive explanation for the origins and various manifestations of Orthodoxy's ambivalence vis-a-vis pluralism. However, in so far as they most effectively capture the historicized nature of such ambivalence, these conditions are central as support for the exploration of Orthodoxy's relationship with pluralism as argued here and, above all, to any inquiry into the possibilities for a transformation in the encounter of Orthodox churches with conditions of pluralism in the 21st century.

3. From ambivalence to resolution: Orthodoxy's changing engagement with pluralism

As an effort to contribute to systematic inquiry into the nature and implications of Orthodoxy's engagement with the ideas, institutions and practices of pluralism, this presentation has made two claims: first, that the nature of Orthodoxy's engagement with pluralism is clearly defined in terms of ambivalence; and second, that the origins of such ambivalence lie in three, inter-related, confining conditions. These claims raise the obvious question of the possibilities for a move beyond ambivalence in Orthodoxy's encounter with pluralism. By way of conclusion, it is logical to offer some concluding observations about indicators of transformation, with theoretical and empirical dimensions, in Orthodoxy's encounter with pluralism. These indicators underscore the importance of democracy in both enabling and challenging Orthodox actors and institutions to overcome the confining conditions noted above and, through the momentum of steady incremental changes, to achieve the kind of revolutionary breakthrough that could alter the path of Orthodoxy's engagement with pluralism in the third millennium.[80]

The indicators of incremental change in each of the confining conditions that have shaped Orthodoxy's encounter with pluralism over the last two millennia must be situated within the tendencies of democratization and globalization that are radically redefining the possibilities for religion as a force in world affairs at the current historical moment. The combined effects of globalization and democratization have created a new operational environment for Orthodoxy, one whose essential feature is pluralism in the form of competition. The unprecedented porousness and flexibility of territorial and cultural boundaries, the renegotiation and redefinition of both material and non-material conceptions of security, and the associated reconsideration of legal-constitutional relations between religion and state, have emerged as intrinsic components of the processes of globalization and democratization, and in every respect imply a competitive, pluralized, operational space for Orthodox ideas, practices and actors.

It is in the responses to the evolving operational environment for religion noted above that one finds indications of incremental changes in Orthodoxy's conception of and response to pluralism. Indeed, the Greek case is instructive, in so far as it underscores the ways in which democracy-building is being interpreted by Orthodox actors as a discursive and practical opportunity for Orthodoxy to engage in conversation, within civil society and with the state. Whether on questions about the reconfiguration of church-state relations through constitutional reform, the designation of religion on national identity cards as an expression of collective identity, or the authenticity of Greece's claim to Europeanness, Orthodoxy has been both subject and object of a series of debates whose parameters are the democratization experience.[81]

Beyond the Greek context, there is significant evidence that Orthodox actors view democracy and globalization as competitive, pluralizing conditions that offer opportunities, rather than simply challenges to Orthodoxy. Debates about the ecclesiastical relationship between Orthodox churches in America and mother churches abroad have been cast increasingly in terms of optimizing the capacity of indigenized Orthodox churches to function successfully in the American religious marketplace,[82] while the Ecumenical Patriarch of Constantinople has identified the realities of pluralism, rooted in virtues of diversity and tolerance, as "the fundamentals for a Christian life"[83] that must be celebrated and commended by Orthodoxy.

In short, the competitive, pluralizing impulses at the core of democratization and globalization have been met by Orthodox actors in ways that suggest a discursive and practical move beyond the long-standing view of pluralism as a threat to Orthodoxy, towards a conception of pluralism as an opportunity for Orthodoxy to renegotiate its position in the contemporary world. Embedded in and consequent to this reconceptualization of pluralism are the signs of incremental change in the institutional dynamics of Orthodox churches. Indeed, some of the most controversial episodes of church-state reform in Greece since 1974 have been informed by contests of power between hierarchical, clerical and lay strata within the Orthodox Church in Greece, as ecclesiastical actors conceived of church-state negotiation as an opportunity to redress institutional dysfunctionalities understood as causal to the Church's marginalization in public life.[84]

Beyond the Greek case, there is especially compelling evidence that the particularities of pluralism at the current historical conjuncture are understood to offer unprecedented opportunities for overcoming institutional constraints and limitations on Orthodoxy's role in the public sphere. Pressures for institutional reorganization have emerged in diverse ecclesiastical contexts. In the Patriarchate of Jerusalem, ethnic tensions between Arab and Greek members of the ecclesiastical structure have been mapped onto an institutional power struggle between, respectively, lay and clerical strata, on the one hand, and hierarchs on the other.[85] Meanwhile, demands for a recalibration of institutional power, through the implementation of conciliar structures rooted in Orthodox theology, have been especially acute within the context of Orthodox churches in America, where "the Orthodox ministry of the laity [has been identified as] a serious and sensitive issue that needs to be studied on a pan-Orthodox and ecumenical level".[86]

In terms of the interpenetration of church-state relations and the associated conflation of religious and political (national) forms of collective identity, there is also interesting evidence of incremental change in the analytical frameworks and, therefore, applied solutions under consideration in countries with both Orthodox majority and minority populations. In particular, the priority of citizenship, as both national and transnational construct, has emerged as a discernible theme in discussions by public intellectuals interested in the links role of Orthodoxy in a globalized world.[87] Indeed, political and cultural elites dealing with Orthodoxy, in Greece and other European countries, have begun to contextualize their discussions about church-state relations within the larger problematic of balancing respect for the religious specificity of national history with a commitment to democratic principles of equality.

In this sense, questions about the tension between religious and civic dimensions of collective identity in Orthodox countries, as explored emblematically in Nikolas Gvosdev's discussion of Orthodoxy and national identity in post-Soviet Russia[88] and in my own work on the marginal role of Orthodoxy in the reiterative formulation of American collective identity,[89] have begun to engage well beyond the intellectual, ecclesiastical and geographic boundaries of Orthodoxy.[90] Similarly, discussions that situate church-state questions within the broader problematic of the crisis of modernity, such as Theodoros Zakas's work on the ontological and political content of the subject,[91] suggest Orthodoxy's turn towards theoretical debates and empirical studies about the possibility of multiple modernities.[92]

The evident reconceptualization of pluralism as an opportunity for Orthodoxy in a world shaped increasingly by processes of globalization and democratization is suggested in the incremental changes in the confining conditions that have accounted for Orthodox churches' ambivalent stance towards pluralism up until the present. Furthermore, the diversity of participants, including public intellectuals, lay and ordained strata, and political and public-policy elites, in reconsidering the implications of pluralism for Orthodoxy points to a possible rupture in Orthodoxy's ambivalent path of engagement with pluralism. However, the degree to which such a rupture occurs, as well as the direction that a path redirection may take, remains an open question. The capacity for Orthodoxy to compress "thoroughgoing or revolutionary changes as distinct from incremental change" in its engagement with pluralism will depend on how Orthodox thinkers and actors draw on and actualize the theological resources of the faith, with its intrinsic affinities for pluralism's principles of tolerance, freedom and equality. In this respect, the outcome of Orthodox churches' struggle to renegotiate their engagement with pluralism will affect the hope for peace in the 21st century, by offering Orthodoxy's contribution to what Richard Falk has called an affirmation of universality simultaneous with a respect for particularities.[93]

NOTES

[1] I am especially grateful to Dr Alexandros K. Kyrou for his thoughtful criticism of several incarnations of this text, and likewise to Dr Andrew Walsh for his comments on the comparative differences amongst and within Orthodox churches in their approaches to pluralism and their conception of democracy.

[2] Studies of what has come to be termed "desecularization", or the various processes and structures that reflect either the survival or revival of religion in conditions of modernity, have proliferated in the social sciences since the last quarter of the 20th century. These studies are preoccupied with explaining the predictive failure and, according to some arguments, the normative weaknesses of the classical thesis of secularization, which equated modernity with secularity conceived in terms of the structural-functional differentiation of state and religion, religious decline, and privatization. Representative works include Peter L. Berger, *The Desecularization of the World: Resurgent Religion and World Politics*, Grand Rapids MI, Eerdmans, 1999; Jose Casanova, *Public Religions in the Modern World*, Chicago, Univ. of Chicago Press, 1994; and Mark Juergensmeyer, *The New Cold War? Religious Nationalism Confronts the Secular State*, Berkeley CA, Univ. of California Press, 1993. Discussions of desecularization have also made their way into popular magazines, such as "Oh, Gods!" in *The Atlantic*, 298.2, Feb. 2002, pp.37-45.

[3] The rush by international relations theorists and practitioners to gain purchase on the role of religion in world affairs, particularly since the terrorist attacks on the United States on 11 September 2001, is understandable in terms of the fact that international relations scholar-practitioners have consistently either under-estimated or overlooked religion as a force for change in international affairs. Readable discussions of changes in this tendency in the academic study of international relations are offered by Scott Thomas, "Taking Religious and Cultural Pluralism Seriously: The Global Resurgence of Religion and the Transformation of International Society", *Millennium: Journal of International Studies,* 29.3, 2000, and Scott Thomas, "The Global Resurgence of Religion and the Study of World Politics", *Millennium: Journal of International Studies,* 24.2, summer 1995.

[4] The most paradigmatic, if over-cited, work in this genre is by Samuel Huntington, *The Clash of Civilizations and the Remaking of World Order*, New York, Simon & Schuster, 1996.

[5] An interesting, provocative exploration of the links between religion and violence is undertaken by Mark Juergensmeyer, *Terror in the Mind of God: The Global Rise of Religious Violence*, Berkeley CA, Univ. of California Press, 2000.

[6] Excellent overviews of this issue from diverse disciplinary and methodological perspectives include Simone Chambers and Will Kymlicka eds, *Alternative Conceptions of Civil Society*, Princeton NJ, Princeton UP, 2001; Johan D. van der Vyver and John Witte, Jr eds, *Religious Human Rights in Global Perspective: Legal Perspectives*, Grand Rapids MI, Eerdmans, 2000; and Paul Weithman, *Religion and the Obligations of Citizenship*, Cambridge, Cambridge UP, 2002.

[7] See notes 1, 3, 4 for details that elucidate this claim.

[8] For a superb treatment of the equation of modernity and, more specifically, assumptions about the secular nature of modernity, with the system of international relations introduced at the peace conference at Westphalia in 1678, see Daniel Philpott, *Revolutions in Sovereignty: How Ideas Shaped Modern International Relations*, Princeton NJ, Princeton UP, 2001. Philpott's arguments are usefully read as companion to works on the possible need to transform the Westphalian system, such as Gene M. Lyons and Michael Mastanduno eds, *Beyond Westphalia? State Sovereignty and International Intervention*, Baltimore, Johns Hopkins UP, 1995; Susanne Hoeber Rudolph and James Piscatori eds, *Transnational Religion and Fading States*, Boulder CO, Westview, 1997; and William H. Swatos ed., *A Future for Religion: New Paradigms for Social Analysis*, London, Sage, 1992. Related explorations of the limitations of a state-centred approach in conceptualizing the relationship between modernity and secularity include Jose Casanova, *Public Religions in the Modern World*, Chicago, Univ. of Chicago Press, 1994; Rudolph and Piscatori eds, *Transnational Religion and Fading States*. In the previous list of representative debates on the survival and/or revival of religion in late 20th century world affairs, Orthodox Christianity is absent, whether in terms of contributions from Orthodox thinkers or as object of analysis and potential theoretical utility.

[9] According to Merriam-Webster Online, pluralism is defined in the following terms: (1) the holding of two or more offices or positions, as benefices, at the same time, (2) the quality or state of being plural, (3a) a theory that there are more than one or more than two kinds of ultimate reality, (b) a theory that reality is composed of a plurality of entities, (4a) a state of society in which members of diverse ethnic, racial, religious, or social groups maintain an autonomous participation in and development of their traditional culture or special interest within the confines of a common civilization, (b) a concept, doctrine, or policy advocating this state. See http://www.m-w.com/cgi-bin/dictionary.

[10] Vassilios N. Makrides, "Byzantium in Contemporary Greece: the Neo-Orthodox Current of Ideas", in David Ricks and Paul Badalino eds, *Byzantium and the Modern Greek Identity*, Aldershot, UK, Ashgate, 1998, p.142. Leading thinkers in the revival of Orthodox studies and, more generally, in the *aggiornamento* of Orthodox theology include Greek Orthodox thinkers such as Savvas Agourides, Nikos Nissiotis, Stelios Ramfos, John Romanides and Christos Yannaras, as well as Russian Orthodox thinkers such as Vladimir Lossky, John Meyendorff and Alexander Schmemman. These authors are prolific, so that, while a meaningful sampling of their works is precluded by space constraints, representative works include Vladimir Lossky, *The Mystical Theology of the Eastern Church*, repr. Crestwood NY, St Vladimir's Seminary Press, 1976; Stelios Ramfos, *Hroniko Enos Kainourgiou Hronou*, Athens, Indiktos, 1996; and Christos Yannaras, *To Prosopo kai O Eros*, Athens, Papazisis, 1976.

[11] A useful note on the lack of systematic social and political theory from an Orthodox perspective is provided by Nikolas K. Gvosdev, *Emperors and Elections: Reconciling the Orthodox Tradition with Modern Politics*, Huntington NY, Troitsa Books, 2000. The disciplinary boundedness to theology and philosophy, and associated distance from political and social theory, is reflected in representative works such as Paul McPartlan, *The Eucharist Makes the Church: Henri de Lubac and John Zizioulas in Dialogue*, Edinburgh, T & T Clark, 1993, and Paul M. Collins, *Trinitarian Theology and the West: Karl Barth, the Cappodocian Fathers, and John Zizioulas*, New York, Oxford UP, 2001. For titles that might fall under the general category of "Orthodox studies", see, for example, Vigen Guroian, *Incarnate Love: Essays in Orthodox Ethics*, Notre Dame IN, Univ. of Notre

Dame Press, 1987; Alexander Schmemman, *Church, World, Mission: Reflections on Orthodoxy in the West*, Crestwood NY, St Vladimir's Seminary Press, 1979.

[12] See notes 8 and 9. English-language work that moves deliberately beyond the disciplinary boundaries of theology, in an effort to engage with the social sciences and humanities, include Nicos C. Alivizatos, "A New Role for the Greek Church?", *Journal of Modern Greek Studies*, 17.1, May 1999; Efterpe Fokas, "Greek Orthodoxy and European Identity", in Achilleas Mitsos and Elias Mossialos eds, *Contemporary Greece and Europe*, Aldershot, UK, Ashgate 2000; P. Kitromilides and Th. Veremis eds, *The Orthodox Church in a Changing World*, Athens, Hellenic Foundation for European and Foreign Policy, 1998; P. Kitromilides and Th. Veremis eds, "Paradigms, Power and Identity: Rediscovering Religion and Regionalizing Europe", *European Journal of Political Research*, 30.2, Sept. 1996; Pedro Ramet ed., *Eastern Christianity and Politics in the Twentieth Century*, Durham NC, Duke UP, 1987; Andrew Walker and Costas Carras eds, *Living Orthodoxy in the Modern World: Orthodox Christianity and Society*, Crestwood NY, St Vladimir's Seminary Press, 2000; John Witte, Jr and Michael Bourdeaux, *Proselytism and Orthodoxy in Russia: The New War for Souls*, Maryknoll NY, Orbis, 1999.

[13] Emmanuel Clapsis, *Orthodoxy in Conversation*, WCC Publications, 2000, p.136.

[14] Emblematic of the voicelessness and seeming marginality of Orthodoxy as a participant in and contributor to pluralism is the complete absence of any mention of Orthodoxy in a book widely discussed in academic and policy circles – Diana Eck, *A New Religious America: How A 'Christian Country' Has Become the World's Most Religiously Diverse Nation*, San Francisco CA, HarperCollins, 2001.

[15] The notion of a global wave of democracy, begun in 1974 and reinforced by the demise of communist regimes in Europe in 1989, is analyzed in qualitative and quantitative terms in Samuel P. Huntington, *The Third Wave: Democratization in the Late Twentieth Century*, Norman OK, Univ. of Oklahoma Press, 1991.

[16] Freedom House, "Freedom in the World 2001-2002", New York, Freedom House Publishing, 2002, www.freedomhouse.org.

[17] According to the survey, Orthodox countries are those which lie in the historic heartland of Orthodoxy, or what Dimitri Obolensky referred to as the Byzantine Commonwealth, in *The Byzantine Commonwealth: Eastern Europe, 500-1453*, London, Phoenix, 1971. Likewise, Orthodox countries are those where any one or a combination of the following features obtain: Orthodox Christians form a majority of the population, Orthodoxy is legally identified as the state religion, Orthodoxy has exercised a formative role on the political and cultural development of the country and Orthodox Christians play a key role in social and governmental affairs. For a discussion of the designation of Orthodox countries as part of the overall methodology employed in the Freedom House survey, see http://www.freedomhouse.org/research/freeworld/2002/methodology.htm.

[18] According to the study, 80 percent of Orthodox countries ranked as free or partly free, which is well within the norm for the overall global record, which identifies 75 percent of the world's countries as free or partly free. See Nikolas K. Gvosdev, "Orthodoxy and Freedom: the Global Picture, 2002", in *Orthodox News*, www.orthodoxnews.com. For individual country rankings, see http://www.freedomhouse.org/research/freeworld/FHSCORES.xls.

[19] For representative works that speak to the ambivalent posture of Orthodox thinkers and, in the Freedom House formulation, Orthodox countries vis-a-vis pluralism, see Dimitris Christopoulos ed., *Nomika Zitimata Thriskeutikis Eterortitas stin Ellada*, Athens, Centre for Research on Minority Groups, 1999; Mient Jan Faber ed., *The Balkans: A Religious Backyard of Europe*, Ravenna, Longo, 1995; Gvosdev, *Emperors and Elections*.

[20] The literature on the pluralist qualities and possibilities of democratic regimes is expansive and highly contentious. For an excellent compendium of the debates on democracy and pluralism, see Seyla Benhabib ed., *Democracy and Difference: Contesting the Boundaries of the Political*, Princeton NJ, Princeton UP, 1996; Will Kymlicka, *Multicultural Citizenship*, Oxford, Oxford UP, 1995; and Chantal Mouffe ed., *Dimensions of Radical Democracy: Pluralism, Citizenship, Community*, London, Verso, 1992.

[21] The definition of democracy remains a vexing theoretical task and practical challenge. For representative discussions on the procedural minima on which most scholars of democra-

tic theory concur, see Robert A. Dahl, *Democracy and its Critics*, New Haven CT, Yale UP, 1989; David Held, *Models of Democracy* , Stanford CA, Stanford UP, 1987; Huntington, *The Third Wave;* Gary Marks and Larry Diamond eds, *Reexamining Democracy: Essays in Honor of Seymour Martin Lipset*, London, Sage, 1992. Well-developed discussions about the taxonomy of phases of democratization are available in Richard Gunther, P. Nikiforos Diamandouros and Hans-Jurgen Puhle eds, *The Politics of Democratic Consolidation: Southern Europe in Comparative Perspective*, Baltimore, Johns Hopkins UP, 1995; and Juan J. Linz and Alfred Stepan eds, *Problems of Democratic Transition and Consolidation: Southern Europe, South America, and Post-Communist Europe*, Baltimore, Johns Hopkins UP, 1996.

[22] Stephanos Stavros, "Human Rights in Greece: Twelve Years of Supervision from Strasbourg", *Journal of Modern Greek Studies*, 17.1, 1999, p.10.

[23] The religious pluralization of the EU has resulted from the conflation of three tendencies, namely, the EU enlargement process, along with demographic patterns within the EU and, emigration / immigration patterns affecting the EU. There is an expanding literature that explores the reiterative mapping of Europe in terms of compatible versus incompatible cultural and geographic cartographies, and the religious diversification and pluralization of Europe has emerged as an analytic salient in such research. For representative works, many of which place particular emphasis on the links between state, religion and implications for democracy, see G. Delanty, *Inventing Europe: Idea, Identity, Reality*, London, Macmillan, 1995; Efterpe Fokas, "Greek Orthodoxy and European Identity", in Mitsos and Mossialos eds, *Contemporary Europe*; A. Hofert and A. Salvatore eds, *Between Europe and Islam: Shaping Modernity in Transcultural Space*, Brussels, Presses Interuniversitaires Européennes, 2000; B. Nelson, D. Roberts and W. Veit eds, *The Idea of Europe: Problems of National and Transnational Identity*, Oxford, Berg, 2000; Elizabeth Prodromou, "Paradigms, Power, and Identity: Rediscovering Orthodoxy and Regionalizing Europe", *European Journal of Political Research*, 30.2, 1996; C. Shore, "Inventing the 'People's Europe': Critical Approaches to European Community 'Cultural Policy'", *Man*, 28.4, 1993; H. Vermeulen ed., *Immigrant Policy for a Multicultural Society: A Comparative Study of Integration, Language, and Religious Policy in Five Western European Countries*, Brussels, Migration Policy Group, 1995/6; and William Wallace, *The Transformation of Europe*, London, Royal Institute of International Affairs, 1990.

[24] An excellent synopsis – and subsequent critique – of the conventional sociological conceptualization of secularity is the basis of the classical thesis of secularization is provided by Jose Casanova, *Public Religions in the Modern World*. Accordingly, secularity is a condition defined by the structural-functional separation of the domains of the profane (state) and the sacred (religion), the decline of traditional religious beliefs and behaviours, and the relegation of religion to the private sphere.

[25] I use the term "Orthodox space" as a loose designation including Orthodox churches, organizations and actors around the world.

[26] Greece's democratization project began with the transition from authoritarianism in 1974, and has continued with successful consolidation in the 1980s into the persistence of democracy. For a representative and comparative discussion of the qualitative preoccupations of the persistence phase of democratization in Greece, see Gunther, Diamandouros and Puhle, *op. cit.*

[27] Globalization itself remains a highly contested term amongst scholars and policy-makers, particularly since the processes of globalization are not easily specified as dependent versus independent variables. However, there is little disagreement that globalization has meant expanding networks of interdependence at the sub-national, interstate, and transnational levels, and there is increasing convergence amongst scholars and policy-makers that globalization poses significant challenges to democracy. For interesting debates on the nature and consequences of globalization, see John Beynon and David Dunkerly eds, *Globalization: The Reader*, New York, Routledge, 2002; David Held, *Democracy and the Global Order: From the Modern State to Cosmopolitan Governance*, Stanford CA, Stanford UP, 1995; David Held, Anthony McGrew, David Goldblatt and Jonathan Perraton, *Global Transformations: Politics, Economics and Culture*, Stanford CA, Stanford UP, 1999; Noreena Hertz, *The Silent Takeover: Globalization and the Death of Democracy*, New York, Free Press, 2002; Mary Kaldor, *New and Old Wars: Organized Violence in a*

Global Era, Stanford CA, Stanford UP, 1999; James H. Mittelman, *The Globalization Syndrome: Transformation and Resistance*, Princeton NJ, Princeton UP, 2000; Marc F. Plattner and Aleksander Smolar eds, *Globalization, Power and Democracy*, Baltimore, Johns Hopkins UP, 2000; and Joseph P. Stiglitz, *Globalization and Its Discontents*, New York, Norton, 2002.

[28] Comprehensive overviews useful in contextualizing Greece's democratization trajectory within the context of local, regional, and global dynamics of change include Mitsos and Mossialos, *op. cit.*, as well as Graham Allison and Kalypso Nicolaides eds, *The Greek Paradox: Promise versus Performance*, Cambridge MA, MIT Press, 1997.

[29] For a compelling exploration of the centrality of the twin tolerations with regard to the role of religion in democratic regimes, see Alfred Stepan, "Religion, Democracy, and the 'Twin Tolerations'", *Journal of Democracy*, 11.4, Oct. 2000. He argues that sustainable democracy requires the establishment and consistent protection by constitutional and legal methods of twin tolerations, which are as follows: first, "religious institutions should not have constitutionally privileged prerogatives that allow them to mandate public policy to democratically elected governments", and second, "at the same time, individuals and religious communities... must have complete freedom to worship privately[, as well as]... to advance their values publicly in civil society,... as long as their actions do not impinge negatively on the liberties of other citizens or violate democracy and the law". See *ibid.*, pp.39-40.

[30] Stepan's logic of focusing on constitutional provisions as the optimal mechanism, or at the very least, the necessary point of departure for an inquiry into the relationship between religion and democracy, see note 27, is echoed by Stavros in "Human Rights in Greece". Stavros expands the focus on the constitutional provisions dealing with religious freedom to include an evaluation of the judicial system as it affects religious freedom as a fundamental human right.

[31] Useful treatments of the pluralism in EU approaches to the regulation of relations between the state and religion are offered by Stephen V. Monsma and J. Christopher Soper, *The Challenge of Pluralism: Church and State in Five Democracies*, and W. Cole Durham, "Perspectives on Religious Liberty: A Comparative Framework", in van der Vyver and Witte, Jr eds, *Religious Human Rights*.

[32] For example, in the case of the Church of England, what Monsma and Soper term a partial establishment model is built on a "cultural assumption that religion has a public function to perform... [so that]... it is appropriate for the state and church to cooperate in achieving common goals". Monsma and Soper, *The Challenge of Pluralism*, p.121. Similar assumptions inform the rights and functions accorded to the Presbyterian Church of Scotland. In both cases, the church carries out coronations "and all other state functions where prayer or religious exercises may be required and the Church of England is the only religious body with reserved seats in the House of Lords". *Ibid.*, p.129.

[33] The German models means that German citizens seeking access to sacramental, educational, and in some cases social service benefits from these two churches must accept to pay a 9 percent surcharge "on their tax bill in the form of a Church tax and thereby become a member of the church". See Stepan, "Religion, Democracy, and the 'Twin Tolerations'", p.41. Germany has four types of schools at the kindergarten-through-twelve level: inter-denominational Christian, Catholic of Protestant confessional public schools, secular (i.e. non-denominational) public schools, and private confessional schools. This typology is consistent with article 7, section 3 of Germany's constitution, which declares that religious instruction shall be part of the curriculum in state schools, except for secular (i.e. non-denominational) schools, and which allows that churches, rather than the state, control the content of the religious curriculum and parents determine of which classes their children will take.

[34] For an excellent, readable treatment of the equal treatment approach to regulation of state-religion relations, see Stephen V. Monsma and J. Christopher Soper eds, *Equal Treatment of Religion in a Pluralistic Society*, Grand Rapids MI, Eerdmans 1998.

[35] The Dutch constitution was revised in 1983 in line with the concept of equal treatment. See Monsma and Soper, p.63.

[36] The Dutch approach to religious dis-establishment has developed the relationship between religion and the state in a manner consistent with the pillarized, consociational structures

of the country's democracy. Based on the country's historical experience, the four pillars in the Netherlands are Reformed, Catholic, socialist and neutral (liberal).

[37] Stepan, "Religion, Democracy, and the 'Twin Tolerations'", p.54.

[38] A very useful discussion that places Greece's prevailing religion formula within a comparative EU context is provided by Nicos C. Alivizatos, "A New Role for the Greek Church?"

[39] There is a serious debate over the interpretation of the term "prevailing religion" in Greece, although amongst the four major interpretations now part of the battle of the jurisprudents, the most commonly accepted is that the prevailing religion is that which represents the overwhelming majority of the population. For a very useful summary of the competing interpretations of prevailing religion, see Kyriakos N. Kyriazopoulos, "The 'Prevailing Religion' in Greece: Its Meaning and Implications", *Journal of Church and State*, 43.3, summer 2001. Furthermore, precise numbers on the portion of the country's population that is Greek Orthodox are difficult to obtain, with disagreements deriving from problems in identifying citizens and permanent residents, inaccuracies in and lack of consensus over counting criteria, and methodological disagreements over treatment of nominal and secular (lapsed) Orthodox Christians. Nonetheless, most reliable sources agree that between 94 percent and 97 percent of the population identify, at least nominally, with the Orthodox Christian faith. See http://www.state.gov/g/drl/rls/irf/2001/5653.htm for the State Department's International Religious Freedom Report (2001) for Greece.

[40] Kyriazopoulos: "The 'Prevailing Religion' in Greece", p.512.

[41] George Th. Mavrogordatos, "Church–State Relations in the Greek Orthodox Case", paper presented to the workshop on "Church and State in Europe", Copenhagen, Denmark: ECPR Joint Sessions, 14-19 April 2000, p.2.

[42] The works by Huntington, Wallace and Mavrogordatos are representative of a broader collection of social science literature and popular writings that use Greece as evidence of Orthodoxy's intrinsic incompatibility with democracy and modernity. For paradigmatic works, as well as useful bibliographic resources, see Samuel Huntington, *Foreign Affairs* articles; Victoria Clark, *Why Angels Fall: A Journey Through Orthodox Europe from Byzantium to Kosovo*, New York, St Martin's, 2000; and William Wallace, "From Twelve to Twenty Four? The Challenges to the EC Posed by the Revolutions in Eastern Europe", in Colin Crouch and David Marquand eds, *Towards Greater Europe? A Continent Without an Iron Curtain*, Cambridge MA, Blackwell, 1992.

[43] See Helena Smith, "The Ayatollah Replaces Zorba", *New Statesman*, 21 Aug. 2000; and Takis Michas, *Wall Street Journal of Europe*, 23 Oct. 2001.

[44] For a summary review of the links between policy discussions, academic debates, and media coverage on Orthodoxy and democracy, see Prodromou, "Paradigms, Power, and Identity".

[45] Some representative criticisms of the weaknesses in what can best be termed as a civilizational approach to Orthodoxy and modernity and, most specifically, Orthodoxy and modernity, include Fokas, "Greek Orthodoxy and European Identity"; Gvosdev, *Emperors and Elections*; Aristotle Papademetriou, "Byzantium, Orthodoxy and Democracy", unpublished paper at the conference on "Orthodoxy and Democracy: Challenges after the Cold War", New York, Columbia University, the Harriman Institute, 2001; Elizabeth Prodromou, "Orthodoxia, Ellinismos kai Politiki Koultoura sti Sighroni Ellada: Kainouries Prossegisei h Esoterikopoiisi Dedomenon Paradigmaton?" in *Elliniki Epitheorisi Politikis Epistimis*, 5, April 1995; and Stepan, "Religion, Democracy, and the 'Twin Tolerations'".

[46] The full text of the Greek constitution is available at http://www.mfa.gr/syntagma. Articles relevant to the broad basket of rights encompassing freedom of religion and conscience include articles 3, 4 and 13. These constitutional articles also deal with those freedoms and liberties that are increasingly associated with the still evolving concept of religious human rights. Excellent discussions of the conceptual and methodological challenges associated with the definition and study of religious human rights can be found in, respectively, Durham, "Perspectives on Religious Liberty", and David Little, "Studying 'Religious Human Rights': Methodological Foundations", in Van der Vyver and Witte eds, *Religious Human Rights*.

[47] Kyriazopoulos, p.512.

[48] For a discussion of this legal designation, see Section II: Status of Religious Freedom, in the Oct. 2001 *International Religious Freedom Report* of the US Department of State, http://www.state.gov/g/drl/rls/irf/2001/index.cfm?docid=5653.

[49] *Ibid.*

[50] The stipulation on public order has its roots in the pre-second world war environment in Greece, as do several other constitutional provisions – most notably, those dealing with national military service and consciencious-objector status. Thoughtful treatments of the historical context in which those articles were developed, as well as their impact on religious human rights in post-1974 Greece, is provided in Alivizatos, "A New Role for the Greek Church"; Christos L. Rozakis, "The International Protection of Minorities"; and Stephanos Stavros, "Citizenship and the Protection of Minorities", in Kevin Featherstone and Kostas Ifantis eds, *Greece in a Changing Europe: Between European Integration and Balkan Disintegration*, Manchester, Manchester UP, 1996; and Stavros, "Human Rights in Greece".

[51] Designation as a legal personality of public law places religious actors under effective non-profit status for purposes of taxation, while designation as a legal personality of private law regulates religious actors according to taxation provisions for corporations, according to the provisions of the Greek civil code.

[52] Members of minority religious groups that are classified as private entities also cannot be represented in court as religious entities and cannot will or inherit property as a religious entity. See Stavros, "Human Rights in Greece".

[53] Alivizatos, "A New Role for the Greek Church?", p.26.

[54] Once again, I use the Freedom House formulation.

[55] A useful, if at times polemical, treatment of litigation in the ECHR against Greece in cases dealing with rights of religious freedom for religious minorities is provided by John Warwick Mongtomery, *The Repression of Evangelism in Greece: European Litigation vis-à-vis a Closed Religious Establishment*, Lanham MD, Univ. Press of America, 2001.

[56] For a comprehensive list of religious minorities in Greece, see the State Department's International Religious Freedom Report (2001) for Greece, at http://www.state.gov/g/drl/rls/irf/2001/5653.htm.

[57] Stavrou, "Human Rights in Greece", p.5. According to Stavrou, Greece has been condemned on numerous occasions by the Strasbourg organs for the protracted nature of court proceedings on matters of religious human rights, but he cautions that the temporal parameters are "not particularly surprising for a country whose courts are chronically understaffed and usually lack the necessary technical resources". *Ibid.*

[58] Stavrou provides a useful distillation of the historical origins of and contemporary problems deriving from the Metaxas laws dealing with religion. See *op. cit.* Useful alternative sources on the same point include Alivizatos, "A New Role for the Orthodox Church?" and Adamantia Pollis, "Greek National Identity: Religious Minorities, Rights, and European Norms", *Journal of Modern Greek Studies,* 10, 1992.

[59] Indeed, critics charge that although the constitution provision against proselytism apparently includes the established religion, the Church of Greece is able to proselytize in many indirect forms that function collectively to limit diversity and freedom of operation by religion in the public sphere in Greece. Religious education has been a domain of particular contestation over the interpretation and application of the proselytism prohibition. Religious education in public schools is available to, and compulsory for, only Orthodox students. See Alivizatos, "A New Role for the Greek Church?", pp.27-30.

[60] See Otto Kirchheimer, "Confining Conditions and Revolutionary Breakthroughs", *American Political Science Review,* 59, Dec. 1965, pp.964-74.

[61] *Ibid.*, p.964.

[62] *Ibid.*

[63] Geoffrey Pridham, "Confining Conditions and Breaking with the Past: Historical Legacies and Political Learning in Transitions to Democracy", *Democratization,* 7.2, summer 2000, p.40.

[64] My thinking on the permeation of culture by religion, particularly in terms of the penetration of national cultures and conceptions of national identity by Orthodoxy, has been

deeply affected by the work of Daniele Hervieu-Leger on secularity, Catholicism and French culture. For a representative treatment of her work on the subject see Daniele Hervieu-Leger, "The Twofold Limit of the Notion of Secularization", in Linda Woodhead ed., with Paul Heelas and David Martin, *Peter Berger and the Study of Religion,* New York, Routledge, 2001.

[65] For an especially critical and pessimistic interpretation of the confining conditions rooted in Orthodoxy's historical evolution, see Michael Radu, "Religion in World Affairs: The Burden of Eastern Orthodoxy", *Journal of International Affairs,* 10.10, winter 1997.

[66] An excellent reference collection for the impacts of the Byzantine and Ottoman imperial regimes on Orthodoxy's perception of pluralism includes the following sources: Obolensky, *The Byzantine Commonwealth*; George Ostrogorsky, *History of the Byzantine State,* Oxford, Blackwell, 1968; and Steven Runciman, *The Great Church in Captivity: A Study of the Patriarchate of Constantinople from the Eve of the Turkish Conquest to the Greek War of Independence,* Cambridge, Cambridge UP, 1968.

[67] A useful, synoptic reference for the experience of Orthodox churches under communist rule in Europe is found in Pedro Ramet ed., *Eastern Christianity and Politics in the Twentieth Century,* Durham NC, Duke UP, 1988.

[68] For a policy-making summary of the various types of oppression and threat confronted by Orthodox minority populations in the aforementioned regions and zones, see the International Religious Freedom Reports by the US Department of State. For the 2002 reports, see http://www.state.gov/g/drl/rls/irf/2002/.

[69] See Ramet ed., *Eastern Christianity.*

[70] Alexei D. Krindatch, "Orthodox (Eastern Christian) Churches in the United States at the Beginning of a New Millennium: Questions of Nature, Identity, and Mission", *Journal for the Scientific Study of Religion,* 41.3, 2002, p.543.

[71] Mark Stokoe, in collaboration with Leonid Kishkovsky, *Orthodox Christians in North America, 1794-1994,* Syosset NY, Orthodox Christian Publications Center, 1995. There is an interesting and growing literature on Orthodoxy in North America, one of whose primary considerations is the sources of and possibilities for resolution of the institutional dysfunctionalities that have marked Orthodox churches' experiences in the New World. Emblematic of the diversity of this literature are sources including *ibid.*, as well as Alexander Boglepov, *Toward an American Orthodox Church: The Establishment of an Autocephalous Orthodox Church,* Crestwood NY, St Vladimir's Seminary Press, 2001; John H. Erickson, *Orthodox Christians in America,* Oxford, Oxford UP, 1999; Theodore Saloutos, "The Greek Orthodox Church in the United States", *International Migration Review,* 7.4, 1973; and Stephen J. Sfekas and George E. Matsoukas eds, *Project for Orthodox Renewal: Seven Studies of Key Issues Facing Orthodox Christians in America,* Chicago, Orthodox Christian Laity, Inc., 1993.

[72] I have summarized the origins and implications of church–state interpenetration for Orthodoxy's performance in democratic contexts in Elizabeth H. Prodromou, "Toward an Understanding of Eastern Orthodoxy and Democracy Building in the Post-Cold War Balkans", *Mediterranean Quarterly,* 5.2, spring 1994, pp.126-35.

[73] See note 16 above.

[74] I have written about this elsewhere, in "Democratization and Religious Transformation in Greece: An Underappreciated Theoretical and Empirical Primer", in Walker and Carras eds., *Living Orthodoxy in the Modern World.*

[75] The conception of pluralism and, especially, democracy as a phenomenon that both produces and derives from pluralism, has been intrinsic to efforts by Orthodox churches in the United States – as well as recent debates about the best strategies – to engage with a public sphere that can easily be characterized as a religious free market. See Leonidas C. Contos, *2001: The Church in Crisis,* Brookline MA, Holy Cross Orthodox Press, 2001; and Sfekas and Matsoukas eds, *Project for Orthodox Renewal.*

[76] See Prodromou, "Toward an Understanding", for a summary discussion and some standard references on the use of Orthodox churches for state legitimation purposes under communist regimes in Eastern Europe.

[77] Yannis Stavrakakis, "Religion and Populism: Reflections on the 'Politicized' Discourse of the Greek Church", discussion paper no. 7, London, The Hellenic Observatory and the European Institute at the London School of Economics and Political Science, 2002, p.14.

[78] For an abbreviated definition and discussion of the Schengen (Agreement) Convention, see http://www.europa.eu.int/scadplus/leg/en/cig/g4000s.htm#s1. For a broad treatment of changes in Greece's demographic profile and, therefore, in the content of the nation, see John S. Koliopoulos and Thanos M. Veremis, *Greece: The Modern Sequal, from 1831 to the Present*, New York, New York UP, 2002; see esp. pp.207-209, but more broadly, pp.200-76.

[79] Stavrakakis, "Religion and Populism", p.21.

[80] I draw here from Kirchheimer's discussion of the differences between incremental change and revolutionary breakthroughs in "Confining Conditions", pp.964-68.

[81] There is a sizeable literature on each of these three issues. Representative treatments include Fokas, "Greek Orthodoxy and European Identity"; P. Kitromilides, N. Kokosalakis, A. Manitakis, P. Nikolakopoulos, C. Yannaras and S. Zoumboulakis, "Church and Nation: A Discussion", in *Synaxi*, 2001; and Ioannis Konidaris, *O Nomos 1700/1987 kai H Porsfati Krisi stis Sheseis Ekklesias kai Politeias*, Athens, Ant. N. Sakkoulas Publishing, 1988.

[82] See the discussions in Sfekas and Matsoukas, *op. cit.* as well as the autobiographic treatment of this issue in Frank Schaeffer, *Dancing Alone: The Quest for Orthodox Faith in the Age of False Reason*, Brookline MA, Holy Cross Orthodox Press, 1994.

[83] "Statement of His All Holiness Ecumenical Patriarch Bartholomew for the Forthcoming United Nations Durban World Conference against Racism, Racial Discrimination, Xenophobia, and Related Intolerance", at http://fmpro.goarch.org/patriarchate/.

[84] Summary treatments of these episodes are available in Ioannis M. Konidaris, *H Diapali Nomimotitas kai Kanonikotitas kai H Themeliwsi tis Enarmoisews Tous*, Athens, Ant. N. Sakkoulas Publishing, 1994, pp.31-35 and 156-93; Prodromou, "Democratization and Religious Transformation in Greece"; and Yiorgios Tsananas, "*Éxasfalish Proupothesewn apo thn Plevra tis Ekklhsias gi thn Anabathmish twn Shesewn tis me thn Politeia, Thewrish Theologikh,* " in *Dikaio kai Politikh,* 15, 1988.

[85] See for example, "The Task Force to Support the Orthodox Christians in the Patriarchate of Jerusalem", at http://www.orthodoxnews.com/stories/gmm070699a.shtml.

[86] Clapsis, "The Laity in the Orthodox Church", in *Orthodoxy in Conversation*, p.80.

[87] *Pagkosmiopoiisi & Orthodoxia. Keimena Ergasias11*, Athens, *Instituto Dimokratias Konstantinos Karamanlis*, March 2001.

[88] Nikolas K. Gvosdev, "The New Party Card? Orthodoxy and the Search for Post-Soviet Russian Identity", in *Problems of Post-Communism*, Nov.-Dec. 2000, pp.29-38.

[89] Elizabeth H. Prodromou, "Religious Pluralism in 21st-Century America: Problematizing the Implications for Orthodox Christianity". Unpublished paper, presented at the 14th annual conference of the Orthodox Christian Laity, on "Orthodox Christian Diversity in America and the Unity We Need", Chicago, Oct. 2001.

[90] Research dealing with the (lack of) impact of Orthodoxy on the religious dimensions of national identity and, more specifically, on the penetration by religion of national cultures, have comparative implications for, amongst others, cases such as Daniele Hervieu-Leger's inquiry into the "permeation of culture by Catholicism in a country [that is, France,] where reference to the beliefs, norms and values imparted by the Roman Catholic Church is negligible". See Hiervieu-Leger, "The Twofold Limit", p.122.

[91] Theodoros I. Zakas, *H Ekeipsh tou Ypokeimenou: H Krisi tis Neoterikotitas kai H Ellinikh Paradosi*, Athens, Domos, 1996.

[92] A comprehensive overview of the discussion of multiple modernities as theoretical construct and empirical reality is provided in *Daedalus*, "Multiple Modernities", 129.1, winter 2000.

[93] Richard Falk, "Religion and Globalization", see pp. 67-76 of this volume.

The Challenge of a Global World

EMMANUEL CLAPSIS

At the eighth assembly of the World Council of Churches in Harare (1998), the Christian churches recognized the pervasiveness of globalization as an economic, cultural, political, ethical and ecological issue in the life of the world. They asked themselves, "How do we live our faith in the context of globalization?"[1] Since Harare, the challenge of globalization has assumed central importance in the efforts of the Christian churches to live and witness the gospel in the modern world.[2] Orthodox theologians, usually reluctant to address issues of social structures, have begun to reflect on the challenge of globalization and its cultural and social implications. Metropolitan Kirill of Smolensk, in an article published in *The Ecumenical Review*, described the socio-economic and cultural context in which the Christian churches find themselves:

> The epoch of mono-ethnic and mono-confessional states is fading into the past... the world has become open, diffusive and interpenetrating. How should Christians, and the communities which identify themselves as Christian, respond to this challenge of our time?[3]

If the epoch of mono-ethnic, mono-confessional and mono-cultural states is fading into the past, Christian churches – which refuse to succumb to privatization and aim to transform the life of the world – must find new ways to witness their faith in the public life of the modern world. This quest reflects their desire to contribute their insights towards the formation of the common good without misrecognizing or suppressing the multiple cultural, ethnic and religious others who also wish to contribute to the formation of the common good.[4] Orthodox theologians and church hierarchs repeatedly have acknowledged that Orthodoxy promotes a culture of justice and peace that respects the inviolate and God-given gift of freedom, which allows people to affirm and cultivate their particularity.[5] They have recognized that, in the context of an open and mutually penetrable world, isolationism and withdrawal from public life for the purpose of preserving religious and ethnic purity is a betrayal of the Church's mission. This presentation is a contribution to a process of understanding the challenges that the global world is posing to the Christian churches.

Questioning the world

Questioning the ostensibly unquestionable premises of our way life is, as Zygmunt Bauman has stated, "the most urgent of the services we owe to our fellow humans and ourselves".[6] The cost of not questioning either the performance of the Church in the world or the rapidly changing structures of the world is human suffering and alienation. If the Christian churches are not merely agencies of cultural legitimation, there is an inescapable need for them to participate in the process of questioning the modern world, raising the right questions, and developing the right pastoral strategies towards the creation of a just and peaceful world.

The recognition that late modernity, through its rationality and technological advances, has transformed the world into a highly mobile and interconnected society obliges the churches to reassess their operating premises for their active presence and witness in the world, and more specifically in the public realm. The churches, in responding to this rapid cultural change, may either:

1) choose to stay in the past, refusing to be critically engaged with the evolving social structures and cultures;
2) resort to militant opposition against apparent or imaginary threats by the emerging cultural realities perceived as hostile to the purity and the integrity of their identity;
3) accept passively the emerging globalized world by abandoning their particular identity and becoming agents of cultural change; or
4) engage critically the emerging social structures and cultures in light of the irreducible elements of their religious identity.

Their responses will reflect, if not fear and uncertainty in face of uncharted social realities, their particular understandings of culture and how the gospel and the essential and irreducible elements of the churches' faith and life relate to cultures, either in the past or in the present.

From the study of the gospel and culture(s), we have learned that there are no particular cultures void of God's presence, and that all cultures are in need of redemption because of the pervasive presence of evil in each of them.[7] The pervasiveness of evil in God's good creation is a warning that in every cultural movement, while the grace and providence of God is actively present, evil is also there working against God's cause and his love for the world. Furthermore, the eschatological nature of the Christian faith does not allow the churches to be identified completely with, to ignore, or to reject uncritically any human cultures. It is also important to note at the beginning the operating view of culture that I have adopted in this presentation. I maintain that a culture provides the system and the frameworks of meaning which serve both to interpret the world and to provide guidance for living in the world. A culture embodies beliefs, values, attitudes and rules of behaviour. It includes the rituals, the artifacts and the symbolization that bind people to communities and enable them collectively to embody and express their histories and values. From this perspective, religion is the central expression of every human culture and it contributes to cultural vitality and growth.

Conflicts of identity

The present resurgence of identity politics is a sign that identities are in crisis because of cultural changes and transition. Robert J.C. Young has noted, "Fixity of identity is only sought in situations of instability and disruption, of conflict and change."[8] Thus, it is not surprising that identity should be an issue at a time marked by the pressures of globalization. An identity is the people's source of meaning and experience. It arises out of the process of the construction of meaning on the basis of cultural attributes, which attain priority over other sources of meaning. Multiple identities generate multiple meanings and they are a continuous source of stress and conflict.

Manuel Castells[9] deciphers three forms and processes of identity-building in the modern world. First, the "Legitimizing Identity", which is introduced by the dominant institutions of a society to extend and rationalize their domination vis-a-vis social actors. Second, the "Resistance Identity", which is generated by those actors who are in devalued positions or conditions, and/or are stigmatized by the logic of domination. Such people, through the crafting of their resistance identity, are building trenches of resistance and survival on the basis of principles different from, or in opposition to, those permeating the institutions of society. And third, the "Project Identity" by which social actors, on the basis of whichever cultural materials are available to them, build a new identity that redefines their position in society and, by so doing, seek the overall transformation of social structures. Social conflicts naturally arise from the simultaneous presence of these three different identity-building processes within us and in the world. Those who operate with an essentialist view of culture and identity inevitably view changing social realities as a threat to their identity, and they adopt attitudes of exclusion often associated with violence and suppression of the multiple others. Those, however, who perceive culture and identity as historical constructs adopt a much broader understanding of cultural change, provided that the distribution of power and resources in the new socio-economic order which such change may bring about is relatively equitable or serves their interests.

It is my contention that, through the distinctions that Manuel Castells has provided, it is possible to illuminate the social dynamics of the complicated structure and processes of identity construction in any modern society, and even in the life of the Church. For my purpose, in this presentation, it is enough to note that our faithfulness to the Christian gospel demands that we recognize the pre-eminence of the Project Identity over the other two forms and processes of identity formation. Cultures as essential and imaginary historical constructs will be forever matters of contestation in the context of a pluralistic world. However, in every culture there is an essential element of particularity, which is embodied and communally expressed through those symbols, artifacts and rituals that reflect historical circumstances, needs and challenges. The exaltation of a particular culture must not become an excuse to ignore the structures of domination that operate in all cultures. This process of discernment and critical appreciation of all cultural identities is, and will continue to be, a highly contested and complex matter.

In what follows, I will attempt to converse with social scientists in my quest to understand the "global world" which the advances of late modernity are creating in an irreversible and intractable manner. This conversation reflects my strong conviction that theologians should ground their moral judgments in sound social scientific analysis. I am aware of the contested nature of any social analysis, and the difficulties of relating social analysis to theological reflection, but to continue to speak about the world with carelessness and ignorance is, in my judgment, irresponsible and leads the churches, at least in the public sphere, into a state of irrelevance. This presentation is only a modest attempt to contribute to such a dialogue for understanding the world as it is presently experienced.

Globalization: the social structural context of late modernity

Since the early 1990s the notion of globalization has been used extensively to refer to and describe a multidimensional socio-economic and cultural process that has brought forth a new world order. Some of its most salient characteristics are the global diffusion of democratic institutions and practices, the intensification of patterns of worldwide economic, financial, technological and ecological interdependence, and the weakening of state sovereignty. The roots of the complex and multidimensional phenomenon that we call globalization are simultaneously cultural, economic and political. In the process of trying to understand what globalization is, J. Rosenau proclaims that the world has entered a "historical breakpoint" in which "present premises and understandings of history's dynamics must be treated as conceptual jails".[10] Globalization has become the notion, the concept, or the key idea by which we understand the transition of human society into the third millennium.[11]

Globalization, because of its complexity as a process and its wide use as a concept, has assumed multiple meanings. A helpful description of the dynamics of globalization is provided by Antony McGrew:

> Globalization refers to the multiplicity of linkages and interconnections that transcend the nation-state (and by implication the societies) which make up the modern world system. It defines a process through which events, decisions and activities in one part of the world can come to have significant consequences for individual and communities in quite distant parts of the globe. Nowadays, goods, capital, people, knowledge, images, communications, crime, culture, pollutants, drugs, fashions and beliefs all readily flow across territorial boundaries. Transnational networks, social movements and relationships are extensive in virtually all areas of human activity from the academic to the sexual. Moreover, the existence of global systems of trade, finance and production binds together in very complicated ways the prosperity and fate of households, communities, and nations across the globe.[12]

This complex multiplicity of linkages and interconnections of globalization creates new social structures and ways in which nations and states, as well as religious, ethnic and racial communities, interact and constitute a society:

> Globalization involves the systematic inter-relationship of all the individual social ties that are established on the planet. In a fully globalized context, no given relationship or set of relationships can remain isolated or bounded. Each is linked to all others and is systematically affected by them.[13]

Globalization increases the inclusiveness and the unification of human societies by relativizing the multiple communal and personal identities by which particular communities and people give meaning to their existence. This relativization results from the inevitable linkage and connectivity that all social, political, racial, religious and ethnic communities have with one another, and which all of them share with the greater unity of the human family. In some instances those cultural, ethnic, racial and religious communities may feel that their own particularity is at risk, and become hostile towards the multiple others with whom they inhabit the same social space.

In describing current socio-economic and cultural processes, globalization must be recognized as ambivalent in nature. It is both potentially good for humanity and a possible social disaster of staggering proportions. The process of globalization is contingent and dialectical in nature, in the sense of embracing contradictory dynamics, unevenly experienced across time and space. Anthony Giddens explicitly acknowledges that globalization "is a dialectical process" because it does not bring about "a generalized set of changes acting in a uniform direction but consists in mutually opposed tendencies".[14] Globalization simultaneously universalizes while it particularizes. It intensifies homogenization as well as differentiation. It integrates as well as fragments, it centralizes as well as decentralizes, and it juxtaposes as well as syncretizes. The inherent contradictions of globalization defy the master-oppositions between inside and outside, friends and enemies, and good and evil, by which we order the life of the world and our life in the world. It belongs to the category of "undecidables". According to Zygmut Bauman, "Oppositions enable knowledge and action; undecidables paralyze. They brutally expose the fragility of the most secure of separations. They bring the outside into the inside, and poison the comfort of order with suspicion and chaos."[15]

The churches seem to have difficulty accepting the ambivalence of globalization. They seem to have adopted the bifurcation of "good or evil", "inside and outside", "friendly and adversarial" which seem to have been surpassed in the ending of the modern period. In the world of choice, liberation and alienation, order and disorder, meaning and meaninglessness are inextricably connected. They are the reverse sides of the same coin. As Peter Berger states: "To want the first without the second is one of the recurring fantasies of the modern revolutionary imagination; to perceive the second without the first is the Achilles' heel of virtually all conservative viewpoints."[16] Contingency breeds multiple possibilities that cause anxiety, uncertainty and disorder. Yet from another perspective, as Bauman states, "the unsteadiness, softness and pliability of things may also trigger ambition and resolve: one can make things better than they are, and need not settle for what there is since no verdict of nature is final, no resistance of reality is unbreakable".[17]

These responses are legitimate expressions of the globalized world. The churches, in their responses to globalization, must move beyond the bifurcation of reality into good and evil and recognize that in the created world good and evil simultaneously may coexist and differentially operate in all social realities and processes. This compels the churches to develop the skills of discernment that presuppose a recognition of the complexities and the ambivalences of social realities and the need to constantly assess them from a theological perspective. In other words, the churches, in their theological witness in the public realm, aim to lessen the evil and suffering that the world in its present conditions generates without pretending that their actions are in every instance a reflection of God's intentions for the world.

One may wonder whether the universal aspects of the Church's faith will contribute towards the development of a just, peaceful and relational world or will be a source of exclusion, suppression of difference and violence? Will the apparent or imaginary threats that the multiple others pose to the churches' cultural and religious particularity lead them to adopt hostile and violent attitudes against the multiple others? I believe that the Orthodox Church, by giving primary emphasis to the universal aspects of the Christian gospel, the doctrine of creation, the work of the Holy Spirit in the world, and the cosmic significance of the eucharist, can and should contribute to the creation of a culture of peace.

One of the most crucial tasks of the churches in the globalized world is to generate, sustain and enhance what the social scientists call "social capital".[18] Social capital "refers to connections among individuals – social networks and the norms of reciprocity and trustworthiness that arise from them".[19] Of course, social capital is generated by many civic organizations, family ties, and ethnic, racial or other friendly connections, but as Robert Putnam emphasizes, "faith communities in which people worship together are arguably the single most important repository of social capital".[20] The churches generate human solidarity not only through their beliefs but also through the social ties which they embody: "Connectedness, not merely faith, is responsible for the beneficence of church people... religious involvement is certainly associated with greater attention to the needs of our brothers and sisters".[21]

Some forms of social capital are, by choice or necessity, inward looking, and they tend to reinforce exclusive identities and form homogeneous groups. They offer emotional as well as material benefits to individuals who have chosen for their own advantage to be connected to the wider community. Other forms of social capital are outward looking and encompass people across diverse social cleavages. The former category, which may be termed "bonding social capital", is good for under-girding specific reciprocity and mobilizing solidarity. The latter category, which may be termed "bridging social capital", can generate broader identities and reciprocity, whereas bonding social capital bolsters our narrower selves. Bridging networks, in contrast, are better for linkage to external assets and for information diffusion. Christian spirituality needs to integrate bonding and bridging social capital by connecting spiritual enlightenment, personal peace and illumination with social involvement and solidarity with God's creation and the whole human family. The churches need to move beyond the spiritualized, privatized interpretations of faith which are so pervasive, and which do not readily lead to engagement with social, economic and political realities.

Homogenization versus heterogenization

Another aspect of globalization that creates anxiety and becomes a challenge for the churches is the cultural implications of globalization. Will globalization homogenize all cultures and impose the hegemony of American consumerist culture and American values as they are projected by Hollywood, news coverage and MTV? The idea and dream of a global culture has been espoused in the past and in the present by many religious communities, political ideologies, nations and empires. It was understood in the past, as it is perceived now: as promise and threat, as dream and nightmare. A particular culture, nation, race or empire may have placed itself at the centre of things and declared itself to be for all intents and purposes "the world". Whoever opposed or did not conform to their reading of "reality" was misrecognized, suppressed, liquidated or ignored.

At the eighth assembly of the World Council of Churches in Harare, the Christian churches together recognized globalization as an "inescapable fact of life" and acknowledged the need to study its dynamics:

> Christians and churches should reflect on the challenge of globalization from a faith perspective and therefore resist the unilateral domination of economic and cultural globalization. The search for alternative options to the present economic system and the realization of effective political limitations and corrections to the process of globalization and its implications are urgently needed.[22]

The Christian churches feared that globalization is eroding democratic governance and that it exacerbates inequality and injustice. They repudiated the kind of community that globalization creates and the anthropology that it advances: "The vision behind globalization is a competing vision of the *oikoumene*, the unity of humankind and of the whole inhabited earth." It is grounded in an anthropological reduction that views "human beings as individuals rather than persons in community, as essentially competitive rather than cooperative, as consumerist and materialist rather than spiritual".

The Orthodox churches, through the Ecumenical Patriarch Bartholomew, have also expressed similar views. In a speech delivered at the annual Davos meeting of the World Economic Forum in 1999, the Ecumenical Patriarch stated that the Christian Church envisions and generates another form of globalization that he called "spiritual ecumenicity". In his view, Christian ecumenicity differs substantially from globalization. The former is based on love for one's brother and sister and respects the human person, whom it seeks also to serve. The latter is primarily motivated by the desire to enlarge the market and to merge different cultures into a new, singular one, in accordance with the convictions of those who are in a position to influence the worldwide public. The Patriarch insisted that globalization as a means of making humanity homogeneous, of influencing the masses and bringing about a single, unified and unique mode of thought, cannot be accepted. The Archbishop of Athens, Christodoulos, argued that globalization leads to "a common vision and outlook based on the choices of the powerful" that removes people from "local traditions, religions, languages, forms of expression" and leads them towards the construction of a new age where none of these will be distinguishable. Globalization is identified with syncretism, the merging of religions, cultures and traditions that have existed in history.[23]

In the view of Patriarch Bartholomew and Archbishop Christodoulos, globalization has become a cultural phenomenon. The market seems to have changed from an exchange mechanism to a medium of a new culture. It imposes its way of thinking and acting, and stamps its scale of values upon behaviour. The question that arises from such remarks is whether globalization leads indeed to homogenization, the collapse of all local cultures into a global culture and, furthermore, whether the homogenized global culture really advances the interests of economic capital in economically, politically and technologically powerful nations or empires. This view is often referred as "McDonaldization", and it entails the notion that the irresistible forces of sameness, standardization and bureaucratic rationality are crushing difference and variety.[24] This homogenized global culture is projected as the American culture of consumerism that serves the needs of the purveyors of neo-liberal capitalism.

Is it plausible to claim that a single hegemonic "homogenized" global culture is emerging? The most obvious evidence of this claim is the "convergence" and standardization evident in cultural goods around the world. Certain styles, brands, tastes and practices in clothing, food, music, film, television and architecture now have global currency, and they can be found virtually anywhere in the world. They are signs of the emerging global culture that serves the needs of economic capital and reduces humanity to a commodity of consumption.[25] But does this distribution and presence of uniform cultural goods actually signify anything other than the power of some capitalist firms to command wide markets around the world? When we assume that the global presence of their goods is itself a token of convergence towards a capitalist monoculture, we utilize a rather impoverished concept of culture – one that reduces culture to its material goods. The argument of cultural imperialism can only be advanced if interaction with these cultural goods penetrates deeply into the way in which people construct their "phenomenal world" and make sense of their lives. The problem with the cultural imperialism argument is that it merely assumes such penetration. It makes a leap of inference from a simple presence of cultural goods to the attribution of deeper cultural or ideological effects. Movement between cultural and geographical areas always involves interpretation, translation, mutation, adaptation and "indigenization" as the receiving culture brings its own cultural resources to bear, in dialectical fashion, upon "cultural imports".

The argument that globalization promotes a particular way of life that favours the interests of economic capital is strong among those who notice the commodification of culture. There can be little doubt that a large proportion of cultural practices in modernity have become commodified – turned into things which are bought and sold. The activity of shopping has become in Western societies one of the most popular cultural practices. The shopping element is structured into almost any contemporary leisure activity. Of course, this is merely a problem for the most affluent parts of the world. For the populations of the third world, the routine consumer experience remains much less seductive. Members of these populations are primarily preoccupied with the daily and weekly struggle to make ends meet on a tight family budget.

Social scientists, while they recognize the homogenizing force of globalization, point out that, simultaneous with this force, we have the resurgence of particular cultures, which use globalization's new means of communication to assert themselves and to resist the impact of homogenization in their context. For Roland Robertson, this homogenization-versus-heterogenization dispute is the core feature of globalization, the process that universalizes the particular and particularizes the universal. In globalization, we experience trends that simultaneously promote sameness and difference. Anthony Giddens, in his influential book *The Consequences of Modernity*, defines globalization as "the intensification of worldwide social relations which link distant localities in such a way that local happenings are shaped by events occurring many miles away and vice versa".[26] This complex connectivity means that, in the globalized world, all local cultures are connected with one another and that, in a broad sense, their complex connectivity can be described as a world culture.

Yet, globalization creates a network of cultures and does not lead to a single culture that embraces everyone on earth and replaces the diversity of cultural systems that have flourished up to now.[27] This, however, does not mean that globalization is sensitive to the need to maintain cultural differences and resist cultural domination. Globalization is an uneven process, far more complex than can be grasped in the single story of the unilinear advance of Western culture. We can superficially advance and embrace the thesis of homogenization only by ignoring the complexity, reflexivity and sheer recalcitrance of actual, particular cultural responses to modernity.

Our belief that globalization will not lead to a unified global culture in any conventional sense does not mean that national cultures are likely to remain significant poles of cultural identification for the foreseeable future. The style of cultural experience and identification is bound to be affected by the complex and multiform inter-relations, penetration and cultural mutations that characterize globalization. In this process, different and highly complex identities are developing, and different modes of cultural identification are arising. All particular cultures and identities in a globalized world are involved in a highly complex and dialectical process of reconfiguring themselves in conversation with the multiple others, as ideas and cultural forms invade their living space. In that process a new cosmopolitan culture may emerge and at the same time a "class of civilizations" may burst out, since particular cultures may oppose, misrecognize, suppress and colonize others less powerful and rich in economic, political, social and technological capital.

De-territorialization: the cultural conditions of globalization

John Tomlinson, in his important book *Globalization and Culture*, suggests that globalization fundamentally transforms the relationship between the places we inhabit and our cultural practices, experiences and identities.[28] The sociologist Zygmunt Bauman, reflecting on this matter, states that perhaps the last quarter of the 20th century "will go down in history as the Great War of Independence from Space".[29] Social relationships in the pre-modern world were primarily face-to-face inter-actions, but with the advances of modernity, social relationships were freed from the constrictions of locality.

The compression of space and time that modern communication technology has promoted does not mean that locality is not important for the creation and the sustenance of human culture, experience and identity, but it makes possible the effect of distant social forces and processes upon all localities. We continue to live in familiar and comforting localities, but the distant others have invaded our space and, thus, we live in an ambivalent cultural setting which generates uncertainty and power-lessness.

In such a context, the homeliness of the local community erodes.[30] The impact of distant forces may have direct effects on people's immediate material condition and environment. For example, European Union regulations may impact (positively or negatively) on local people and communities. People experiencing the impact of such events – on their jobs, their mortgage payments or savings – are of course liable to feel generally more insecure in planning their lives and less confident in their national government's ability to control events. The way that distant events are "delivered" to our homes by globalized media technologies contributes to a loss of cultural certainty. Being informed implies having available a range of perspectives on events beyond that of one's "home culture". Regardless of whether the experience of different events may contribute to a cosmopolitan cultural disposition, it also represents a loss of cultural certainty. It threatens the existential "comfort" involved in having the world "out there" presented to us from the point of unchallenged national or local perspectives.

The increasing traffic between cultures suggests that the dissolution of the link between culture and place is accompanied by an intermingling of disembedded cultural practices producing new hybrid forms of culture. Hybridity is the mingling of cultures from different territorial locations. The idea of hybridization captures the general phenomenon of cultural mixing which is unquestionably increasing with the advance of globalization, and which describes the sort of new cultural identifications that may be emerging in the transnational cultural space. The complex transmutations of cultural practices and forms as they pass rapidly and effortlessly across national boundaries through a transnational cultural economy provide perhaps a model for what a future "globalized popular culture" may turn out to be. Such a "globalized popular culture" certainly will be different in character from the integrating, "essentializing" nature of national cultures, and looser in texture, more protean, and relatively indifferent to the maintenance of sharp discriminations of cultural origins and belonging.

This emerging social reality generates anxiety for the Christian churches since they are striving to maintain their particular identity faithful to God's revelation as it was understood, lived and communicated through them. The intermingling of cultures acutely raises the problem of syncretism as an unavoidable social reality, which affects the reconstruction of all identities – personal, communal, religious and cultural – in the globalized world. Syncretism has been understood to be identical with betrayal of the Christian faith. It signifies the harmonization of Christianity with its environment at any cost. Once we recognize the need for the Christian Church to connect itself with its immediate historical environment, history will teach us that in the process of communicating the gospel in different cultural settings, there are continuous disagreements and lack of clarity as to what constitutes authentic and inauthentic inculturation of the Christian faith.

It is important to remember that the Church has evolved in history by embracing elements from other cultures and religions, but it has also resisted the incorporation or acceptance of certain elements from other cultures, religious faiths and philosophies. Robert Schreiter suggests that "syncretism" can be a useful term to describe the formation of religious identity in the present world, but with the explicit understanding that, at times, the new identity under examination will be in accord with, and will even enrich, the religious tradition. At other times, it will not be in accord, and may threaten the religious tradition, and so it must be rejected. In the context of globalization, it is unavoidable that the identities of religious communities will evolve. The crucial issue that the churches should grapple with is how identities are constructed and what theological criteria we use to ascertain the quality of the constructed identities. As Schreiter states:

> The meaning of the term "syncretism" will no doubt remain a contested issue, and for many will continue to bear a negative connotation. And it deserves to be contested, for it is about nothing less than the faithful transmittal of the word that God has entrusted to us. At the same time, a better understanding of the complexity of intercultural communication, of the struggles for human and Christian cultural identity today, and an appreciation of the manifold, faithful ways in which Christianity has already manifested itself in history should ease our anxieties to some degree. They should make us more generous in listening to our brothers and sisters, more circumspect in how we speak, and always conscious of the treasures we bear in vessels of clay.[31]

Economic globalization and the churches

Who partakes of globalized culture and who is excluded from it? The impact of distant events on locality is uneven and highly differentiated from locality to locality. What appears as globalization for some means localization for others; signalling a new freedom for some, while upon many others it descends as an uninvited and cruel fate. Thus, the uses of time and space are sharply differentiated, as well as differentiating. Being local in a globalizing world is a sign of social deprivation and degradation. The discomfort of localized existence is compounded by the fact that, with public spaces removed beyond the reaches of localized life, localities are losing their meaning-generating and meaning-negotiating capacity. They are increasingly dependent on sense-giving and interpreting actions, which they do not control.[32] As Bauman illustrates,

> The mobility acquired by "people who invest" means the new, indeed unprecedented, disconnection of power from obligations: duties towards employees, but also towards the younger and weaker, towards yet unborn generations, and towards the self-production of the living conditions of all. In short, it indicates freedom from the duty to contribute to daily life and the perpetuation of the community.[33]

He further reminds us that, in the global world, "capital can always move away to more peaceful sites if the engagement with 'otherness' requires a costly application of force or tiresome negotiations".[34]

Most of the objections raised against globalization focus upon its economic aspects and the international institutions that have written the rules which mandate or push things like the liberalization of capital markets (i.e., the elimination of the rules and regulations in many developing countries which are designed to stabilize the flows of volatile money into and out of the country). The main thrust of economic globalization, according to Barry K. Gills, aims at the creation of a situation in which private capital and "the market" alone determine the restructuring of economic, political and cultural life, making alternative values or institutions subordinate.[35] Rather than capital and the "economy" being embedded in society and harnessed to serve social ends, the "economy" becomes the master of society and of all within it, and society exists to serve the ends of capital and its need for self-expansion:

> As states compete for the favours of transnationally mobile capital, the "race to the bottom" threatens to increase the rate of exploitation of labour at a global scale. The deregulation of finance and decentring of production contribute to the destabilization of national societies and their political frameworks. As state capacity decreases, the structural power of capital increases, as do social and class conflicts. All states and societies seem under pressure to make ever greater concessions to capital, including greater capital mobility, flexibilization of labour, lower social burdens and higher (indirect) social subsidies for capital, the upshot of which is a redistribution of wealth from labour to capital. All states are potentially vulnerable to sudden capital movement, whether by productive or "speculative" capital.[36]

According to Joseph E. Stiglitz, the winner of the 2001 Nobel Prize in economics, the free-market ideology, as it has been adopted by the IMF and the World Bank since the 1980s, has produced ambivalent social and economic results.[37] In some instances it has promoted economic growth and democratization, but in others it has created economic disruption, income inequality and job insecurity, which lead to decreased growth and more social conflict.[38] A great divide between the "haves" and the "have-nots" has left increasing numbers in the third world in dire poverty, living on less than $1 per day. Despite repeated promises of poverty reduction made over the last decade of the 20th century, the number of people living in poverty has actually increased by almost 100 million. In 1990, 2.718 billion people were living on less than $2 per day; in 1998, the number of poor living on less than $2 per day was estimated at 2.801 billion. Almost half of these people live on less than $1per day.[39] Economic globalization is blamed for the increasing poverty around the world, and the heightened sense of vulnerability and insecurity which people experience in intensely mobile modern societies.

Stiglitz, in his remarkable book *Globalization and Its Discontents*, gives some explanation of the causes of inequality that economic globalization seems to have generated. He argues that capital market liberalization has been pushed despite the fact that there is no evidence showing that it spurs economic growth. Quite the contrary, free-market ideology has been followed by increased misery, high unemployment, insecurity, social unrest and chaos. In his view, what is wrong in the current state of globalization can be turned around. For Stiglitz, the root of the problem is that the complex process of globalization has created

> a system that might be called global governance without global government, one in which few institutions – the World Bank, the IMF, the WTO – and a few players – the finance, commerce, and trade ministries, closely linked to certain financial and commercial interests – dominate the scene, but in which many of those affected by their decisions are left almost voiceless.

He believes that,

> It's time to change some of the rules governing the international economic order, to think once again about how decisions get made at the international level – in whose interests – and to place less emphasis on ideology and to look more on what works... There is an enormous cost to continuing global instability. Globalization can be reshaped, and when it is, when it is properly, fairly run, with all countries having a voice in policies affecting them, there is a possibility that it will help create a new global economy in which growth is not only more sustainable and less volatile but the fruits of this growth are more equitably shared.[40]

The staggering statistics of increased poverty and social inequality that the World Bank has provided us elevates social inequality as one of the central moral issues of our times. While it is difficult for a theologian or for the churches to make a judgment on matters of economics, it is important to insist upon the socially contested and historically open nature of all forms of political and economic ideologies, "globalization" foremost among them. In addition, disapproval and critique of the "free-market ideology" must be grounded, not upon ideological prejudice against it, but on its empirical performance.

Christian churches, along with many other civil organizations, have expressed strong opinions against the performance of economic globalization and the ideology of the "free market". The World Council of Churches in its preliminary assessments of globalization has focused its attention on the fallacies and the injustices that the "free market" ideology has generated.[41] Ecumenical Patriarch Bartholomew, at the 1999 annual Davos meeting of the World Economic Forum, expressed the objections of the Orthodox Church against the injustices of economic globalization:

> Globalization tends to evolve as a means of expanding economic dominance of the financial giants over poor nations and people. It proves to be a new vision for some and a new threat for others; a vision which promises much to a few and very little to many; a vision impressive to some extent in its conception and in its realization.[42]

For the Orthodox Church, economic progress is morally justifiable only when all the members of the global community participate in it and benefit from it. Pope John Paul II, in his address to the members of the Foundation for "Ethics and Economics", admitted that globalization may provide great possibilities for economic growth and production but "it does not in itself guarantee a fair distribution of goods among the citizens of different countries".[43] He suggests that,

> To give positive bearings to developing globalization, a deep commitment to building a "globalization of solidarity" is needed by means of a new culture, new norms and new institutions at national and international levels. In particular, it will be necessary to intensify the collaboration between politics and the economy, to launch specific projects to safeguard those who might become the victims of the globalization process throughout the world.

Similar positions have been taken to a greater extent by the World Alliance of Reformed Churches (WARC) and the Lutheran World Federation[44] which have undertaken specific study projects on globalization in their quest to develop the pastoral strategies of their churches on this complex but very important issue.

There is an emerging ecumenical consensus about the need to address the injustices and the suffering that economic globalization generates. The churches, through the World Council of Churches and through the witness of their specific traditions, participate in the search for alternative visions to economic globalization. The Justice, Peace and Creation committee of the WCC, meeting in Potsdam, Germany, in January 2001, adopted a policy on economic globalization. It stated that its work on this matter should be built upon the strength of existing initiatives by churches, ecumenical groups and social movements, support their cooperation, and encourage them to take action and form alliances with other partners in civil society working on issues pertinent to globalization.[45]

The general, as well as the unique, contributions of the churches in the movement of resistance against the perils of economic globalization may be clear to some churches, but not to others. The churches do not endanger their particularity if they participate in "movements from below" that aspire to minimize violence, to maximize economic well-being, to realize social and political justice, and to uphold environmental quality. The tactics and the priorities of such movements of resistance, because of their global scope, combined with the unevenness of economic and political conditions will, as Richard Falk indicates, be diverse, adapted to local, national and regional circumstances.[46] Such movements of resistance, from an Orthodox perspective, must not only provide opportunities for the structural transformation of the world in a fragmentary way, but they also should be grounded in, and motivated by, a new vision of what it means to be a human person in a globalized world.

NOTES

[1] Diane Kessler ed., *Together on the Way: Official Report of the Eighth Assembly of the World Council of Churches*, WCC Publications, 1999, p.183.

[2] For sociological and theological reflections and insights on globalization see: Roland Robertson, *Globalization: Social Theory and Global Culture*, London, Sage, 1992; Jon Sobrino and Felix Wilfred eds, *Globalization and Its Victims*, London, SCM Press, 2001; Anna L. Peterson, Manuel A. Vasquez and Philip J. Williams eds, *Christianity, Social Change, and Globalization in the Americas*, New Brunswick, Rutgers UP, 2001; Max L. Stackhouse and Peter J. Paris eds, *God and Globalization* vol. 1, *Religion and the Powers of the Common Life*, Harrisburg PA, Trinity, 2000; Max L. Stackhouse and Don S. Browning, *God and Globalization* vol. 2, *The Spirit and the Modern Authorities*, Harrisburg PA, Trinity, 2001; Max L.Stackhouse and Diane B. Obenchain, *God and Globalization*, vol. 3, *Christ and the Dominion of Civilizations*, Harrisburg PA, Trinity, 2002; Cynthia D. Moe-Lobeda, *Healing a Broken World: Globalization and God*, Minneapolis, Fortress, 2002; Richard Falk, *Religion and Humane Global Governance*, New York, Palgrave, 2001; Hans Küng, *A Global Ethic for Global Politics and Economics*, New York and Oxford, Oxford UP, 1998; Hans Küng ed., *Yes to a Global Ethic*, New York, Continuum, 1996; Lisa Sowle Cahill, "Toward Global Ethics", *Theological Studies* 63, 2002, pp.324-44; Thomas R. Kopfensteiner, "Globalization and the Autonomy of Moral Reasoning: An Essay in Fundamental Moral Theology", *Theological Studies* 44, 1993, pp.485ff.; Richard Marzheuser, "Globalization and Catholicity: Two Expressions of One Ecclesiology", *Journal of Ecumenical Studies* 32, 1995, pp.179-93. Simon Coleman, "Charismatic Christianity and the Dilemmas of Globalization", *Religion* 28, 1998, pp.245-56; John B. Cobb, "Can a Globalized Society be Sustainable?," *Dialog* 36, 1997, pp.7-16; R.C. Abraham, "Globalization:

A Gospel and Culture Perspective", *International Review of Mission*, 85, 1996, pp.85-92; T. Howland Sanks, "Globalization and the Church's Social Mission", *Theological Studies*, 60, 1999, pp.625-51; William T. Cavanaugh, "The World in a Wafer: A Geography of the Eucharist as Resistance to Globalization", *Modern Theology*, 15, 1999, pp.181-96; David L. Schindler, "Homelessness and the Modern Condition: The Family, Community, and the Global Economy", *Communio*, 27, 2000, pp.411-30; June O'Connor, "Making a Case for the Common Good in Global Economy: the United Nations Human Development Reports 1990-2001", *Journal of Religious Ethics*, 30, 2002, pp.157-73; Douglas A. Hicks, "Thinking globally: making sense of a shrinking world", *Christian Century*, 118, 2001, pp.14-17; George M. Thomas, "Religion in Global Civil Society", *Sociology of Religion*, 62, 2001, pp.515-33; Jose Casanova, "Religion and Globalization at the Turn of the Millennium", *Sociology of Religion*, 62, 2001, pp.415-50; Tevita Banivanua and Donal McIlraith, "Globalization", *Pacific Journal of Theology*, 24, 2000, pp.1-108; Michael Ignatieff, "The Big Story: What Is the Moral Meaning of Globalization?", *Religion and Values in Public Life* (Harvard Divinity Bulletin) 7, winter-spring 1999, p.3.

[3] Metropolitan Kirill of Smolensk and Kaliningrad, "The Orthodox Church in the Face of World Integration: The Relation between Traditional and Liberal Values", *The Ecumenical Review*, 53/4, 2001, p.479.

[4] I have attempted to address this challenge in my book *Orthodoxy in Conversation: Orthodox Ecumenical Engagements*, WCC Publications/Brookline MA, Holy Cross Orthodox Press, 2000, pp.127-50.

[5] Archbishop Anastasios of Albania, *Παγκοσμιότητα και Ορθδοξία*, Athens, Akritas, 2001; Georgios Mantzarides, *Παγκοσμιοποίηση και Παγκοσμιότητα – Χίμαιρα και Αλήθεια*, Thessalonike, P. Pournara, 2001; Christodoulos Archbishop of Athens and all Greece, *Rooting of Joy and Hope: The Word and the Role of Orthodoxy in the European Union*, Athens, Synodal Committee for Matters Pertaining to the Media, Information and Public Relations, 2001; Institute Konstantinos Karamanlis, *Παγκοσμιοποίηση και Ορθοδοξία*, Athens, 2001; Constantinos Vas. Zorbas, *Δοκίμια για την Παγκοσμιοποίηση*, Katerine, Tertios, 1999.

[6] Zygmunt Bauman, *Globalization: The Human Consequences*, New York, Columbia UP, 1998, p.5.

[7] H. Richard Niebuhr, *Christ and Culture*, New York, Harper Torchbooks, 1951; Kathryn Tanner, *Theories of Culture: A New Agenda for Theology*, Minneapolis, Fortress, 1977.

[8] Robert J.C. Young, *Colonial Desire: Hybridity in Theory, Culture and Race*, London, Routledge, 1995, p.4.

[9] Manuel Castells, *The Information Age: Economy, Society and Culture – The Power of Identity*, vol. 2, Oxford, Blackwell, 1997, pp.6-12.

[10] J. Rosenau, *Turbulence in World Politics*, Brighton, Harvester Wheatsheaf, 1990, p.5.

[11] Malcolm Waters, *Globalization*, London, Routledge, 1995, p.1.

[12] Antony McGrew, "A Global Society", in Stuart Hall, David Held, and Tony McGrew eds, *Modernity and Its Future*, Cambridge, Polity, 1996, p.66. See also: Malcolm Waters, *Globalization*, London, Routledge, 1995; David Held, Antony McGrew, David Goldblatt and Jonathan Perraton, *Global Transformations: Politics, Economics and Culture*, Cambridge, Polity, 1999; Mike Featherstone ed., *Global Culture: Nationalism, Globalization, and Modernity*, London, Sage, 1990; Robertson, *Globalization: Social Theory and Global Culture*; Jonathan Friedman, *Cultural Identity and Global Process*, London, Sage, 1994; Fredric Jameson and Masao Miyoshi eds, *The Cultures of Globalization*, Durham NC, Duke UP, 1998; Frank J. Lechner and John Boli, *The Globalization Reader*, Oxford, Blackwell, 2000; Thomas L. Friedman, *The Lexus and the Olive Tree*, New York, Anchor, 2000; Andrew Hurrel and Ngaire Woods eds, *Inequality, Globalization, and World Politics*, New York, Oxford UP, 2000; Marc F. Plattner and Aleksander Smolar eds, *Globalization, Power, and Democracy*, Baltimore and London, Johns Hopkins UP, 2000; Kostas Vergopoulos, *Παγκοσμιοποίηση η Μεγάλη Χίμαιρα*, Athens, A.A. Livani, 1999.

[13] Malcolm Waters, *Globalization*, London, Routledge, 1995, p.15. For a description of how globalization is reshaping human lives see Anthony Giddens, *Runaway World*, New York, Routledge, 2000.

[14] Anthony Giddens, *The Consequences of Modernity*, Cambridge, Polity, 1990, p.64.

[15] Zygmunt Bauman, "Modernity and Ambivalence", in Featherstone ed., *Global Culture:* p.146. See also his monograph *Modernity and Ambivalence*, New York, Cornell UP, 1991.

[16] Peter Berger, *The Heretical Imperative*, New York, Anchor / Doubleday, 1979, p.23.

[17] Zygmunt Bauman, "Identity in the Globalizing World", in *idem, The Individualized Society*, Cambridge, Polity, 2001, p.141.

[18] Partha Dasgupta, Ismail Serageldin eds, *Social Capital: A Multifaceted Perspective*, Washington DC, World Bank, 2000.

[19] Robert D. Putnam, *Bowling Alone: The Collapse and the Revival of American Community*, New York, Simon & Schuster, 2000, p.19.

[20] *Ibid.*, p.66.

[21] *Ibid.*, p.67.

[22] Kessler ed., *Together on the Way*, p.183.

[23] Christodoulos Archbishop of Athens and all Greece, *Rooting of Joy and Hope*, 2001, p.14.

[24] Benjamin Barber, *Jihad vs. McWorld*, New York, Times Books, 1995. Many sociologists and anthropologists have observed that the spread of McDonald's fast-food restaurants as well as various brand-name goods and services sold and distributed on a worldwide basis involves subtle differences from one country to another. James L. Watson, *Golden Arches East: McDonald's in East Asia*, Stanford CA, Stanford UP, 1997; John Tomlinson, *Cultural Imperialism?*, Baltimore, Johns Hopkins UP, 1991.

[25] "The cultural-ideological project of global capitalism is to persuade people to consume above their 'biological needs' in order to perpetuate the accumulation of capital for private profit; in other words, to ensure that the global capital system goes on forever. The culture-ideology of consumerism proclaims, literally, that the meaning of life is to be found in things that we possess. To consume, therefore, is to be fully alive, and to remain fully alive we must continuously consume." Leslie Sklair, "Social Movements and Capitalism", in Jameson and Miyoshi eds, *The Cultures of Globalization*, p.269.

[26] Giddens, *The Consequences of Modernity*, p.64.

[27] Ulf Hannerz, "Cosmopolitans and Locals in World Culture", in Featherstone ed., *Global Culture*, p.237.

[28] John Tomlinson, *Globalization and Culture*, Chicago, Univ. of Chicago Press, 1999, p.106.

[29] Bauman, *Globalization: The Human Consequences*, p.8.

[30] The oppositions "here" vs "out there," "near" vs "far away" that recorded the degree of taming, domestication and familiarity of various fragments (human as much as inhuman) of the surrounding world have collapsed. "Near" primarily refers to what is usual, familiar, a space inside which one can feel at home. "Far away" is a space which one enters only occasionally or not at all, in which things happen that one cannot anticipate or comprehend. The "near–far" opposition has another crucial dimension: that between certainty and uncertainty, self-assurance and hesitation. Whatever it has come to be known as, the "local community" is brought into being by this opposition between "here" and "out there", "near" and "far away". It was primarily the availability of means of fast travel that triggered the typically modern process of eroding and undermining all locally entrenched social and cultural totalities.

[31] Robert J. Schreiter, *The New Catholicity – Theology Between the Global and the Local*, Maryknoll NY, Orbis, 1997, p.83.

[32] Bauman, *Globalization: The Human Consequences*, p.3.

[33] *Ibid.*, p.9.

[34] *Ibid.*, p.11.

[35] Barry K. Gills, "Introduction: Globalization and the Politics of Resistance", in Barry K. Gills ed., *Globalization and the Politics of Resistance*, New York, Palgrave, 2001, p.7.

[36] *Ibid.* The Greek economist Kostas Vergopoulos has expressed similar positions in *Παγκοσμιοποίηση η Μεγάλη Χίμαιρα*, Athens, Nea Synora – A. A. Livanis, 1999.

[37] Joseph E. Stiglitz, *Globalization and Its Discontents*, New York, Norton, 2002. For further criticism of economic globalization see: Barry K. Gills ed., *Globalization and the Politics of Resistance*, New York, Palgrave, 2000; Hurrel and Woods eds, *Inequality, Globalization, and World Politics*; Richard Falk, *Predatory Globalization – A Critique*, Cambridge, Polity, 1999; David Held and Mathias Koening-Archibugi eds, *Taming Globazation – Frontiers of Governance*, Cambridge, Polity, 2003.

[38] Ethan B. Kapstein and Dimitri Landa, "The Pluses and Minuses of Globalization", in Plattner and Smolar eds, *Globalization, Power, and Democracy*, p.133. Similar positions have been expressed by Bruce R. Scott in his article "The Great Divide in the Global Village", *Foreign Affairs*, 80/1, 2001, p.161.

[39] World Bank, *Global Economic Prospects and the Developing Countries 2000*, Washington DC, World Bank, 2000, p.29.

[40] Joseph E. Stiglitz, *Globalization and Its Discontents*, New York, Norton, 2002, p.22. For further criticism of economic globalization see: Gills ed., *Globalization and the Politics of Resistance*; Hurrel and Woods eds, *Inequality, Globalization, and World Politics*.

[41] Richard Dickinson, *Economic Globalization: Deepening Challenge for Christians*, WCC – Unit III Justice, Peace and Creation, 1998; Kessler ed., *Together on the Way*, p.255.

[42] Address given by All Holiness the Ecumenical Patriarch Bartholomew at the 1999 annual Davos meeting of the World Economic Forum. Similar reservations against globalization were expressed by the Russian Orthodox Patriarchate in its recent pronouncement of the social teachings of the Russian Orthodox Church. The Russian Orthodox Church points out that many of the positive fruits of globalization are available only to nations comprising a small portion of humanity, but having similar economic and political systems, while other nations, comprising five-sixths of the world's population, have found themselves on the margins of the world civilization. The Russian Orthodox Church advocates that "the challenge of globalization demands that contemporary society should give an appropriate response, based on concern for peaceful and dignified life for all people and combined with efforts for their spiritual perfection. It favours the development of a world order based on the principles of justice and the equality of people before God, and would exclude any suppression of their will by the centres of political, economic and informational influence." See *The Orthodox Church and Society: the Basis of the Social Concept of the Russian Orthodox Church*, Moscow, Christ the Savior Cathedral, 2000, p.66.

[43] 17 May 2001.

[44] Lutheran World Federation / The Church and Social Issues, *Engaging Economic Globalization as a Communion*, a working paper, Geneva, Lutheran World Federation, 2001.

[45] The Justice, Peace and Creation Team of the WCC, *Economic Globalization: a Critical View and an Alternative Vision*, dossier 6, Geneva, 2001, p.2.

[46] Richard Falk, *Predatory Globalization: A Critique*, Cambridge, Polity, 2000, p.135. I am particularly intrigued by his citation of the specific conditions that are in the process of shaping the political oppositional forms to what he calls "globalization-from-above" (pp.131-36).

Religion and Globalization

RICHARD FALK

I am very moved and impressed by the strength and vitality of the strong, deep community of Holy Cross that seems able to combine the achievements of tradition while it partakes so fully of modernity. And in a way, it is itself a metaphor of what I would call a utopian globalization, a globalization that finds a creative way of establishing a deep sense of community while coexisting in a world that is increasingly interconnected and which depends for its survival and its development on an ever-greater sense of human solidarity, that possesses the moral and political capacity to combine an appreciation of particularity with an embrace of universality. On one level, the most profound challenge is to sustain a sense of individual and group identity, while having the moral energy to affirm the relevance of compassion for the suffering and aspirations of those who do not share our specific identity or our material and cultural circumstances. Such attitudes are particularly needed with respect to those several billions who are being victimized, deprived of basic human needs, by the way the world is currently organized.

Comprehending the overall challenge of globalization is difficult, no matter what our point of departure. There exists a multiple task of comprehension and presentation. Partly it involves the social scientist, particularly in this renaming of international political life, which expresses a very widely shared judgment that something has fundamentally changed that requires us to use a different political language if we are to understand the world adequately. But exactly what is it that has fundamentally changed? That is what I think is elusive, and people assume contradictory understandings of the nature of the character of this discontinuity that validates adoption of the terminology of globalization.

Is it primarily the new technologies, especially information technology and the way in which computers and the internet have changed how knowledge and communication occur on the planet? Or is it the sense of growing interconnectedness, the real time awareness of the unfolding of history before our eyes? Or is it primarily the rise of markets and banks and corporations as global actors that demand to be given increasing attention in our perception of what the real world is like? Or is the sense of a new reality better generalized as primarily expressed through the compression of time and space? There exists now a sense that an acceleration of history makes it much more illuminating to emphasize time rather than space as a primary category of understanding. And particularly for those who have tried to understand international political life, spatial understanding, territorial understanding, has long been treated as far more fundamental; that is, international society can be effectively comprehended as the relations among territorial communities. But increasingly, because of this acceleration of the unfolding of history, this sense of speed and momentum, there is an increasing focus on time as a dimension of political reality. And when we focus on the future and on what is going to happen in the future, it also makes us more aware of the past. And so there is a kind of recovery of the past that paradoxically is linked to this increasing preoccupation with the future, as with change generally.

But instead of this shift from space to time, should we, in trying to grasp what is new, focus on the emergence of what some have called global civil society? By this is meant the rise of transnational, social movements that have initially been concerned with protecting the environment and promoting human rights, and also with helping third-world countries get out from under the burden of debt; more recently they have increasingly focused their energies on the importance of establishing global democracy. These civic activists have also called for the extension of the values of liberal democratic society from internal political life to international institutions which, with the rise of the global economy, have become more important in their impact on human lives and on society.

And finally, is the phenomenon we are calling "globalization" better conceived as a displacement of territorially organized sovereign states by non-territorial networks of actors that are difficult, if not impossible, to situate in space? Is the fundamental reality of our time one in which the territorial state is being superseded by communities that are smaller than the state, and by these networks that can operate without a secure territorial base? Or should such an extended reach lead us to consider these networks as larger than even the largest state, and as potential modes of global governance as well as instruments of subversion in relation to territorial forms of governance? Such networks are very flexible, and can arrange their operations in such a way as to become almost invisible. They have become very important for both positive and negative aspects of the contemporary world.

We initially became aware of networking as a revolutionary innovation in the organization of complex undertakings with respect to the impact of information technology on the structure of corporate management, giving rise to economic globalization. Only gradually did the negative sides of networking become appreciated, and then initially in connection with transnational crime, and later in the context of global terrorism. In this connection, I would mention in passing that the trauma of 11 September 2001 can be interpreted as the darkest side of globalization, where the kind of networking that proved such a powerful organizational tool for the development of the world economy suddenly became an incredibly destructive lever of power on behalf of those who were challenging the existing statist world order. They proved capable, with minimal resources and the most modest military capabilities, and without the kinds of power that is associated with states, to produce an extraordinary level of damage, psychologically and materially, on the most powerful country in human history.

Power and the global battlefield

These momentous developments force us to rethink some fundamental concepts. We need to ask anew, "What is power?", in the setting of world politics. What is the nature of power if this kind of intense political threat can be mounted and harm can be inflicted from distant caves in Afghanistan against the dominant political actor in the world, what some have called the sole surviving superpower in the aftermath of the cold war? These events dramatically change our understanding of the way in which the world is organized, including the extent to which the state (or community or way of life) that is under attack is itself led to ignore the territorial organization of the world in devising its defensive strategy of response. The United States, in responding to the attacks of 11 September, has essentially defined the entire world as a battlefield against the global terrorist network of al Qaeda and is extending and projecting its power in such a way as to refuse to be inhibited by the sovereign rights of other states.

The mutual globality of this great terror war is complemented by American efforts to develop weapons that operate from space and are able to control events, or at least destructively to impose this control on events anywhere on the planet. The weaponization of space is a metaphor for a post-territorial form of global domination and global empire that appears to represent the American approach to global and national security at this point. Such an approach was already emerging as a goal of American global policy, but 11 September lent an urgency to this project as it exposed the acute vulnerability of the United States to suicidal tactics that could turn normal instruments of peaceful modern interaction into weaponry of mass destruction. In a sense, the shock of such vulnerability lent an air of practical necessity to the emergent post-cold war American ambition to provide global security from a vantage point of military domination. But however explained, this American project is as subversive of the modern reliance on a territorial world order as are the undertakings of the global terrorists.

For all these reasons, globalization, if considered on its own, is a very bewildering confluence of developments. My definition of the term is essentially the cumulative impact of these various features of post-modernity that I have been describing: as a totality, they make it appropriate to say that something sufficiently new has happened as to make it desirable to use a different language to talk about the world as it now operates and functions.

Some commentators on the world scene have relied upon the terminology of "post-modern" rather than "globalization", thereby stressing that the idea of modernity, at least for the secular sensibility, had been a world that was essentially organized around territorially sovereign states. And if we are no longer in such a world, we are in some sense in a post-modern circumstance. The essence of that post-modernity is this emphasis on time, and on the interplay of non-territorial actors, especially the potency of networks, whether operating as criminal networks, as terrorist networks, or as the networks of multinational corporations, high finance, media or entertainment. In both formulations, the territorial state persists as the most influential political actor, but its primacy is being drawn into question by this multi-faceted challenge, whether it is called globalization or post-modernity.

Hostility to modernity

It seems to me that there are several aspects of the relevance of religion to globalization that should be noted. First of all, there has most unexpectedly occurred in this period a growing awareness of a religious resurgence taking place throughout the world. It became first evident to most observers of the contemporary world in the late 1970s, at the time of the Iranian revolution. We became aware of an entirely unexpected and truly revolutionary challenge directed at what was thought to be one of the strongest secular governments of modernist persuasion in the non-Western world. This revolution was mounted by an essentially non-violent religious movement headed by a religious figure who seemed to belong more to the pre-modern world of traditionalism than to the modern world of science and technology. The Islamist victory in the Iranian revolution came as a great shock to the political leadership of the world, especially in Washington which had previously assumed that all serious threats to the established order were associated with Marxist/Leninist influences, ultra-secular in character. If 11 September 2001 was a shock to the American citizenry as a whole, the Iranian revolution was only slightly less of a shock to the policy-makers and those who were thinking about the way the world was functioning and how power was organized.

Until the Iranian revolution, religion was thought of as an ally of the West in the struggle against communism. Such a presupposition followed rather automatically from the avowedly anti-religious orientation of Marxist thinking. Religious movements were assumed to be on the side of the West in the cold war, and were promoted as such, in Iran and in other countries, especially those in the Islamic world. The prevailing thinking was that the danger to the kind of stability the West was seeking came only from the secular left, from Marxism and communism. And in a sense, the geopolitical strategists of the day were blind-sided, to use a football phrase; they did not see the potency or the animus of this religious challenge, that had deep roots in many societies and not only in Islamic countries. The Iranian revolution and 11 September were radical expressions of hostility to most of what modernity represented.

Other examples in the last three decades include: a resurgent political Islam coupled with the rise of Hindu nationalism in India, the second most populous country in the world; the further spread of Islamic militancy; the emergence of Christian evangelism as a central political reality in the West. Even in communist China, the great challenge to the existing order was being mounted by an essentially religious movement, the Falun Gong.

So throughout the world in this period, the secular imagination was unready for this development because the modern mind had so completely subscribed to the basic message of the Enlightenment in Europe. This message was that history should be conceived as a linear process in which the public order of humanity would be increasingly shaped and improved by the forces of science, technology and instrumental reason. And the privatizing of religion, an essential part of the politics of the Enlightenment, was regarded as a freeing of the creative forces of society to solve the problems of humanity. The prosperity and strength of Europe created the impression that the marginalization of religion from the perspective of public space had been responsible for the extraordinary progress and dominance of the Western nations. It was expected that this process would continue indefinitely, gradually benefiting the whole of humanity. As a result, religion was essentially viewed as an expression of backwardness, and was being superseded as an historical force. And so this religious resurgence was not something that could easily be comprehended by the modern mind, especially when it turned in such hostile anti-modern directions that treated the West as the source of the decay of civilization and as the prime enemy of human wellbeing and the religious life. In the West, religion had been reconciled to the public / private accommodation that was institutionally embodied in the separation of church from state.

Understanding religion correctly

This anti-secular religious backlash has, I think, created confusion among those who are still governing the economic and political life of the planet. That is to say, the disruption of the positive sides of modernity is a consequence of this re-emergence of religion as a strong presence in the public space. In other words, religion is reduced in the understanding of many secularists to religious extremism with a political edge, and therefore religion, in general, is blamed for the destructive encounter that now seems to dominate our understanding of the struggle that is occurring in the world.

This is a very unfortunate line of interpretation, in my view. It implies that religion, as such, is a menace to moderate and progressive government and to a hopeful destiny for human society. What makes this anti-religious turn so dangerous is that in our planetary circumstance, perhaps as much as any time in human history, there exist crucial potential roles for religion and spirituality as emancipatory forces. The need for religion is particularly great in relation to economic globalization, because one of the consequences of the ending of the cold war, and the struggle between East and West, was that socialist values and socialism as an ethical challenge to market materialism disappeared. In other words, the exclusion of socialism from the arena of ideas and public policy created a kind of moral and political vacuum as far as concern for the suffering of those who are victimized by economic adversity is concerned. Attempts were made to fill this vacuum to some extent by expressing the economic philosophy of globalization in its extreme market form, as the shaping of economic policy: in other words, the purpose of politics was to facilitate economics, and the function of the economy was to use capital efficiently, which in the end via the trickle-down effects of economic growth would eventually overcome poverty.

This economistic way of thinking, which is sometimes called the Washington Consensus, and is sometimes referred to as neo-liberalism, is an extreme ideology that is not organically linked to the technologies embedded in globalization. In other words, ideas with more ethical content, other than those associated with neo-liberalism, could be brought into the policy domain for the purpose of shaping global life so that all the peoples of the world derive benefits. The role of socialism had been to challenge capitalism to show a moral face, or else risk being displaced as the basis of economic development. This encounter between socialism and capitalism contained a creative tension in Western society. And with the loss of that creative tension, a moral vacuum has occurred and a form of cruel capitalism has been taking hold in many parts of the world, although unevenly.

The prevailing ideology has several maxims: Let the market prevail. Let growth provide social solutions. Let the poor depend both on their own efforts and on the eventual trickle-down effect, the so-called invisible-hand effect. Past experience strongly suggests that these positive social effects claimed for unbridled capitalism do not occur without strong government regulation and social intervention. In such a setting, I argue that only religion can provide a source of moral renewal and ethical perspective that can fill this vacuum in a constructive manner and lay the foundations for what I would identify as "humane globalization". Such an alternative globalization would not be indifferent to the poor. It would not be indifferent to investment and development in areas of the world that are not currently attractive to investors, like sub-Saharan Africa and the Caribbean. Religion, in its moderate and universal outlook, has the opportunity to re-establish the creative tension that was lost with the collapse of socialism. To fill the vacuum with religious extremism is, of course, also a possibility that has been given a frightening currency by the 11 September attacks and the violent aftermath manifest in many parts of the world.

Religion must work with civil society

I would not claim that positive forms of religion can fill this vacuum by themselves, without secular collaboration. The most hopeful scenario in this regard is the converging perspectives of what I referred to earlier as global civil society, those civil society actors that are challenging globalization from below, a challenge that became dramatic on the streets of Seattle in December 1999, and since then at successive meetings of international financial institutions like the IMF, the World Bank and the World Trade Organization. These anti-globalization demonstrations were essentially expressing the point that the people of the world (and not considerations of capital efficiency) should be the fundamental criterion for whether an economic policy is working or not, and beyond this that the people of the world needed to participate as subjects in the process by which policy was being made that affected their lives. So this new anti-globalization politics was partly a search for equity and partly a search for global democracy.

These demands had a resonance within the wider, more passive community. Indeed, even leading figures in business and finance began to respond positively to these criticisms of unregulated globalization, at least at the rhetorical level. The famous and notorious hedge-fund master and currency specialist, George Soros, who had made billions manipulating monetary markets, shocked the financial community by contending that market fundamentalism was as dangerous to the world as communism had been. And the head of the World Bank, James Wolfensohn, also abandoned neo-liberal language, making statements that exhibit a sudden social responsibility on the part of international financial institutions to address world poverty as an urgent priority, and not just to conceive of their function as to facilitate economic growth and capital expansion.

These defections from the neo-liberal creed represented an important contribution to a climate of opinion that supported global reform. And so my essential point here is that it is the constructive activation of the religious perspective, which alone has the capacity to represent the masses of humanity in conjunction with the emergence of civil society as a moral agent, that provides us with the political foundations for a more hopeful future based on an alternative, ethically accountable, form of globalization. For this reason, among others, it is very important not to allow religion to become associated in the secular mind with the sorts of extremism and fanaticism that engages in suicidal terrorism as exemplified by the events of 11 September, and subsequently.

So the challenge that faces democratic societies, especially the United States, is to discover how to bring religion back into the life-world in its creative, transformative and uplifting aspects at this historical moment. There is a moral consensus that joins the main religious perspectives, in their inclusive expression and recognition of this responsibility, to respond at this historical moment to the challenge of human suffering, a challenge that endangers the entire created order of the planet, including climate and the environment.

The issue that arises most vividly as a result of this moral consensus, which can also be treated as consensus of civilizational world-views, is this: How do you make this consensus politically relevant in light of two obstructing factors? The first of these is the fear that making religion politically relevant is an encouragement of political extremism and intolerance, and is a step backward from modern secularism and rationality. The second is that religion is only useful as the expression of pious sentiments that contribute to social peace and individual serenity, but do little to overcome conditions of injustice and oppression.

Religion must not retreat from the public space

Such concerns make us aware of the complexity and ambiguity of the religious heritage. It is, of course, true that religion has been a historical force on both sides, and contains both dimensions. Religion can either be an expression of intolerance, or a nexus for solidarity. So how does one strengthen the public role of those aspects of religious perspective that emphasize nonviolence, human solidarity and celebration of others that seek a spiritual destiny for human society? How are those forces used in positive ways at a time when society fears religion as a vehicle of extremism? There is a tendency, because of that fear, for the more moderate constructive dimensions of religion to retreat from the public space, and of course to the extent that such a retreat occurs it reinforces the general societal image that what religion is really about is this kind of exclusivity and dominance that is incompatible with a peaceful and satisfying form of globalization. And I would say that one of the ways that religion can re-enter the public space without being challenged in this way, without the problematics of this misunderstanding that is so culturally prevalent at the moment, is to direct much more of its energy at the legitimate social and political grievances of those who are suffering in various parts of the world.

To illustrate symbolically what I mean by such a call, let me refer to two very obvious forms of legitimate grievance that enjoy a widespread prominence at present. I think a response to each enables demonstrations of the sincerity and seriousness of the religious perspective, defeating the other harmful impression that if religion is not extremist, it is mere piety with no capacity to overcome human victimization. I know these are gigantic generalizations that have numerous exceptions.

The first of these is the need to address poverty as an urgent priority for political actors everywhere, including here in the USA, in the most affluent of societies. The scandal of half the world living on $2 per day, while a tiny minority accumulates ever more millions and billions, is an intolerable condition from ethical and spiritual perspectives, as well as being politically destabilizing. I choose as my second illustration the ordeal of the Palestinian people, whose exploitation and domination has been allowed in a way that is shameful for all of us. It is a struggle that I think should engage Christian communities everywhere, at least in part because the status of Jerusalem has long been at the centre of that struggle in one way or another, but predominantly because the victimization of the Palestinian people is such an assault upon what it is that Christianity should aspire to in the world.

Let me end by venturing even further into the religious domain, and I do so with fear and trembling. I assume this risk so as to convey as clearly as I know how the vital articulation of a religious perspective towards globalization. There is a passage in the letter to the Hebrews that begins, "Now faith is the assurance of things hoped for, the conviction of things not seen." The writer goes on (in chapter 11) to depict the journey of men and women of faith that made them no longer content with the world as they saw it: "They could no longer return to the country from which they had come. But now they desired a better, that is, a heavenly country." I consider the spiritual challenge of this conference to embody the moral and political courage to start such a journey of faith towards a better, that is, a heavenly country. In my own way of expressing this, we need to become what I have previously called "citizen pilgrims", persons of religious persuasion embarked on a journey through time to create in the future a humane globalization. That is, we act on faith without evidence and hope for what seems currently to be unattainable, and set forth on such a journey that crosses and denies all boundaries. It is part of the writer to the Hebrews' understanding that what these individuals of faith were seeking by pursuing a heavenly country was a pilgrimage to the future. And so it is as citizen pilgrims that I believe we can best address these profound concerns about the relevance of religion to the understanding and reform of globalization as now embodied in the economic and cultural life of the world.

Human Rights and Responsibilities in a Pluralistic World

DAVID LITTLE

Picking up on the idea of "responsibility" in the title I was assigned, let me suggest two ways in which religious bodies, such as the Orthodox churches, can be "responsible" in regard to human rights in a pluralistic world.

The first is that they take responsibility for embracing and promoting human rights, once they have examined thoughtfully the reasons why we have human rights in the first place, and why human rights are so important. Second, I recommend that Orthodox clergy and laity, along with other religious practitioners, become actively involved in helping to think through sensitive issues in the human-rights field, such as the treatment of new religious movements and the subject of proselytism. I shall take up these two points in order.

Why human rights are important

It is widely believed, in the West and outside it, that human rights are the outgrowth of a peculiarly 18th-century European cultural movement called the Enlightenment. Accordingly, human rights are interpreted as being militantly secularist, as well as excessively individualistic and bourgeois in the sense of idolizing private property and of elevating individual interest above economic and social welfare and responsibility. If this account were true, it would explain why many religious communities, including some members of the Orthodox tradition, either reject or are deeply sceptical of the language and ideals of human rights.

However, the reality is much more complicated. For one thing, the Enlightenment was not all of a piece. The French Enlightenment, with its emphasis on atheism and anti-clericalism, did have a strong secularist bent, but the English Enlightenment did not. John Locke, one of the parents of modern human-rights ideas, was a devout Christian believer, who defended the freedom of religion and conscience, as much to ensure the purity of religion as to protect the state from church domination. That emphasis became a hallmark, I would argue, of the American tradition of religious freedom, which owed so much to Locke. Amazing as it may sound, Locke gave as a reason for prohibiting suicide the belief that human beings are ultimately God's property, and not their own!

More importantly, the whole idea of an individual right as something "natural", something inborn and claimable by all human beings, whatever their religion, language, culture or place of birth, is much older than the Enlightenment. It found its origins in the Christian Middle Ages, as early as the 12th century. What was absolutely revolutionary about the idea, and what underlay everything else, was that, ultimately, it extended to every human being, simply as a human being, "an inherent right of self-defence... *against any oppressive authority*, even an oppressive pope".[1]

Above all, the original notion of individual rights was a resistance doctrine against arbitrary authority. There were, it was assumed, certain things that existing powers, whether religious, social, political or economic, simply may not do to any individual, no matter who the power might be. Individuals have a right to protest against gross injustice and, in extreme circumstances, to take things into their own hands, individually or in concert. The implications of the doctrine eventually touched a wide range of issues, including religious freedom, political expression and organization, as well as the protection of "life, liberty and estates" against both economic and political tyrants.

Over the centuries, and well before the Enlightenment, this doctrine of the right of individual resistance was widely applied. It was advocated, often by fervent religious believers, on behalf of religious minorities in Europe and America, on behalf of the indigenous peoples of the Americas against European colonialism, and on behalf of "all orders and sorts" of English citizens who, faced in the 1640s with economic oppression, demanded, as they said, "the recovery of our natural human rights and freedoms", since it is "against the radical law of nature... that any [person] should be deprived of a human subsistence".[2]

There is no denying, of course, that the doctrine of individual rights became, in certain times and places, wedded to excessive individualism and to the idolatry of private property. Such excesses can be found in Locke, and in others, and they still undoubtedly inspire a large following in contemporary American society. But that is by no means all there is to the rights tradition. In reality it is a capacious storehouse containing a rich variety of appeals and proposals, many of them invoked on behalf of oppressed peoples, often from strong religious motivation.

All these appeals and proposals must be carefully explored and examined before any religious community is entitled to disparage or reject the tradition out of hand. My guess is that, on inspection, many of the sentiments and concerns registered in the name of individual rights over seven long centuries are in fact strongly consonant with the deepest convictions of many religious communities around the world, including, I would imagine, the Orthodox tradition.

What is more, there is a strong reason to believe that human-rights language today constitutes an effective common idiom for articulating severe grievances, and consequently provides a basis for shared ideas of peace and justice in the public sphere among different communities with different, and sometimes conflicting, ideals and convictions.[3]

One critical reason that human-rights protections, including the protection of religious freedom, are so important at this moment is that what we could call the threat of communal domination is so potent under modern conditions. That threat was, of course, most dramatically and perniciously manifested in the form of German and Japanese fascism of the 20th century, a movement that found expression outside as well as inside the West. But it has also been exemplified in various forms of state socialism, past and present and, again, in non-Western as well as Western settings. More recently, the threat has taken the shape of ultra-nationalism, as found in the former Yugoslavia and elsewhere.

The central threat is, of course, the same one that the age-old rights tradition has combated, namely, arbitrary authority. But it is many times more sinister under modern conditions because of advances in the technology of domination. Human rights developed after the second world war, not so much because of the dominance of Western liberalism but precisely in response to the expanded capacity on the part of the modern state for exercising arbitrary authority. After the experience of fascism, it would be difficult to dispute the need of each and every human being, regardless of creed, background, race or gender, to have protection against arbitrary injury, confinement and discrimination, against the suppression of speech, assembly, political, cultural or religious expression, or against economic abuse and neglect – all justified in the name of a supreme set of communal values and ideals.

One of the main problems we face worldwide is that under the impulses of nationalism, or related political and economic interests, governments, often armed with an impressive capacity to regulate and suppress, ally themselves with one from among a wide diversity of ethnic, religious, racial or cultural groups within a society, and give special favours and advantages to the members of that group over all others. As case after case demonstrates, the potential for conflict and bloodshed is palpable. It is not hard to understand why, again and again, members of minorities reach out, regardless of culture or country, for human-rights protection against religious and other forms of discrimination of that sort.

It cannot be denied that the problems are not only political and civil, but also economic and cultural. Many religious communities understand that point well enough. Fortunately, the human-rights vocabulary, consistent, as we saw, with the earlier rights tradition, includes protections not only of physical integrity, and of civil, political and legal rights, but also of economic and cultural rights. That these are manifestly not promoted and enforced as resolutely and persistently as the other rights is a good reason for religious communities, if they are so disposed, to take up the cudgels and begin to agitate for change. To take up that cause, along with promoting other human rights, would be one way of discharging the "duties to the community" that the Universal Declaration in article 29 imposes upon "everyone".

So far as the general purpose and impact of human-rights language is concerned, it is by now very difficult to refute the statement contained in the preamble to the UN Declaration against Intolerance that "the disregard and infringement of human rights and fundamental freedoms... have brought, directly or indirectly, wars and great suffering to [human]kind".

New religious movements and proselytism

A key problem exercising the human-rights community these days concerns the question of the limits of proselytism as posed by the growing presence of what are called "new religious movements".[4] In the discussion, the right of free religious expression and the right to change one's religion are frequently pitted against the right of privacy and the right to protection against coercive intrusion, or "improper pressure", in matters of religion or belief. A whole series of laws has either been recently passed, as in Russia,[5] or vigorously reasserted, as in Greece,[6] affirming the right of traditional religions to restrict the efforts, usually of religious minorities, including "new religious movements", to propagate their faith. Some of these laws have been adjudicated by the European Court of Human Rights,[7] and while recent decisions in regard, for example, to Greek anti-proselytism laws have ruled in favour of the rights of minorities to engage in the dissemination of their views, the tensions between minorities and established or majority religions raised by the issue of proselytism have hardly been resolved.

In a recent publication, Natan Lerner enunciates some of the remaining areas of tension, and suggests points at which different rights seem to conflict with one another:

> [I]n a democratic society people should be free to disseminate their religious
> views. They should not be silenced simply because some people prefer not to

hear those views. There is, however, a right to privacy, and uninvited speech should not necessarily prevail over this right.

[P]roselytism involving material enticement – money, gifts, or privileges – should be considered a form of coercion and, thus, may be limited by law. Such material enticements exceed the area of freedom of speech and expression. However, borderline cases may not be easy to judge.[8]

Should all forms of educational and welfare assistance freely offered by religious groups be considered illicit forms of "material enticement", and thus banned by law? Is it fair for state-supported churches to provide various forms of material assistance while non-established churches are prohibited from such activities?

In the discussion of these problems, new religious movements have typically been classified, rather disparagingly, as "sects" and "cults". In Western, Eastern and Central Europe and elsewhere, there has been in recent years a rather extensive and persistent "anti-sect" or "anti-cult" campaign. From the perspective of the human-rights community, these campaigns, in general, have not represented the appropriate way in which to think about the problems of proselytism and the treatment of new religious movements.

The attitude to such campaigns on the part of the human-rights community has been compellingly stated by the UN Special Rapporteur on Religious Freedom, Abdulfattah Amor:

> The term "sect" seems to have a pejorative connotation. A sect is considered different from a religion, and thus not entitled to the same protection. This kind of approach is indicative of a propensity to lump things together... which is hard to justify and harder still to excuse, so injurious is it to religious freedom. Sects... are not above the law. The state must ensure that the law – particularly laws on the maintenance of public order and penalizing swindling, breach of trust, violence and assaults... the illegal practice of medicine, abduction and corruption of minors, etc. – is respected. In other words, there are many legal courses open and they afford plenty of scope for action against false pretences and misdirection. Beyond that, however, it is not the business of the state or any other group or community to act as the guardian of people's consciousnesses and encourage, impose or censure any religious belief or conviction.[9]

Directly supportive of the Special Rapporteur's opinion on "sects" and other religious minorities is the Comment by the UN Human Rights Committee on article 18 of the International Covenant on Civil and Political Rights. In expressing its concern over "any tendency to discriminate against any religion or belief for any reason", the Committee suggests as a special danger that groups will be treated with prejudice because "they are newly established, or represent religious minorities that may be the subject of hostility on the part of a predominant religious community". The implication is that under conditions of nationalist fervour which, as we saw above, naturally cater to majority beliefs and ideals, governments must go to extra lengths to guarantee freedom and equality for religious minorities.

Conclusion

I have tried to suggest there are good reasons why we have human rights, and why religious bodies ought to embrace and promote them. I have also mentioned some particularly sensitive areas of current human-rights concern that affect religious bodies directly – the problems of proselytism and the treatment of new religious movements and religious minorities. These problems, and others like them, are of urgent concern, and call for the active involvement of religious bodies, like the Orthodox communities. To reflect on the importance of human rights and to contribute to the lively discussions going on around the world are an important way, I suggest, of manifesting "responsibility" "in a pluralistic world".

NOTES

[1] Brian Tierney, "Religious Rights: An Historical Perspective", in John Witte, Jr and Johan D. van der Vyver eds, *Religious Human Rights in Global Perspective: Religious Perspectives*, The Hague, Martinus Nijhoff, 1996, p.29. Cf. Brian Tierney, *The Idea of Natural Rights: Studies on Natural Rights, Natural Law and Church Law, 1150-1625*, Atlanta, Scholars, 1997.

[2] Richard Overton, "An Appeal to the People" (1647), in A.S.P. Woodhouse, *Puritanism and Liberty*, Chicago, Univ. of Chicago Press, 1947, p.333.

[3] See Ted Robert Gurr, *Peoples vs. States: Minorities at Risk in the New Century*, Washington DC, United States Institute of Peace Press, 2000, which argues, based on considerable statistical evidence, that there has been an overall decline in ethno-political armed conflict around the world in part because of the spread of adherence to cultural and religious freedom and equality, particularly in regard to minorities.

[4] See John Witte, Jr, "Soul Wars: The Problem of Proselytism in Russia", *Emory International Law Review*, 12.1, winter 1998; John Witte, Jr and Michael Bordeaux eds, *Proselytism and Orthodoxy in Russia*, Maryknoll NY, Orbis, 1999; Paul E. Sigmund, *Religious Freedom and Evangelization in Latin America*, Maryknoll NY, Orbis, 1999; and Natan Lerner, *Religion, Beliefs, and International Human Rights*, Maryknoll NY, Orbis, 2000, pp.80-118.

[5] "The 1997 Law of the Russian Federation on the Freedom of Conscience and Religious Association", see *Emory International Law Review*, *op. cit.*

[6] See Lerner, *Religion, Beliefs*, pp.110-16.

[7] *Ibid.*

[8] *Ibid.*, p.117.

[9] Implementation of the Declaration on the Elimination of All Forms of Intolerance and of Discrimination based on Religion or Belief, submitted by Mr Abdelfattah Amor, Special Rapporteur, in accordance with Commission on Human Rights Resolution 1996/23; E/CN.4/1997/91; 30 Dec. 1996, paras 94, 99.

Human Rights and the Orthodox Church

CHRISTOS YANNARAS

What is the meaning of the term "human rights"? The adjective "human" attributes something to all humans in general. "Rights" belong to each human individually, unconditionally and without exceptions. Each individual existence, being human, is a bearer of rights. The word "right" refers to the claim-demand of an individual, a claim which is made possible by some commonly accepted (and therefore mandatory for all) code of law. The code of law ("social contract") assures that the right is a legal, that is, mandatory upon all, individual claim.

The legal safeguarding of individual rights through codes of law is a fundamental attribute of modernity. It is theoretically grounded on the philosophy of the 18th-century Enlightment. The notion of "right" has been known in the West since the Middle Ages, even if it is unclear when exactly the term was first used. However, in the Middle Ages the rights concerned specific individuals or specific social classes. The radical innovation of modernity lies in the fact that modernity made rights "human", that is, common to all humans, without discrimination.

The protection of human rights became the symbol of modern Western civilization. Together with the adoption of advanced technology, the undertaking of legal commitments (international treaties) for the protection of individual rights is considered in the modern world to be the proof of a civilized society. Of course, the countries that have signed these international treaties and have integrated them into their own legal systems are not always consistent with the obligations to which they have been committed. Human rights are even less respected in the field of international relations and the strategies of the great powers.

This means that the protection of human rights remains a moral problem. And morality always and immediately begs the question: Who and with what authority defines morality, who commits people to obey its rules? Is it God and his law, as expressed by the religious institutions? With such a view, the European West lived (in the so-called Middle Ages) a very negative historical experience. Religious ethics became linked, in the consciousness of people, to situations of social injustice, torture, arbitrariness, nightmarish punishments and ideological terror-ism.

The medieval experience led modernity to the polemical rejection of any metaphysical grounding of morality and right. The denial of meta-physics encouraged the absolute affirmation of nature (physics). The idea was that normative principles and rules of justice should not be deduced from the hypothetical "law of God" which was arbitrarily handled by religious institutions, but by the logic of the laws of nature which was objective and controllable.

Humankind is by nature a logical existence; reason is a natural char-acteristic of everyone. Consequently, we should be able to deduce nor-mative moral principles from the logical definition of the common good and interest. Of course, provided that every person is committed, by their own will, to the common (natural) logic, every person would responsi-bly accept the conditions of the "social contract".

This is how the notion of "natural right" penetrated modernity with an astonishing growth of domains and sectors. With it came also the idea of a "natural" right for every "natural" person prior to social, class, eco-nomic or other differentiations. Religion was rigidly separated from social organization, thus becoming a personal matter; the separation of the "sacred" from the "secular" (church and state) is nowadays consid-ered an institutional *sine qua non* of Western societies. Of course, from the end of the 18th century already, in an atmosphere of enthusiastic affirmation of nature and rejection of metaphysics, the Marquis de Sade had foretold that the logic of nature was not always benign and that, on the contrary, crime was inherent in the human biostructure. The horror of inhuman behaviour, the complete destruction of any sense of individ-ual rights, reached its culmination during the 20th century. Even today, when the global hegemony of the West is hailed as the triumph of the defence of human rights, practices of genocide, ethnic cleansing, slaugh-ter of innocent people, torture, policing and censorship, even slavery, lie on the everyday agenda of the international arena. Suffice to recall the tragedies of the Palestinians, Kurds, Serbs, or of northern Cyprus to real-ize that the West usually decides which people have human rights and to which people these should by definition be denied.

The ancient Greek paradigm

There is a crucial question which specialists of human rights leave without answer. How and why did ancient Greece, which created poli-tics (both as "art" and "science"), as well as the magnificent achieve-ment of democracy, entirely ignore the idea of "human rights"? The same question could be asked about Roman justice, which crucially influenced every new form of codification of right in Europe and also ignored the notion of "human rights". Should one conclude that Classical Antiquity, about which Europe is so proud, was indifferent to the protection of human life, honour and dignity?

I will try to give a short answer concerning ancient Greece, because this is relevant to my main subject.

Ancient Greece's radical innovation in human history was that it transformed simple cohabitation into the achievement of a city, that it transformed necessary (for utilitarian reasons) collectiveness into an "exercise of truth". The city is the state of social relations which results when the aim and axis of collectiveness is metaphysical and not utilitarian. This aim is the imitation of "what truly exists", of the way of existence "according to the truth", the way of incorruptibility and immortality. And this way is the "common" (i.e. universal) logic, the logic of harmony and order, which makes the Universe a cosmos (ornament).

The imitation of the community of relations "according to the truth" is the art and science of politics, of the way of transforming collectiveness into a city. This cannot be an individual effort or an individual aim; it is by definition a social event, a "common exercise". The people who participate in this exercise are citizens: they share the supreme honour of realizing, by their life and their relations, "truth", the mode of existence of "what truly exists".

In modernity, "individual rights" protect an individual from the arbitrary exercise of power. But in ancient Greece, the power meant all citizens together (the *demos*) – the "state" (*kratos*, power) belonged to the *demos* (democracy). Every citizen "has reason and power": from the moment that he is a citizen, he (women, slaves and other groups were excluded in ancient Greece) is by definition capable of holding any political office (this is why citizens were selected randomly and not elected).

Because a political function is "sacred" (it serves the truth), a citizen's body is sacred too. In ancient Greece, bodily punishment (whipping, hitting, etc.) was unthinkable for a citizen; it was unthinkable to insult a citizen's body. It was also unthinkable to have an executioner: Socrates, who preferred death to exile, drank hemlock of his own will – there was no executioner to kill him.

One can therefore understand that the safeguarding of "individual rights" was entirely useless in the ancient Greek world – the whole idea was incompatible with the Greek version of politics. The honour of being a citizen provided many more privileges than those conventionally provided (through the civil code) by the protection of individual rights.

The ancient Greek paradigm helps us to understand the attitude of the Orthodox Church (if we exclude the ideological "Orthodoxism" of our era and its institutional representations) vis-a-vis the "human-rights" issue. It is no accident that the first apostolic Christian communities borrowed from the ancient Greek political event the term *ecclesia* in order to express and reveal their identity and their specific difference from any other "religion".

In the ancient Greek "assembly of the people", Greek citizens did not assemble primarily to discuss, judge and take decisions, but mainly to constitute, concretize and reveal the city (the way of life "according to the truth"). In the same way, Christians would not assemble primarily to pray, worship and be catechized but mainly to constitute, concretize and reveal, in the eucharistic dinner, the way of life "according to the truth", incorruptibility and immortality: not the imitation of the secular "logic", but of the Trinitarian Society of Persons, the society which constitutes the true existence and life, because "He is Life" (1 John 4:16). Participants in this ecclesiastical event, even robbers, publicans, prostitutes or sinners, do not need to establish individual rights. Being a participant and a member of the body of the Church means that one exists only in order to love and be loved – a situation far from any need for, or expectation of, self-protection through legislation which would be "mandatory for all".

This historical transformation of the ancient Greek political event into the eucharistic body of the Christian Church had two basic consequences.

The first was that the Greek political model was the historical flesh which realized and revealed the radical difference between Church and religion. The Church is an event and a way of communion between persons, a way of love: that is, freedom from the existence of nature, freedom from the physical limitations of time, attrition and death. On the contrary, religion is an individual event, subject to the natural need of every person to worship and to appease the unknown and transcendent – it is an individual effort towards individual faith, individual virtues, individual justification, individual salvation.

In the first case (the Church) individual identity is realized and revealed through self-transcendence and self-offering. This is the identity of what we call a person, that is, an existence with an active creative otherness, which is the fruit of relations of communion, love, and freedom from the ego. In the second case (the natural religion and the religionized versions of Christianity in both West and East), the individual seeks his or her justification and salvation, the safeguarding of their egocentric metaphysical protection, through virtues and good actions.

Consequently, the opinion that, in European history, religious individualism preceded the egocentrism of a religionized (from Charlemagne and after) Christianity and set the pattern for the absolute importance of individual rights in modernity, is not arbitrary. When the tyranny of metaphysics was rejected, the aim of individual metaphysical salvation was replaced by the aim of a secularized (legal) protection. And thus was born the political system of so-called "representative democracy", which lies at the antipodes of ancient Greek democracy (in the same way that religionized individualized Christianity lies at the antipodes of the Orthodox Church).

The second consequence of the transformation of the ancient Greek political event into the eucharistic body of the Christian Church is the preservation and revealing of the difference between metaphysics and ideology: the various forms of "theocracy" have no relation at all to ancient Greek politics as an "exercise of truth", nor with the ecclesiastical realization of the image of the Trinitarian communion. Theocracy is the use of metaphysics (as a supreme authority) in order to impose normative principles of behaviour or aims of power by force upon the collectivity (for example, the Djihad of the Islamic tradition, or the phrase "in God we trust" on every American dollar). But any use of metaphysics for secular aims transforms metaphysics into ideology, into a psychological illusion.

In the cases of ancient Greek democracy and of the Orthodox Church, the social event cannot become subject to ideological rules or aims, as its dynamic realization is an aim in itself. Relations that realize the communion of life are in both cases the unique objective of collectiveness, as they constitute the way of "that which truly exists" (even if this way refers to two different models).

Metaphysics is subject to ideology (leading to such phenomena as "theocracy", "kingship by the grace of God", papo-caesarism, caesaro-papism or fundamentalism) when it evacuates metaphysics' ontological content (i.e. the question about existence, about the cause and purpose of being). Metaphysics without ontology serves individual psychology (the priority of individual feelings, sentimental "certainties", "convictions" which protect the ego), and metaphysics borrows these psychological "certainties" and "convictions" from ideologies.

The Orthodox ecclesiastical tradition and the human person

Samuel Huntington, in his famous book the *The Clash of Civilizations* (a book with astonishing inaccuracies and monumental interpretative arbitrariness), blames contemporary societies whose culture has often been developed by the Orthodox tradition for their incapacity to assimilate the principles of the protection of individual rights. In his view, the difficulties of these societies to adapt to the current demands of

Western ideologies such as "pluralism", or to the claim for "tolerance of differences", are a result of this incapacity.

Certainly, the Orthodox ecclesiastical tradition ignores the idea of collectivity as *societas*, as a "blending together of individuals in the pursuit of common interests". It ignores collectiveness as an arithmetic sum total of non-differentiated individuals, it ignores human co-existence as a simple cohabitation on the basis of rational consensus, it ignores the ideal of societies of unrelated individuals. We have briefly seen the conception of the social and political event that is carried by the Orthodox ecclesiastical tradition and the infinite value of the human person that this conception entails.

However, the understanding and respect for the principle of the protection of individual rights, which was introduced by Western modernity, also exists in the Orthodox literature. The more (a society or persons, the revealing of personal uniqueness, otherness and freedom through social relations) does not invalidate or destroy the less (the legal, institutional and uniformed protection of every individual from the arbitrariness of power). The Orthodox acknowledge that the historical existence of such experiences as the Western Middle Ages proves that the protection of individual rights is a major success and a precious achievement.

Nevertheless, we would be doing violence to historical memory and critical thought if, simultaneously, we did not recognize that, compared to the ancient Greek city or the Byzantine (and meta-Byzantine) community, the protection of human rights is a pre-political achievement. It is an undisputable achievement, but an achievement which has not yet attained (perhaps not even understood) the primordial and fundamental meaning of politics: politics as a common exercise of life "according to the truth", politics constituted around the axis of ontology (and not self-interested objectives).

The notion of "individual right" is not a mere production of the philosophy of the Enlightenment, a notion that is characteristic of the civilization of modernity. In the present historical reality, individual rights are the primary constructive material for the realization of the modern "paradigm", our contemporary way of life. In the functioning of politics and economy, in "social struggles", or in individual existential problems (like euthanasia), the notion of "individual rights" is presupposed as the self-evident criterion of any action, planning or logical validity.

Parallel to that, a huge international literature points out and analyzes the undeniable crisis of the modern cultural "paradigm". Scholars generally recognize the "historical end" of many fundamental coordinates of modernity such as the end of ideologies, the end of the parliamentary system or the end of rationalism. And it is not just a theoretical speculation. Every citizen of the so-called "developed" societies has a direct everyday experience of the rapid decline and alienation of the fundamental coordinates of modernity.

The commercialization of politics, its submission to the laws of publicity and the brainwashing of the masses, has literally abolished the "representative" parliamentary system. Politicians do not represent citizens and their interests, but the economic capitals of electoral propaganda and the interests of fund-providers. In the international sphere, the networks of economic and political interests lead to social corruption which increases dramatically through the immorality of the media and their functioning according to "hype" and "readability". The arms trade sustains wars and conflicts, and the drugs trade destroys the youth. Faith in the rationalism of the "social contract" collapsed long ago; only the logic of the antagonism of interests seems to prevail.

Symptoms of such a magnitude are never products of a mere moral decline; they are clear proofs of the end of a cultural "paradigm". The "paradigm" of modernity was grounded on the egocentrism of "human rights". A communion-centred version, based on the protection of human existential truth and authenticity might bear the arrival of a new cultural "paradigm".

BIBLIOGRAPHY

Kelsen, Hans, *General Theory of Law and State*, Cambridge MA, Harvard Univ. Press, 1949
Kelsen, Hans, *Hauptprobleme der Staatsrechtslehre* 2nd ed., Aalen, Scientia Verlag, 1984
Papaioannou, Kostas, *La consécration de l'histoire*, Paris, Champ Libre, 1983
Kondilis, P., *Die Aufklärung im Rahmen des neuzeitlichen Rationalismus*, Hamburg, Klett-Cotta, 1981
Romilly, Jacqueline de, *La loi dans la pensée grecque des origines à Aristote*, Paris, Belles Lettres, 1971
Yannaras, Christos, *Philosophie sans rupture*, Genève, Labor et Fides, 1984
Yannaras, Christos, *Person und Eros*, Göttingen, Vandenhoeck und Ruprecht, 1982
Yannaras, Christos, *The Church in Post-Communist Europe*, in *Mediterranean Quarterly* 9/4, fall 1998
Yannaras, Christos, *The Inhuman Character of Human Rights* (in Greek), Athens, Domos, 1998

Violence and Religion in Pluralistic Societies

KONRAD RAISER

Why do we need to reflect about religion and violence?

The Harare assembly of the World Council of Churches proclaimed the period 2001-10 as an Ecumenical Decade to Overcome Violence. The issue of violence in its various manifestations and the question how churches in cooperation with other religious communities can contribute to the building of a culture of peace and reconciliation will therefore be in the forefront of ecumenical discussion. The focus on violence is related to the rapid increase of conflicts in the decade since the end of the cold war. In addition to "traditional" interstate conflicts and the many new civil conflicts, we are witnessing a generalized spread of acts of violence within society: violence against women, refugees, foreigners, racial minorities, disabled persons, violence by and among youth, ethnic clashes, and so on.

Particularly in situations of civil conflict and unrest, religious traditions and affiliations are mobilized to lend legitimacy to the claims of conflicting parties. Examples are Indonesia, Sudan, Nigeria, Northern Ireland, India and the former Yugoslavia. Religion, together with ethnicity and nationalism, serves as an identity marker in order to define group membership and draw lines of distinction. In public perception such conflicts can easily be perceived as religious conflicts.

The events of 11 September 2001 have exacerbated the situation. The attacks are broadly perceived as expressions of a confrontation between militant Muslim fundamentalism and Western (Christian) culture – or more broadly as a conflict between Christian and Muslim civilization. They seem to validate the thesis of a "clash of civilizations". The language of "jihad" and "crusade" has gained broad currency. Through all of this, religions are suddenly thrust into the centre of global politics.

Confronted with these developments, many political and economic actors on the global scene have begun to look for help in managing the dangerous dynamic of violence which seems to have been unleashed.

There are increasing appeals to religious communities and their leaders for public initiatives of moderation, moral orientation and reconciliation. In response, a series of high-level inter-religious encounters have been organized since 11 September, in Brussels, Assisi and Alexandria, for example, issuing declarations which affirm a strong commitment to peace and inter-religious understanding. None of these declarations, however, has dared to reflect about the links between religion and violence. Most religions, and particularly those considered as "world religions" with a history of missionary expansion, have been implicated in actions of war or the use of violence for religious purposes. So far there has been very little self-critical reflection about these features in the history of religions. This is partly due to the strong tendency, in particular during the latter half of the 20th century, to assign religion to the private sphere and thus weaken any intentional effort to reflect about the ambiguous role and the influence of religions on public life. The present context of globalization has initiated wide-ranging changes in the religious field which call for a new approach also in inter-religious dialogue. All religions have to come to terms with the reality of religious plurality.

Violence in the perspective of religion

As I now concentrate on the specific challenge offered by the theme, that is, a reflection about the ambiguous relationship of religion and violence, it will become apparent that in my approach I have received essential inspiration from René Girard, the French philosopher and anthropologist. I consider his contribution to the discussion to be of vital significance, even though it would need to be complemented by other perspectives such as those of the social and political sciences.

All religions have at their core a message of life, of peace and justice, of harmony and right relationships in community. However, for this very reason, religions have to face up to the pervasive presence of violence in human life and its destructive power. Violence, from a religious perspective, is a manifestation of evil and all religions are struggling with the question where this evil comes from and how it can be overcome. There can, therefore, be no authentic affirmation of peace within any religious tradition without facing up to the challenge of violence in human community life.

Any religious perspective on violence inevitably reflects basic assumptions and convictions about the human condition. Aggression – and therefore the potential of becoming violent – is obviously part of the human condition. Animals, including predators, apparently have an instinctive inhibition against killing members of their own kind. This is not the case with human beings: violent behaviour is a possibility in human life which can be activated at any time. But the human condition not only includes the potential that rivalry in social relationships can lead to violent attacks or even elimination of the rival; it also manifests the capacity for sympathy and mutuality. Religions are not only concerned with moral and ethical guidance of human behaviour and the tension between these two poles, but also with the need to interpret the origin of this potential for violence in the human condition and to formulate moral, ritual and legal rules for limiting the resort to violence.

Primal religions respond to the question of the origin and the limitation of violence by way of myths which bind together the human and divine dimensions of reality. Myths are a reflection of fundamental human experience and represent the inner core of cultures, including religion, in their response to violence. Understanding and interpreting the language of such foundational myths is therefore essential for clarifying the relationship of religion and violence.

René Girard has undertaken the most penetrating analysis of these mythical interpretations of the origins of violence.[1] Girard sees the roots of the potential of violence in the mimetic relationship between humans who imitate each other, responding to actions, initiatives and wishes of the other by mirroring their behaviour. This basic rivalry which aims at reducing or eliminating the difference between me and the other is potentially conflictual and can increase to the point of one attacking, expelling, eliminating and killing the other. Ancient myths abound in scenes of such rivalry between brothers or members of a family or group with a violent outcome. Revenge for unwelcome actions of the other can take the most extreme form of mimetic violence. René Girard interprets religious myths as ways to come to terms with this potential of mimetic violence which would destroy the life of a given community if it cannot be contained. This is the origin of religious prohibitions of the use of violence within the same group or family.

The most significant "solution" to the violent potential of the mimetic crisis is the "scapegoat mechanism". In this case the whole group unites by projecting the violent potential onto a chosen victim. The sacrifice of the victim restores and guarantees the peace of the community. The original mythical murder of the victim, according to Girard, is then repeated through ritual sacrifice in order to reproduce continuously the saving effects of the original violent act. Violence thus is being sacralized because of its redemptive capacity. The potential of aggressive violence is being transferred to the victim who is considered guilty, but by the same token becomes the origin of reconciliation. The sacred thus has an inherent ambivalence: it absorbs the violent potential and thus is dangerous; but at the same time it is the source of peace and salvation.

Girard sees in this sacrificial sacralization of violence the fundamental device for the way cultures and religions have responded to the need for containing violence. This "solution", however, works only as long as the myths and the sacrificial symbolism remain active. The process of de-sacralization of the world has begun to weaken the symbolic power of myths, thus bringing to the fore the fact that the traditional structures of societies, cultures and religions are based on an act of integrating violence. Where the scapegoat mechanism has lost its sacred legitimacy, it can no longer guarantee peace.

From a different point of departure, Walter Wink, in his analysis of the powers in social and political life, comes to a similar conclusion.[2] He speaks of the "myth of redemptive violence" which he sees prefigured in the Babylonian creation story (the "Enuma Elish") which depicts the struggle between order and chaos. Creation, according to this myth, emerges from an act of violence among the gods, the murder of Tiamat by Marduk. Creation is constantly in danger of slipping back into chaos, and order can only be maintained through violence. Wink believes that this mythical legitimation and sacralization of violence is present in most ancient cultures and has not lost its appeal even in our de-sacralized world of today:

> The Myth of Redemptive Violence is the story of the victory of order over chaos by means of violence . . . Life is combat. Any form of order is preferable to chaos, according to this myth. Ours is neither a perfect nor a perfectable world; it is a theatre of perpetual conflict in which the prize goes to the strong. Peace through war; security through strength: these are the core convictions that arise from this ancient historical religion, and they form the solid bedrock on which the Domination System is founded in every society.[3]

These analyses refer to religion and violence in a generic sense. They point to the fact that religion has played a central role since the beginning of human history in the effort to come to terms with the potential of violence in human life. By establishing a close link between religious myths and the corresponding rituals, on the one hand, and the pervasive presence of violence in human life, by integrating violence into the sacred, religions aim at containing the destructive influence of violence in order to establish peace and a viable order. Because order and life are constantly threatened by violence, violence is being absorbed into the sacred which is both threatening and life-giving. It is this ambiguity of religion with regard to violence which calls for critical reflection within all religious traditions.

Religious legitimation of violence

The perspective on violence and religion offered by Walter Wink has received unexpected confirmation by the terrorist attacks of 11 September 2001 and the reaction under the banner of the "war on terrorism". Both sides in this struggle tend to use religious language and symbolism to legitimize the use of violence or military force. What we observe is a re-mythologization of a political struggle for power; the struggle is being transferred on to a symbolic level, that is, interpreted as the confrontation between good and evil, between the forces of order and the forces of destruction. While religion is not the primary cause of violent confrontation, religious symbolism and religious sentiments are being invoked and mobilized to legitimize and sanction the use of destructive force and violence. It is this confrontation between militant Islamism and what is considered to be "Christian civilization" which brings the ambiguous relationship between violence and religion dramatically into perspective.

Yet, not only in the context of this global confrontation but also in many more limited civil conflicts, religion has become a major factor in the dynamic of violence which begins to threaten the viability of pluralist societies. Religious loyalties are being invoked by ethnic, cultural or religious minorities to legitimize their resort to violent means in the struggle for recognition. While religious authorities are quick to declare that these are not religious conflicts and to affirm their commitment to peace and tolerance, they are ill prepared effectively to contain the dynamic that has been unleashed through this association of religion with violence. In particular, the invocation of the religious symbolism of sacrifice and martyrdom serves to legitimize the most irrational and brutal violence and destruction which seem to have become ends in themselves. The dramatic performance of suicide attacks calls for a symbolic framework of interpretation even where there is no explicit religious legitimation.

The American political scientist Mark Juergensmeyer has attempted in several publications over the past decade to elucidate this new phenomenon of the religious legitimation of violence.[4] Central to his interpretation is the observation that the secular understanding of the state which is based on rational legitimation by due process and the rule of law is increasingly being perceived as a threat in cultures and societies in which order, law and morality have traditionally been sanctioned by religion. While the secular nation-state emerged from the trauma of religious wars in 17th-century Europe and has been built on the non-religious legitimation of public authority, most cultures outside the "Christian" West have not appropriated this categorical differentiation between state and religion, between the public and the private realm. The secular state represents an understanding of order that is based on the loyalty of citizens to an authority holding the monopoly on the legitimate use of force and thus, eventually, over life and death. This stands in contrast to cultures where religion offers the ultimate framework of order, including the authority in extreme cases to sanction the use of violence for the purpose of defending or maintaining order.

As a consequence of colonization, the Western model of the secular nation-state has been introduced into other parts of the world, where the legitimation of power and authority was traditionally based on religion. Juergensmeyer interprets the emergence of a militant and revolutionary religious nationalism as a response to the failure of the model of the secular nation-state to meet the expectations associated with the efforts of nation-building in post-colonial societies. The further weakening of the authority and effective power of the new nation-states as a consequence of the process of globalization provides an additional incentive to reawaken loyalties to the religious foundations of authority and the moral and legal order of society, especially among the well-educated who are disillusioned about the prospects of secular modernity.

What is at stake in these confrontations is the question of the legitimation of authority and power and especially the ultimate power over life and death: that is, the authority to decide when violence is morally legitimate and when not. All religions have claimed this authority to sanction the moral order and thus to contain violence, including its legitimation in extreme cases where the fundamental order of life is threatened. This is the function of the symbolic violence of sacrifice. The secular state with its rationalization of authority is a fundamental challenge to all religions. When, however, the power of the modern state and the authority of religion are linked, there emerges an increased potential for violence.

Juergensmeyer interprets the emerging global confrontation between various forms of religious nationalism and the secular understanding of the state in the "Christian" West as the struggle between different "ideologies of order" or between different systems of legitimation of authority. In its extreme form, this confrontation can be interpreted as the struggle between good and evil, as a manifestation of the cosmic war to which Walter Wink referred. Then the use of the most extreme forms of violence can be legitimized by invoking the religious symbols of the "holy war" or the "jihad", referring to the continuous spiritual struggle to defend order against the forces of chaos and destruction. All religions provide examples of the legitimation of violence in such situations in line with Walter Wink's concept of the "myth of redemptive violence".

A Christian biblical perspective

There is no question that the religious ambiguity regarding violence is present in the Christian tradition as well. The Bible, which in large parts is common to Christians and Jews, is full of stories of violence and of violent images even with reference to God. At the very least the Bible presents a very realistic picture of the potential of violence in human life.

However, an analysis of the foundational myths about primeval history in the early chapters of the Bible shows a decisive difference to the examples presented by Girard and Wink. In fact, violence is absent from God's creation, which is considered to be good. The potential of violence enters at the moment when the first human beings acquire the knowledge of good and evil, that is, the capacity to judge and to discern. The first occurrence of violence in the murder of Abel by Cain shows a remarkable characteristic: Cain cannot accept the failure of his sacrifice and kills his brother Abel. The following dialogue between Cain and God demythologizes violence: Cain is made responsible for his act, and at the same time God protects him from revenge. As such he and his descendants are presented as the pioneers of human culture, but this first act of divine containment of the potential of violence fails, and violence increases to the point that God attempts through the flood to eradicate violence once and for all. But God recognizes that violence cannot be overcome by means of violence. God's covenant with Noah expresses God's will to maintain life even in the face of enduring violence. God's alternative to violence is the protection of human life through the gift of the law which centres around the prohibition of human beings killing each other. The protection of human life is entrusted to the observance of God's law, which remains the primary means of reducing and limiting the occurrence of violence.

In his analysis of the Decalogue, Frank Crüsemann has shown that the fifth commandment "You shall not kill [or murder]" (Ex. 20:13) forms the core of this basic framework of divine guidance for the protection of human life.[5] All the other commandments regarding interpersonal relations in the family, just labour relationships, and stealing what others need for their living, and truthful public speaking are ordered in pairs like the peel of an onion around this core. Human beings are free to distinguish between good and evil; they can decide against the rivalry of coveting the other's life, property or being tempted by other gods; they are called by God to control their potential of violence for the sake of life.

While the active limitation of violence is the dominant theme of the biblical ethos, the ambiguity appears in passages which present God as the origin of war and violence, and especially in the passages about the wars of conquest connected with Israel's entry into the Promised Land. These wars, which are presented as executing a divine command, especially with regard to placing the ban on the conquered community, have often been characterized as "holy wars", thus seemingly giving a religious legitimation to war with highly questionable consequences in later history of wars fought with religious sanctioning. What is mostly being overlooked, however, is the fact that these wars are taken out of human control: war is not considered as a legitimate means of human politics. The fighting of war is under the exclusive control of God; it is God's ultimate means to save and protect the people who are urged to entrust themselves to God's power who will struggle for them. This becomes the basis of the prophetic criticism of the power politics of the kings of Israel and of the expectation of a final end to war and violence when people will no longer fight against each other but forge their instruments of war into tools for cultivation (Isa. 2; Micah 4).

The other biblical context in which violent language is being used in direct reference to God is the many psalms of lamentation which call on God to destroy an oppressive enemy. These psalms are to be read first of all as a manifestation of the experience of violence, of being exploited, marginalized and treated unjustly. However, based on the faith conviction that revenging the victims of injustice and restoring the weak to their rightful place is in the hands of God, these psalms present their anger and feelings of aggression to God instead of repressing them or acting them out against the enemy. They entrust retribution and retaliation to God as the final judge who will vindicate the victims of violence. This conviction that God takes the side of those who suffer under and become the victims of violence can be regarded as the common thread throughout the biblical tradition.

Very often, Christian interpreters place the response to violence which is found in the realism of the Hebrew Bible in contrast to the renunciation of violence by Jesus, especially in the Sermon on the Mount. Thus a tension or even contradiction is being introduced into the biblical tradition. However, Jesus was as realistic about the logic of violence as the tradition of the Hebrew Bible which nurtured his own faith. He knew that those "who take the sword will perish by the sword" (Matt. 26:52). Violence cannot be overcome by violence, for any violent resistance against violence is subject to the same logic and only continues the cycle of violence. Therefore this cycle, the very dynamic of violence, must be interrupted at its source, the regarding of the other as a rival and potential enemy. The renunciation of violence which Jesus teaches in the Sermon on the Mount is not advice of acquiescence and passive submission, but an encouragement to refuse to respond to violence on its own terms and the effort to transform a situation of confrontation and enmity into a relationship of communication and mutuality. This alternative praxis which actively challenges the logic of violence is rooted in the conviction that God will ultimately overcome the evil of violence and anticipates God's rule of love and compassion.

The greatest challenge for the Christian interpretation of the relationship between religion and violence has been the violent death of Jesus and its significance. Was his death on the cross a necessary part of his mission or was it rather a sign of ultimate failure? Does the violence of his death have a place in God's plan or was it rather the evidence of his having been abandoned? How to understand that God would allow the one who had completely entrusted his life and mission into God's hands to become a victim of violence?

The confession of the Church that God raised Jesus from the dead and thus vindicated him to be acclaimed as the Christ who is present in the life of the Church shifts the eyes of faith away from his death, but it still leaves the question of the relation of this fact of violence and the will of God.

From very early on the Christian community tried to understand the death of Jesus in the light of the prophetic image of the suffering servant of God and especially the passage about the suffering servant in Isaiah 53. Here we have a classical representation of the vicarious suffering of an innocent victim who, as the scapegoat, assures the peace of the community: "Upon him was the punishment that made us whole, and by his bruises we are healed" (Isa. 53:6). Like the suffering of the servant, the violent death of Jesus was interpreted as a vicarious sacrifice to liberate humanity from the powers of sin and death.

This sacrificial interpretation of the meaning of the violent death of Jesus has continued to shape Christian thinking, especially in the form of the medieval doctrine of atonement formulated by Anselm of Canterbury. According to this understanding, God's righteous wrath over human sinfulness demanded satisfaction which could only be achieved through the vicarious self-sacrifice of his innocent son. Here violence is intimately linked with the image of God, bringing us back to the ambiguity of the sacred, as pointed out before.

However, if we approach the question from the biblical image of God who seeks to contain violence, taking the side of and protecting the victims of violence, and if we consider Jesus' own refusal to respond to violence with violent means, but rather to establish an alternative praxis of overcoming enmity and violence by love and forgiveness, we could understand his vicarious suffering and death as God's way to unmask the logic of violence and its sacrificial legitimation and thus to break the cycle of violence and death. The violence which was meant to destroy and eliminate Jesus has lost its mythical sacred power through his very death and resurrection. Thus the link between religion and violence, the possibility of religious legitimation of violence, is abolished. A similar interpretation is reached by René Girard in the second of his books referred to above.

Reception and critical assessment

The experience of these past decades and especially since 1989-90, but also the intensive ecumenical discussions about war and peace, have initiated a critical assessment of the Christian tradition regarding religion and violence. For the longest period, however, and until the devastations of the second world war, the holocaust and the threat of nuclear annihilation, the Christian churches have followed the dominant trend which Walter Wink has characterized as being under the influence of the "myth of redemptive violence". While the early Christian community followed the example of the alternative praxis initiated by Jesus and the apostles and saw in the nonviolent witness of the martyrs the seedbed of the Church, things changed when Christianity became the dominant religion of the Roman empire. The use of war and violence for the purpose of maintaining and expanding the unity of the Church and the empire became an accepted feature. The details are known and do not need to be rehearsed again: the persecuted Church of the first centuries became itself an agent of persecution, first against Jews in the Byzantine empire, then in the form of the militant missionary expansion into northern Europe, leading to the compulsory baptism of whole peoples under the threat of the sword. These were followed by the crusades to liberate the Holy Land from Muslim rule; they found their continuation in the Inquisition and the Reconquista in Spain, and finally the violent incursion of the Conquista into Latin America and the culmination of this dark side of the Christian symbiosis of religion and violence with the wars of religion in the period of the Reformation and post-Reformation in Europe.

The traces of this unholy alliance of religion and violence are still with us in the crusading language of the "war on terrorism", in the justification of the use of war and violence for the purposes of maintaining order and justice ("just war"), in the dualistic view of the human condition and of the world which operates with a clear distinction between good and evil, friend and enemy, often supported by arguments from apocalyptic language about the eschatological struggle between the rule of God and the powers of darkness.

Meanwhile, Christian consciousness and the discussion in the churches have become more careful and critical over against the influence of this tradition. Thus feminist critique has made us aware that behind this mentality lie hidden assumptions regarding human nature and the exercise of power which are supported by a patriarchal image of God. It has further drawn attention to the fact that the traditional subordination of women in church and society, including its potentially violent consequences, has its parallels in the attitude of human domination over nature and its violent exploitation for human interests. Both have their roots in and are being reinforced by what Walter Wink calls the "myth of redemptive violence" which continues to be operative, at least in popular Christian thinking.

Ecumenical discussion on war and peace as well as on violence and nonviolence has put in motion another process of critical assessment. The wide-ranging debate on nuclear arms has led to a revision of the classical attitude to war in the sense that wars fought with weapons of mass destruction contradict the Spirit of Christ and that Christians should refuse to participate in such wars. More recently the Justice, Peace and Integrity of Creation process has sharpened the critical challenge through the commitment to promote the peace of Christ, to adopt active and life-promoting nonviolence as the response to conflict resolution, and to work towards overcoming the institution of war: that is, to de-legitimize war and the use of force as accepted means of politics in interstate relations. For the first time the pacifist witness of the historic peace churches has been taken seriously in ecumenical discussion.

The debates around the Gulf war in 1991 and more recently around the issue of the "protection of endangered populations in situations of armed conflict" or the response to the challenge of international "terrorism" indicate that the self-critical assessment and reorientation in the Christian churches has not yet been completed. The decision of the WCC's Harare assembly to proclaim the period 2001-10 as an Ecumenical Decade to Overcome Violence constitutes a formal commitment of the WCC to further this continuing debate.

The task ahead of us, both in internal Christian critical reflection and in inter-religious encounter and dialogue, is to unmask the logic and dynamic of violence and its dehumanizing and destructive consequences. In the tradition of most cultures and religions the ugly face of violence was covered in mythological terms by associating violence with the powers of the sacred which was experienced as both threatening and redemptive. The rules and laws which were meant to control and limit the potential of violence in the life of human community drew their authority from sacred sources. We have seen that the biblical tradition shared by Jews and Christians began to dissolve this mythological alliance of religion and violence.

Today we are experiencing an unimaginable increase of the destructive potential of violence, on the one hand, which is accompanied by a radical de-sacralization and thus brings to the fore the ugly face and the brutal logic of violence, leading to a "culture of violence". On the other hand, the obvious lack of legitimacy surrounding the use of violence leads to pressure on the religious communities and their leaders to provide again a cover of moral and religious legitimacy, if only for the limited period of a situation of violent confrontation or conflict. This instrumentalization of religion has become a scandal and must be denounced as such. Instead, religious communities and their leaders should, through inter-religious encounter and dialogue, work towards solemn mutual commitments to withdraw any moral or ethical legitimation from the use of violent means in response to conflict or in the pursuit of political, economic, cultural and – even less – religious ends. The unholy alliance between religion and violence must be broken for the sake of life for all.

The consequence must be the development of a critical realism about the dynamics of violence in contemporary life and its roots in a view of human nature as being under the domination of the struggle for survival in which only the strongest and fittest will be able to maintain themselves. This alleged realistic view is a denial both of human freedom and of the human capacity for sympathy and solidarity, for forming communities of mutuality and cooperation. In fact human identity is formed primarily in positive and supportive relationships of reciprocity rather than in antagonistic or competitive relationships of struggle. Human beings have a fundamental need for belonging and for recognition. The formation of group identity over against a common enemy is a transitory phase in the search for a more inclusive and mature form of identity.

All religions are trustees of the wisdom of nurturing and maintaining community and of shaping right and mutually sustainable relationships. Violence in all its forms, whether interpersonal, social or structural, constitutes a break and a denial of community. It reflects the inability or the refusal to live with differences, to acknowledge the otherness of the other. It arises from the urge to shape the other according to one's own image, to dominate or in the extreme case to exclude or eliminate the other as a threat to one's own identity.

It is precisely the encounter with the holy, with God as the transcendent other, which is the source of the basic trust in oneself, in other persons and in the world, and thus the basis of community in the sense of engaging in trusted relationships with those who are and remain different. Violence is not innate in human nature. Humans are capable of transforming the destructive energy of violence into a constructive force nurturing life. The struggle against the "spirit, logic and praxis of violence" includes more than the development and application of ways of peaceful nonviolent means of resolving conflicts. It is a moral and spiritual struggle in which the religious communities have to take the lead, beginning with the critical assessment of their own involvement in the emergence of a culture of violence.

NOTES

[1] René Girard, *Violence and the Sacred*, Baltimore MD, Johns Hopkins UP, 1979, and *Things Hidden since the Foundation of the World*, Stanford CA, Stanford UP, 1987.
[2] Walter Wink, *The Powers that Be: Theology for a New Millennium*, New York, Doubleday, 1998.
[3] *Ibid.*, p.48.
[4] See, in particular, Mark Juergensmeyer, *The New Cold War? Religious Nationalism Confronts the Secular State*, Berkeley CA, Univ. of California Press, 1993.
[5] See Frank Crüsemann, "Damit "Kain nicht Kain wird" – die Wurzeln der Gewalt und ihre Überwindung in biblischer Sicht", in *epd-Dokumentation* 6/2002, pp.34ff.

An Orthodox Comment
on Violence and Religion

STANLEY SAMUEL HARAKAS

An atonement theory cast in social science categories and an Eastern alternative

I was struck, in Konrad Raiser's paper, by the coincidence between the sociological and anthropological interpretation of religion as characterized by the concept of "scape-goating" and the use of Anselm's use of the idea of redemption in Christ as the satisfaction of the demands of a just God requiring satisfaction, through Christ's suffering and crucifixion, in order to accomplish the salvation of the world.

There is no doubt that the New Testament scriptures provide many different images that serve as foundations for the explication of varied theories of the atonement in Christian theology. And Raiser was correct in basing the development of his argument and the selection of one, from among social science models regarding religion, to find a correspondence between it and the Anselmian approach to interpreting the atonement. It rings true for Western Christians, and I am sure that it therefore may be convincing to them.[1]

My observation here is that both in the social sciences and in Christian theology there are alternative theories and interpretations. In particular, from the perspective of Eastern Christianity, the dominant approach to understanding the death and resurrection of Christ is not that of Anselm, cast as it is in legal categories.

The Eastern Christian tradition has kept all the many different images used in the New Testament to illumine the meaning of Jesus Christ's work of salvation, and used them in many different contexts, but the dominant image is the idea that Jesus Christ has conquered death, sin, evil and the devil through his death and resurrection. It is precisely the resurrection of Christ that makes effective and fulfils the crucifixion ("If Christ has not been raised, then our preaching is in vain and your faith is in vain", 1 Cor. 15:14). Hence, as Gustav Aulen called it, the "classic theory" of the atonement, emphasized in the Eastern Church, is cast in the context and struggle of evil and good.

The Johannine "Light and Darkness" motif, so powerfully expressed in the Orthodox Paschal rite celebrating the resurrection with the dramatic presentation of the lit Paschal candle in the darkened church, embodies the "classic theory" of the atonement in liturgy, making it accessible to all. This approach is confrontational and, and one could even say, violent. It would not relate with the particular social science approaches to religion used in the paper. Rather, it would emphasize the conflict between God and the devil, between the Good and evil, between forces directed to the building up of human existence and those which corrupt and harm it. In Latin, *Christus Victor* is the name of the "classic theory" of the atonement. In Greek it is *Iesous Christos Nika* – Jesus Christ is Victorious.

I think that here we have a methodological difference in the approach to peace and violence, making the argument in the paper not as convincing for the Orthodox as it might otherwise be. This observation will be the source of some of the comments which follow, "from an Orthodox perspective".

Some considerations for evaluation

A major concern in the discussion of violence is the fluidity of meanings attributed to the term. Over the years, both within the WCC effort and outside it, the word has been used to describe many different realities. The first definition of "violence" in my Webster's Collegiate Dictionary is, "An exertion of force so as to injure or abuse." So, if this is taken as the fundamental meaning of the word, then the critical question is, What is meant by "exertion of force"? I think that most people interpret this to refer to physical force, a punch in the face, tripping a person, a shot from a gun, or rape – all intended to harm or injure another. The term has been extended to cover words, emotions and sensibilities.

But people also recognize that force may equally be used, not to harm or injure, but simply to accomplish things, such as the thrust of a rocket, or the explosions within the workings of the internal combustion engine. And it can be shown that the force which is inherent in the maintenance of civil order is used by governments of whatever form, to counter chaos, maintain order and, paradoxically, to "keep the peace".

We see this clearly in the scriptures. There is a tendency in some quarters to read the Old Testament as if it has the same level of authority as the New. I do not think that this is the method generally practised in the Eastern Orthodox tradition of biblical hermeneutics. The Old Testament passages dealing with God and Israelite military efforts do not create as much of a problem for reflection on violence since these are seen as an early stage in the history of salvation, now transcended by the New Covenant. Hence, patristic exegesis tended to allegorize or personalize these conflicts in terms of the soul's spiritual struggle against sin and evil.

It is clear that Jesus' teaching on nonviolence, for example, not returning evil for evil and further, returning good for evil, is a powerful and necessary way for the vicious cycle of evil in response to evil to be broken and even reversed. It is also clear that Jesus' teaching is cast primarily in categories of interpersonal relations. It is, however, not correct to call these injunctions the exclusive New Testament teaching. Long before the Emperor Constantine, the edict of Milan, the establishment of Christianity by Emperor Theodosios, the theocracies of Byzantium and the holy Roman empire, the New Testament itself recognized the need and necessity of the use of force to maintain order and, yes, even to use force to injure and abuse those who did harm to others. No matter how much there might be a desire to explain away the teaching, it is part of the revelatory tradition of the New Testament scriptures. The passage in mind is illuminating and needs to be read in its entirety and in its context to ascertain its significance for our discussion of violence and religion in pluralistic societies.

In no less than Paul's epistle to the Romans 13:1-7, we read precisely about the legitimacy of the exercise of violence against those who do evil:

> Let every person be subject to the governing authorities; for there is no authority except from God, and those authorities that exist have been instituted by God. Therefore whoever resists authorities resists what God has appointed, and those who resist will incur judgment. For rulers are not a terror to good conduct, but to bad. Do you wish to have no fear of the authority? Then do what is good, and you will receive its approval; for it is God's servant for your good. But if you do what is wrong, you should be afraid, for the authority does not bear the sword in vain! It is the servant of God to execute wrath on the wrongdoer. Therefore one must be subject, not only because of wrath but also because of conscience. For the same reason you also pay taxes, for the authorities are God's servants busy with this very thing. Pay to all what is due to them – taxes to whom taxes are due, revenue to whom revenue is due, respect to whom respect is due, honour to whom honour is due.

As we all know, this passage has provoked much discussion and has been interpreted in multiple ways to justify almost every kind of Christian theory regarding the state. My purpose in mentioning it here is not to enter into those debates, but rather to show that the New Testament is far from uniform in addressing the question of violence, whether authorized or not. I think that my point will be made clearer if we note that this passage immediately follows in Paul's course of thought in Romans another passage much more reminiscent of Jesus' Sermon on the Mount pronouncements. In Romans 12:18-21, just prior to the passage quoted above, Paul teaches,

> If it is possible, so far as it depends on you, live peaceably with all. Beloved, never avenge yourselves, but leave room for the wrath of God; for it is written, "Vengeance is mine, I will repay, says the Lord." No, "if your enemies are hungry, feed them; if they are thirsty, give them something to drink; for by doing this you will heap burning coals on their heads." Do not be overcome by evil, but overcome evil with good.

The juxtaposition of these two sentiments seems to be contradictory. However, it is rather just one more example of the paradox of truth so often present in Christian teaching. At its heart is the recognition that evil, violence and disorder are endemic to our human condition and our social, economic, political, national and international existence. To say, from whatever vantage point, that human beings are imbued with tendencies to violence and to counter this with assertions that human beings are also capable of gentleness, generosity and compassion in community, does not replace the former by the latter. It simply says that the human condition is a paradox of conflicting forces. In the fallen condition of humanity, self-determination remains, and that means we are capable of practically anything – atrocious violence and compassionate caring. This paradox is built into phrases such as "war on terrorism", the "decade to overcome violence" and calls to "combat racism". They appeal to the element of conflict, struggle and strife. It is easy for this to be turned into a dualistic frame of mind. But that is precisely what does not happen in the scriptures and in the subsequent intellectual history of the Church.

The tension is maintained without reductionism, and there is an acceptance of the unfortunate and difficult need for violence against the forces of violence, while at the same time recognizing that this is far from the will of God and the values of the kingdom of God.

When this is discussed on the level of war, there are three major stances. Pacifism's total rejection of war appeals to the highest values of peace, yet opens the potential for unopposed violence. The just-war tradition, through its argued conditions leading to justifiable war, turns the horrors endemic to war into moral virtues and goods. I hold that neither of these positions reflects the authentic Orthodox tradition regarding war. I have characterized the Orthodox position as elevating peace to a superior virtue, and the waging of some wars at best as a "necessary evil" – necessary, because other, conflicting values also demand support.

That is what makes some conflicts morally unavoidable. Sometimes the violence of war may serve to protect the innocent and limit the destructive consequences of aggression. We are dealing here with a paradoxical affirmation of the higher value of just peace that sometimes requires participation in some uses of force that are violent in order to contain violence.

There is no doubt in my mind that the Church has frequently been co-opted to support wars and violence in ways that do it no honour. Yet, I think that it is also too easy to ignore the truth that the Church has sought frequently to stand at the side of its people in times of oppression, injustice, attack and subjugation. While appealing to peace, reconciliation, justice and simple human compassion, it has stood together with its people in their suffering and defeat. In my understanding, the argument presented by scholars that attributes to religion a universal "scape-goating function", allowing religion to be co-opted by others, has an element of "question-begging" – its conclusion is fore-ordained by its assumptions. Its assumptions include the post-Enlightenment sharp division between secular power and religion. In earlier times and in some places to this day, the civil and the religious existence of a people or nation are not so sharply divided. It is not so much a question of co-opting as a corporate responsibility for the whole of the people. The consciousness is not so much one of either-or as it is one of both-and.

The mind struggles to hold these things together. But when we consider that no person ever achieves the *telos* of divinization, and that all are in the process of spiritual growth and sanctification and are at different levels; when we recognize that what may be difficult but possible in the personal sphere in terms of returning good for evil becomes increasingly difficult and problematic in expanding spheres of social organization, then we comprehend its complexity. Realizing "kingdom values" becomes perhaps impossible in the largest social sphere of international relations without the potential, at least, for the use of violent force. In such situations the paradox becomes ever too real.

Perspectives for a constructive theological position

I think that an honest theological approach to the New Testament paradox must, of necessity, also be paradoxical. We cannot reduce the one side of the equation to the whole. But we can acknowledge that there are higher and more imperative values and lesser and minimum, though empirically essential, values requiring resort, at times, to necessary evils.

Nevertheless, the Church's task is to do everything in its power to minimize and make unnecessary the resort to violence, coercion, the "use of the sword" or the unnecessary use of "necessary evil". Once

Jesus made use of a paradoxical phrase that is pertinent to our conversation. In the gospel of Luke there is this dominical saying: "The law and the prophets were in effect until John came; since then the good news of the kingdom of God is proclaimed, and everyone tries to enter it by force" (Luke 16:16). In the gospel of Matthew a parallel though slightly different *logion* declares, "From the days of John the Baptist until now the kingdom of heaven has suffered violence, and the violent take it by force" (Matt. 11:12).

Both are understood in the framework of the gospel of Jesus Christ by St Cyril of the Alexandria in his *Commentary on the Gospel of St Luke*. He writes:

> Whosoever, therefore, is a hearer and lover of the sacred message takes it by force; by which is meant, that he uses all his earnestness and all his strength in his desire to enter within the hope. For, as He says in another place, "The kingdom of heaven is taken by violence and the violent seize upon it."[2]

In the ascetical tradition of the Orthodox Church, this spiritual violence *(bia)* is the "effort required by our own choice and will to opt for the good, in the face of the temptation to do otherwise".[3] What is true of the *agona* and *askesis*, the struggle and spiritual exercise needed for personal growth towards *theosis*, that is, striving for God-likeness, is equally true in the struggle and effort required to reduce destructive violence in the world.

From this reality comes the ethical imperative. Wherever possible, and even when it appears to be an impossible task, the Church's effort must be to foster the peace that arises from justice and not injustice, the minimizing of inhuman practices of violence wherever possible, the overcoming of conflict with reconciliation and dialogue, the forming of personalities, of communities, of nations and peoples with the spiritual mindset that hammers swords into ploughshares. But it cannot do so in a spirit of naiveté that does not recognize the alternative need for some agencies in society to have the power and resources to subdue what is corrupting and destructive.

I am struck by the paradoxical wisdom of the Orthodox Church in the prayer at the end of the Divine Liturgy, still referred to as the "Prayer behind the Ambon". The priest prays in part, "Grant peace to Your world, to Your churches, to the clergy, to our civil authorities, to the armed forces, and to all Your people." It affirms the need and place of "civil authorities" and of "the armed forces". But what it prays for is that they exercise their roles not in violence or in war, but "in peace".

It also means that in a very religiously, ethnically, politically, economically, socially, racially and internationally pluralistically fragmented world, the Orthodox Church must constantly exercise its own forces, its own *bia*, in its own way, everywhere to limit and reduce unjust violence, the victimization of the innocent, and the inhumanity of war.

It is not without significance that the Standing Conference of Canonical Orthodox Bishops in the Americas has recently made an effort to affirm positively the value and importance of peace. In an encyclical of the Standing Conference of Canonical Orthodox Bishops in the Americas, dated 20 September 2002, the bishops endorsed the United Nations-sponsored International Day of Peace. I conclude these comments with a portion of that encyclical, because I think that through it the positive struggle against unjust violence is emphasized:

> Throughout the world, Orthodox Christians pray daily for peace. These prayers are at the heart of Orthodox worship. The Great Litany, sometimes called the "Litany of Peace" is insistent on the centrality of peace. "In peace let us pray to the Lord", "for the peace from above and for the salvation of our souls, let us pray to the Lord", "for the peace in the whole world, for the welfare of the holy churches of God, and for the union of all, let us pray to the Lord". Prayer is never an isolated action or orientation. As we pray, so we believe. As we pray, so we act. Orthodox Christians seek peace and pursue it in prayer, in faith and in action.

Amen. So be it.

NOTES

[1] For an insight into the variety of social science approaches to religion and the complexity of their practice, see A. Blasi, J. Duhaime and P.-A. Turcotte eds, *Handbook of Early Christianity: Social Science Approaches*, New York, Alta Mira, 2002; especially the first three chapters constituting the first, methodological part of the book.
[2] L.I.C.: *Astoria*, New York, Studion, 1983, p.448. trans. R. Payne Smith.
[3] Stanley S. Harakas, *Toward Transfigured Life: The Theoria of Orthodox Christian Ethics*, Minneapolis, Light & Life, 1983, p.258.

Forgiveness and Reconciliation in Christian Theology

A Public Role for the Church in Civil Society

RODNEY L. PETERSEN

> So if anyone is in Christ, there is a new creation: everything old has passed away; see, everything has become new! All this is from God, who reconciled us to himself through Christ, and has given us the ministry of reconciliation...
> (2 Cor. 5:17-18)

The de-escalation of conflict can have nothing to do with forgiveness and reconciliation – and everything to do with it. When we were filming material for the documentary *Prelude to Kosovo: War and Peace in Bosnia and Croatia*, our group of students and faculty went to the city of Zenica, in Bosnia-Herzegovina, where we had been invited to speak with some local Muslim leaders. After initial presentations we spent an uneasy hour or more on the front porch of the new Islamic pedagogical institute discussing the conflict in Bosnia. After getting almost nowhere, a young professor of *sharia* (Islamic law) turned to me and said, "All we really want is for someone to say 'I'm sorry.'" This having been said, statements of apology having been heard, we proceeded into a more fruitful, if still incomplete conversation.

A similar encounter occurred in Ghana, as Ghanaian nationals confessed to their North American brothers and sisters their sorrow over their ancestors' part in the sale of the ancestors of African-Americans into slavery, part of a slave trade that so decimated West Africa. Needless to say, this encounter with apology drew many other North Americans of whatever colour into an atmosphere of forgiveness and reconciliation.

Each of these episodes draws us to the vitality of our topic. History bears upon the present. An inability to break out of a cycle of victimhood and aggression keeps us locked within a cycle of revenge. The Serb defeat at Kosovo Polje in 1389, enslavement at the Cape Coast castles of West Africa, or other stories we might add from other ethnic settings remind us that a failure to deal with the eddies of history keeps us in their thrall. Forgiveness and reconciliation have much to do with public life. The purpose of this paper is to sketch in the broadest of strokes the importance of the church's public role in civil society.

Forgiveness, reconciliation and restorative justice

We live in one world. This was known in the first century of the Christian era as apostles, missionaries and teachers moved out throughout the Mediterranean world and were blessed by Africans (Acts 13:1) to carry the gospel to the Dark Continent of Europe. It was then, as it is now, a world characterized by economic injustice, political division, racial intolerance, sexual exploitation, and religious competition and division. While the Church has been decisively international through most of its history, as epitomized in the history of mission, ever since the flight of the Voyager I spacecraft in 1977 we have seen this one world differently. This encounter with ourselves is a facet of globalization, a complex phenomenon sometimes discussed with reference to a "globalization from above", meaning a set of corporate and economistic changes, and a "globalization from below", those transnational forces pushing to create a global civil society.[1] Code words, such as "Jihad vs McWorld",[2] bring this home to us with a new immediacy. Regional political instability seems to give visible reality to Samuel P. Huntington's oft-quoted thesis about a "clash of civilizations"[3] such that we fear not only the disruption of our lives but that of the habitats and neighbourhoods of our world.[4] Through the events that have opened the 21st century, new meaning is given to the reality behind the title of the book *Managing Global Chaos*[5] – as if we might achieve at least this penultimate goal in a world erupting with conflict.

One of the remarkable features of this new era of globalization is that when forgiveness and reconciliation occur in the midst of the conflicts or social disruptions characteristic of our times, this occurrence is not a private affair but a public statement of far-reaching political import. In fact, one major critique of Huntington's thesis is that he appears to ignore reconciliation possibilities that may result not only from conscious political choice but also from such aspects of globalization as may promote unifying and hybrid multicultural realities. A more public discussion of the place of forgiveness and reconciliation in civil society, whether through conscious choice or social evolution, can be traced through a number of entry-points in political life. These have come in the context of a religious resurgence welcomed by some but little understood and seen as a potential menace by others.[6] Permit me to cite three of these.

Entry-points for public discussion

While for tactical purposes we might reach back to the work of Gandhi and his successful challenge to British colonialism early in the 20th century, a more focused entry-point for theological reflection comes in the context of the second world war.[7] Some of our most important examples of what living a life of forgiveness might look like are visible in such persons as Dietrich Bonhoeffer, Corrie Ten Boom and Simone Weil.[8] It was in this context that the German theologian Bonhoeffer began to lay the groundwork for a theology of forgiveness in forms of what he called "costly grace" *(The Cost of Discipleship)* and in a pattern of spirituality that committed us to healing relationships *(Life Together)*.[9] The simple trust and evangelical obedience of Corrie Ten Boom left an inspiring legacy in popular piety.[10] It was only through suffering and forgiveness that Simone Weil found the means to a spiritual unity with God.[11] The legacy of the war and its Holocaust gave impetus to the emergence of international institutions designed to promote forgiveness and reconciliation, or at least a more responsive and responsible world order, such as the World Council of Churches, long called for by Orthodox churches and other contributing movements.[12] Organizations like the United Nations and its associated bodies, Initiatives for Change, and other institutions in New York, London, Paris and Geneva in Switzerland and elsewhere were also born in this cauldron of conflict.

More recently, public recognition was given to forgiveness and reconciliation by the way in which Nelson Mandela chose to leave incarceration on Robben Island. Mandela, the African National Congress, and other cooperating parties in South Africa opened up a new level of public discussion about the place of forgiveness and possibilities for reconciliation through the national unity and reconciliation act of 26 July 1995 and the establishment of the Truth and Reconciliation Commission. Other public debates surrounding national tragedies have followed in line: in Northern Ireland, Chile, Argentina, the Middle East, Rwanda and the Balkans, to name but a few. Some of these have found a way forward. Others show continued intransigence. The point is that the political and religious leadership in South Africa has raised the issue of public forgiveness as the only way to a constructive future, the argument of Anglican Archbishop Desmond Tutu in *No Future without Forgiveness*.[13] Harvard legal scholar Martha Minow balances pairs of responses to horrific violence, remembering and forgetting, judging and forgiving, reconciling and avenging as ends on a spectrum of human responses to atrocity that call for therapy, politics, cross-communal reconciliation, recognition of cruelty and lack of closure.[14] This is the left-over debris of national pasts that continues to clog the relationships of diverse groups of humans around the world. Donald Shriver writes that these will never get cleaned up and animosity will never drain away "until forgiveness enters those relationships in some political form".[15] Such debris contributes to the spiralling cycles of conflict analyzed by social scientists.[16]

Our third entry-point is that of the growing awareness in the medical and health-care fields of the effects of cycles of violence on people's psychic lives and in society.[17] Work among health professionals over the past quarter-century has drawn increasing attention to forgiveness as a powerful psychotherapeutic tool. This recognition has often come with respect to trauma studies.[18] The effect of anger upon health and well-being and the role that forgiveness can play in the process of healing is increasingly recognized.[19] Particular studies in interpersonal relations, marriage and the family, and private and social behaviour are pointing to the deep connection between personal psychological health, social bonding and healthy civic life and forgiveness.[20] Learning to forgive one's self, or self-acceptance, and addiction and personal depression, or violent and abusive behaviour are seen to be increasingly connected – and with social and even public policy consequence.[21]

These entry-points for the public discussion of forgiveness and reconciliation have contributed to a wider conversation subsequent to the fall of communism in 1989. Communism was not just a system that crushed economically. It created severe injury to civil society and to the religious communities behind the iron curtain. Priests, rabbis, imams and pastors – as well as the faithful – suffered in the communist prisons for their faith.[22] More central for our purposes, the bipolarity of political life then has given way to a multipolarity today that is shaped by a global religious resurgence that asks for a deeper "politics of meaning".[23] We are coming to experience this as a facet of globalization from below. Historical grievances shape contemporary political life. They look to become invested with religious meaning. Churches, together with other religious communities, must find ways to move these beyond cycles of victimhood and revenge through forgiveness and reconciliation.

What is forgiveness?

In light of entry-points such as these for a public recognition of the value of forgiveness and necessity of reconciliation, how, in brief, are we to understand forgiveness and the terms to which it is linked? As the Church, we might begin with the utterances of Christ on the cross (Luke 23:24).[24] Yet, in our own time, we find a variety of interpretations for the word "forgiveness" with respect to its public significance. While no one has brought the term into public currency more than Anglican Archbishop

Desmond Tutu, others like Chief Rabbi Jonathan Sacks of the United Hebrew Congregations of the Commonwealth, Rajmohan Gandhi, and Dr Zaki Badawi, Chair of the Imams and Mosques Council of Great Britain, have been equally vocal in drawing attention to this term.[25]

For some, forgiveness is a commitment to a way of life and practice.[26] Others find it to be a commitment of the will.[27] It may also imply liberation from the past.[28] Forgiveness for some is a way of focusing on work to be done in the secular realm and world of public policy,[29] for others it might be better channelled towards the motivations that reduce interactions with one who has hurt us.[30] One researcher, Joanna North, writes, "Forgiveness is a matter of a willed change of heart, the successful result of an active endeavour to replace bad thoughts with good, bitterness and anger with compassion and affection." Another, Michelle Nelson, finds there to be stages of forgiveness: detached, limited, and complete along a road towards healing.[31] Journalist and political philosopher Hannah Arendt writes of Jesus as the "discoverer" of forgiveness.[32] And theologian Geiko Müller-Fahrenholz adds, "To understand what forgiveness does to our relationships we need to see the bondage that evil creates."[33] Forgiveness represents a way of breaking through this bondage. It may do so in a paired relationship as one repents and another forgives. It may be without reciprocity as one person chooses no longer to be fettered to the past. It may also become cheapened by triteness and inconsequentiality. It may become a "forgiveness bypass" or failure to deal with a harm caused. Churches, in their relationship with sister communions, can model the "costly grace" of forgiveness. Recent history has given Orthodox churches ample opportunity to lay foundations of forgiveness in different social contexts so as to find the way towards reconciliation.[34]

What is reconciliation?

Reconciliation takes us further. It is the resolution of the violence of separation. Orthodox ethicist Stanley Harakas writes of two aspects to such reconciliation, the "philanthropic" and what might be termed God's creation goodness.[35] There is a human and divine dimension to the term *katallagé* as used by the apostle Paul (2 Cor. 5:16-21; Eph. 2:11-22). While making reference to the monetary exchange in the Hellenistic world, he extended the meaning to imply "the making of what one has into something other" or, by extension, finding oneself to be a new person by virtue of the exchange of another. The biblical record implies agreement after estrangement, seen in the reconciliation of Joseph and his brothers (Gen. 50:15-21), the embrace of Esau and Jacob (Gen. 33:4) and, finally, in Jesus' death on our behalf. Here, one becomes a new creation because a power from without enables one to be other than what one was before. Public reconciliation begins to happen when we participate in positive relations with previous enemies, as we exchange places, become something we were not before our encounter with the other and discover a new level of agreement.

The *Kairos* document, a part of the "Truth and Reconciliation" process in South Africa, talked of "cheap reconciliation", in analogy to Bonhoeffer's "cheap grace", implying reconciliation without justice.[36] It raised the question of the temporal sequencing of justice and reconciliation and whether justice as perceived by all parties can ever be finally determined; hence the need for truth, as we are bound in patterns of victim and perpetrator. In this light, we might speak of "national reconciliation" and wonder about "collective healing" and the pursuit of "political unity", but by whose definition? Beyond the horizon of South Africa, we might ask about what genuine reconciliation looks like in other global settings in which churches have been active, with the Sandinistas in Nicaragua, church life in Cuba, the experience of South Korea and the Philippines, in Columbia, with the Solidarity Movement in Poland, with the Sanctuary Movement in the United States, or among indigenous peoples in Canada or Australia, and perhaps in ways we do not yet see in the Middle East.

In each of these and other settings, justice can be shortchanged on the way towards reconciliation and become impunity.[37] It has been noted that, "Forgiveness happens inside an individual; reconciliation happens within a relationship."[38] If this is the case, in what ways can we characterize such a relationship? For example, four aspects that shape reconciliation are noted by theologian Miroslav Volf: the primacy of the will to embrace or make peace; attending to justice as a precondition of actual peace; the will to embrace as the framework of the search for justice; and embrace, or peace, as the horizon of the struggle for justice.[39] These views, taken from the domain of national life and interpersonal relationships, remind us of the Latin root for reconciliation, *concilium*, or a deliberative process in which conflicting parties meet "in council".[40] When we think of councils of churches, even the World Council of Churches, can we think in terms of reconciliation?

Putting an added spin on these four dimensions of relationship, Mennonite peace activist John Paul Lederach envisions reconciliation as a meeting place where truth, mercy, justice and peace come together (Ps. 85:10). He adds,

> Reconciliation can be thus understood as both a focus and a locus. As a perspective, it is built on and oriented towards the relational aspects of a conflict. As a social phenomenon, reconciliation represents a space, a place or location of encounter, where parties to a conflict meet.[41]

But does forgiveness come before reconciliation? We are drawn to think in the Church, often through the influence of the liturgy, of an order that follows something like this: confession, repentance, forgiveness and reconciliation. Yet, as Charles Villa-Vicencio writes, to focus on the ideal rather than more modest processes can be confusing and counter-productive: "reconciliation as a process preceding and ideally incorporating forgiveness".[42]

What is "restorative justice"?

We would like to think that forgiveness moves towards reconciliation – or that reconciliation incorporates forgiveness – and that reconciliation moves towards patterns of life, based in truth, characterized by mercy, that are just and lead to peace. This would appear to be the conclusion of Ps. 85:10 – the meaningful meeting place of truth, mercy, justice and peace.[43] Such relationships might be called restorative, or we might use the terms "repair-ative" or "transformative" justice. This is to put into practice Micah's minimalist mandate, "to do justice, to love mercy, and to walk humbly with your God" (Micah 6:8).

To be reconciled to another, not merely to tolerate the other, means that change is required on the part of both parties as we seek the restoration of each other, something we or the other may or may not be prepared to do. This perspective about how we might live together draws upon our scriptural assumptions – and also upon the best wisdom traditions of indigenous peoples and other religions or faith traditions.[44] It emphasizes the humanity of both victims and victimizers. It seeks to repair social connections, to foster peace rather than retribution against offenders.[45]

Most agree that restorative justice promotes healing, but the kind of healing depends upon the nature of the breach. One focus is to see crime as more than simply law-breaking, an offence against governmental laws and regulations. Instead, advocates of restorative justice also see crime as causing multiple injuries to victims, the community and the offender.[46] Another lens is to view the criminal justice process as one that should help repair the injuries brought about by crime.[47] Still others protest against the government's monopoly over society's response to crime. Victims, offenders and their communities must also be involved as early as possible and as much as possible.[48]

Whether churches, or their individual members, are able to discover the way to forgiveness or sustain a momentum towards reconciliation that incorporates restorative justice in the face of a *realpolitick* draws us to questions that are fundamental for Christian identity and shape a globalization from below. For example, do we understand ourselves in the first order *as* forgiven? What is the nature of the person that requires forgiveness? How do we understand the way in which forgiveness comes to us? What implications for human community, and pre-eminently the Church, can be drawn from forgiveness and reconciliation? How churches have acted or failed to act in the regions of the world cited above, or elsewhere, provide important case studies that require analysis. They challenge our understanding of what it means to be Church. The work of this chapter only sketches answers to these questions that are, nevertheless, important if churches are to carry an impulse for forgiveness and reconciliation into the public square.

Forgiveness and reconciliation in Christian theology

Churches have a particular role to play in the public character of forgiveness and reconciliation. The kind of healing they can bring to global civil society is not something that will come through a globalization from above. This is most evident as theology finds its way into practice and into patterns of life that are restorative, often in local communities and settings. Such globalization from below can create the conditions for the cessation of conflict and social reconciliation in other areas of public life.[49] While often privatized or "spiritualized" in the past – even removed from the practice of everyday life – contemporary social pressure is demanding that forgiveness and reconciliation find its way in civil society.

Religion marginalized

Churches must take a new look at what was often a rite restricted to the confessional or to private devotional practice and find the means and the language by which to draw these ideas into public discourse.[50] In fairness it must be said that this was not always the choice of religious communities but a part of the exclusion of religion from public life that, in the West, was a consequence of the European Enlightenment and politics subsequent to the peace of Westphalia (1648). As a consequence, forgiveness was often joined to a personal and vertical view of salvation, while justice and the search for reconciliation, or peace, were pursued through prevailing social or religiously neutral philosophy or rhetoric. Those seeking a more integrated spirituality lament this today.

The theological concepts of forgiveness and reconciliation, ways of understanding the doctrine of the atonement, became caught up in a protracted theological conflict in the West as theology sought to clarify itself as a science of the Church in light of the Enlightenment and the reality of social policy. The Social Gospel and Revivalist movements at the end of the 19th century became different ways of dealing with issues of anthropology in the context of theological and materialistic Idealism. So, too, the question of anthropology against issues of historical determinism framed the struggle for theological identity in the East. For example, as a part of a recovery of its own rootedness in history, Orthodoxy in Russia became preoccupied with what Russians call "social thought" (*obshchestvennaia mysl'*), resulting in such social manifestoes as that by Nicholas Chernyshevsky, *What Is to be Done?* (1863), followed by the very different appeal by Leo Tolstoy, *What Is to be Done?* (1883), and then by that of Nikolay Lenin (1902). The perception of religion as social illusion in Marxist/Leninist thought had its counterpart in the West in the de facto marginalization of religious influence in the public square as industrialization and modernization were seen to hold the answer for social ills.

Some of the issues dividing the churches today within the ecumenical movement grow out of the residue of these divisions and conflicts. While there are parallels that can be drawn between churches in the East and West, given the nature of the social history that caught up the churches in the early 20th century we will touch only on developments in the West. Here, Paul Lehmann observed that, at the time of the breakup of New England theology, the decisive nature of forgiveness for Protestants is related to a conception of how grace comes to us. He might, in a certain way, be said to speak for all churches.[51] The real crisis to which Protestantism had been brought by the early 20th century, he felt, was one that focused upon the question of whether man, or humanity, forgives itself or is forgiven. Caught between an arid scholasticism and an evolutionary humanism, a whole line of Protestant thinking which had evolved in relation to the Enlightenment was called into question in Lehmann's day by the dialectical theology of Karl Barth. As Lehmann summarizes,

> The orthodox conception of imputation was predicated upon the insight into the incomparable uniqueness of Christ. The fate of this insight, when the protective doctrine of the two natures and the three offices was replaced by the more intelligible category of the ethical vocation, is almost predictable.[52]

The Church's unique contribution

The Church's unique contribution to forgiveness and reconciliation comes at several points. In the first instance we might cite the classic Christian understanding of the doctrine of forgiveness, that we are forgiven and accepted by God through the person and work of Jesus who is recognized as the Messiah, or Christ. Paul Lehmann continues, ironically, with an edge for any age of narcissistic indulgence, by adding that "The historical uniqueness of Jesus will always be persuasive in a world peopled with potential Christs so long as these remain fascinated by their own possibilities." Without getting into the theological repartee of the early 20th century between Albrecht Ritschl and Karl Barth, the concern of dialectical theology was not to make theology intelligible so much as to permit it to remain faithful to the mystery of an objective truth that speaks to the human condition.[53] And so, Lehmann writes, how is the grace of God thought to be coming to one to forgive one? Grace comes freely. It involves a personal encounter. The forensic character of grace requires the irreversible priority of God in the act of forgiveness. The existence of a community of the forgiven, the Church, is not the continuation of a pre-existing reality but an expression of the absolute freedom of the divine will. This is the first point that must be made about the Church's unique role in the public square. We do not, in the first instance, forgive ourselves but we are forgiven. This theological idea carries implications for human relationships and community.

Second, the Church bears witness to a particular view of human personhood that gives shape to human rights and a particular conception of reconciliation. In his retrieval of the Orthodox idea of personhood, John D. Zizoulas grounds human identity in existential metaphysics, with a phenomenological description of "person" in terms of conscious acts through which one experiences substantial subjectivity. Early Christian theology was drawn to derive a new metaphor for Being with anthropological implications for human self-understanding because of the cosmological revolution of which it was a part. As with Judaism, early Christian theology came to conceive of God, not the world, as being absolute. The biblical doctrine of *creatio ex nihilo* obliged theology to trace ontology back to God, not the world, grounding the person not in necessity as a product of nature or even nurture, but in a form of freedom derivative of divinity. It was out of this perspective that John Paul II worked in the area of higher education in Poland prior to his papacy.[54] This emphasis upon the divine will is what grounds personhood in a free act of divinity, an ecumenical concern as much as it is an Orthodox doctrine and one of increasing scientific inquiry from many disciplines. It is this person who has inalienable rights – "life liberty and the pursuit of happiness" – we are wont to say, but now in the context of global human rights.[55] There is a fundamental discontinuity between God and humankind in the order of creation and also in the work of recreation. God creates. We co-create. God forgives. We can forgive, but we do not self-forgive.[56] All of this is in the service of reconciliation.

Third, this word of forgiveness and reconciliation comes to us through revelation. This is not to speak of religious truth wherever it might be found.[57] It is to say that forgiveness and reconciliation are central to what Jesus was all about.[58] Picking up where Lehmann left off, Stephen N. Williams argues that "the contest between revelation and reason can be significantly read as the conflict between the self-defining subject and the historical enactment of reconciliation".[59] Williams is concerned not only about epistemological questions as they have evolved since the Enlightenment in the West, not doubting that they figure into the story of a contemporary rejection of traditional Christianity. Rather, he finds an alternative way of reading intellectual history since the Enlightenment through a moral rejection of Christianity that only then issued in an epistemological disqualification of Christian belief.[60]

Williams offers due attention to the evolution of epistemology, following a French and English trajectory defined by Descartes, Locke and Tindal more than that of Continental Idealism, as was the case with Lehmann. He finds an opening for renewed thinking about the nature of the atonement as it bears upon forgiveness and reconciliation by turning Friedrich Nietzsche's philosophical scepticism back upon itself as the 20th century moved towards a form of modernity that found renewed space for Pascal's wager for belief in the midst of moral rather than epistemological considerations. Turning, by way of Michael Polanyi and Lesslie Newbigin, Williams offers a reading of the accounts of Jesus that asks us, following Bonhoeffer,[61] to consider again a Christ of faith identical to the historical Jesus who forgives sins not directed against himself, adding conundrum to the nature of his identity. Williams concludes:

> If Jesus did conduct himself in this way, we are at the heart of a puzzle best resolved, as it has seemed for many, by a confession of deity. If he did not, we are into a deeper puzzle about the formation of the earliest Christian traditions.[62]

Looking at the question of forgiveness and reconciliation as a matter of Christian theology, which is really what the Church must do, enables us to see that in matters of public policy we are not simply dealing with religion as a social phenomenon. Theology also matters. Persons grounded in the freedom of God in creation and re-creation, justification by faith through grace, the reality of the work of God as we hear it and practise it in community – these are important areas of ecumenical reflection, and in some cases achievement, even in the face of division over the ethical shape of the Christian life. A commitment to forgiveness and reconciliation on the part of the Church in the context of human rights is also a commitment to dialogue, the importance of which was marked out so well by Mikhail Bakhtin amidst the heterogeneity and contradictions of modernity,[63] a point made forcefully by Jacques Derrida.[64] A commitment to dialogue is a fourth contribution of the Church to public order. Christian anthropology, grounded in a theology of creation and redemption – apart from the world as such – gives courage to work in our deteriorating social order and offers an eschatological horizon of hope. In this light a religious renewal is required if there is to be political renewal.[65]

The Church as the communion of the forgiven

If forgiveness is real and the possibilities of reconciliation manifold, how do we model this reality in civil society? This question draws us to our understanding and practice of what it means to be the Church. It is a question that underscores the importance of churches with different languages, liturgies and governing structures to be in dialogue with one another so as to avoid scandal (John 17:21). It is a question that draws us to the quality of the public witness of the Church in a world marked by the divisions and conflict that are inherent to the kinds of social change we can expect in the 21st century (1 Pet. 2:9-10).

Forgiveness defines the Church

Let us leave for the moment Desmond Tutu and the question of why we should forgive as expressed in *No Future without Forgiveness.*[66] So, too, the sequence through which we travel – encompassing forgiveness, reconciliation and restorative justice.[67] The nature of forgiveness is such that it is difficult to express forgiveness apart from a community that encourages its practice. The community that cultivates forgiveness is the Church. The Church that lives in the world is committed to restorative, repair-ative and transformative justice. This is good news for all races and ethnicities in a pluriform world shaped by contemporary patterns of immigration and migration.[68]

Indeed, the ethnic diversity of the Church itself is a point of increasing remark.[69] This diversity is also reflected in ecclesiology. Such difference as exists might find grounding in Raymond Brown's reflection on the different heritages of the apostles,[70] a compelling point in contrast with the more unitary vision in the West that is derivative of theologians like Augustine, Aquinas and Calvin. For Orthodoxy with its emphasis upon an indigenous character of the Church, it is nevertheless one in so far as it is grounded in the seven councils and divine eucharist.[71] From the perspective of what the Church does, one might speak of different models of the Church.[72] One model that draws many today is that of mystical communion, raising questions about the boundaries of the Church. Karl Rahner's proposal is that if the Church's identity includes openness, then a certain amount of "vicariousness" means that the Church thinks and feels on its own behalf and on behalf of others.[73] This is the third of three types of the Church identified by van Beeck as "pistic", "charismatic" and "mystic" as centred in a Spirit-enlivened Jesus.[74] But the struggle today is with unity in face of the Church's growing diversity. This struggle, often around the question of a common *magisterium* as located in Rome, raises the question of how the Church of Christ is maintained in the truth of the gospel through the Holy Spirit.[75] At this point many issues pertain. Martin Luther, fearful of a theology of glory that ended in self-exaltation, suggested instead a theology of the cross, often yielding an unstable reality. This, for Karl Barth, is the Church as herald,[76] or an assembly that responds to God's word.[77]

In the midst of this controversy over the Church's identity, the Faith and Order Commission of the World Council of Churches defines the Church in the following way in the document, *The Nature and Purpose of the church*:

> 9. The Church belongs to God. It is the creation of God's Word and Holy Spirit. It cannot exist by and for itself.
> 10. The Church is centred and grounded in the Gospel, the Word of God. The Church is the communion of those who live in a personal relationship with God who speaks to them and calls forth their trustful response – the communion of the faithful. Thus the Church is the creature of God's Word which as a living voice creates and nourishes it throughout the ages. This divine Word is borne witness to and makes itself heard through the scriptures. Incarnate in Jesus Christ, it is testified to by the Church and proclaimed in preaching, in sacraments, and in service.[78]

Taking as a point of departure the term *communio sanctorum*,[79] we might fill this out with a sense of Jesus as the expected "prophet", "priest" and "king" long sought in messianic Judaism. Eusebius of Caesarea, Erasmus, and the company of the Reformed in classical Protestantism developed this Christological theme. It has been drawn into ecclesiology as an aspect of ecumenical thinking.[80] Christians, the mystical body of Christ (Rom. 8:17; 12:4; 1 Cor. 6:19; 2 Cor. 2:5), might find their vocation under the rubric of the threefold office *(triplex munus)* of Christ. Heightened in times of crisis, they – and the Church – play a prophetic role as truth-tellers and justice-seekers; find a priestly role in prayer and forgiveness and, in their [servant]-king role they regard one another as images of divine royalty, or God – persons fit for democratic dialogue. But note how "forgiveness" defines the Church: There is no worship apart from forgiveness (Matt. 5:23-24). Forgiveness defines the material identity of the Church (John 20:21-23). Forgiveness, as it tends towards reconciliation, defines (2 Cor. 5:19) vocation. Indeed, it might even be said that just as there are degrees to which we are willing to forgive so, too, there are degrees to which we might find community.

Building sustaining communities

As we think of all of the ways in which religion is criticized today, the work of building community is the Church in its most fundamental sense.[81] This work, as grounded in God's plan for the universe, is good work in so far as this effort finds its way forward through forgiveness, reconciliation and moving towards a restorative justice. This is religion in the service of "humane global governance". Religion, and churches as an aspect of human religiousness, have a role to play in building sustaining community. This is not merely instrumental, but is grounded in the substantial nature of the Church.

We might say that such substantive work is the vocation of the Church in those areas of global challenge that seem most open to "inhumane global governance".[82] So one is compelled to ask, what might forgiveness and reconciliation look like with respect to the polarization of wealth and an apparent global apartheid that sets the Global North against the Global South? Or, how can churches talk about the good news of Jesus Christ and, yet, share in a social reality that evinces wanton neglect of human suffering? Does the "down-sizing" of the Common Good, whether at a local, national or international level, tell us anything about the Church and its commitment to forgiveness and reconciliation? Finally, do we have responsibility for sharing the burgeoning technological innovation now shaping human community precisely because of the ways it bears potential for destructive as well as constructive ends – and bearing implications for forgiveness and reconciliation?

Religion, and Christianity in particular with its theology of forgiveness and reconciliation grounded in an ontology made manifest in Jesus, bears a unique role in fostering hope for humanitarian effort precisely in these days when such hope is flagging in so many quarters.[83] Together with those of good will in the wider religious community, Christians, and their communal expression as churches, can foster a globalization from below towards a more caring global democratic order.[84]

The doctrines of forgiveness and reconciliation remind Christians and their churches of the costly nature of this work. Orthodox churches have a unique role to play in fostering our understanding of forgiveness and reconciliation. They are churches that shape a landscape that reaches from the White Sea to the Black Sea to the Red Sea and across the Mediterranean Sea – and are also found throughout the rest of the world. They are churches with a unique challenge in a region too often characterized by its "clash of civilizations".

NOTES

[1] Many definitions of the term "globalization" have been given in this conference. I will not add to these here except to make reference to those found in Robert Schreiter, *The New Catholicity: Theology Between the Global and the Local*, Maryknoll NY, Orbis, 2000. Schreiter writes of the significance of globalization on local theologies and church life as we have moved from a bipolar to a multipolar world while locating the articulation of theology between global and local flows. Several of the essays in Peter L. Berger and Samuel P. Huntington eds, *Many Globalizations: Cultural Diversity in the Contemporary World*, New York, Oxford UP, 2002, illustrate the role of evangelical Protestantism, Roman Catholic *Opus Dei*, and other Buddhist and Islamic forces shaping global perspectives.

[2] The phrase comes from the title of an article by Benjamin R. Barber in *The Atlantic Monthly*, 269, no. 3, March 1992, pp.53-65.

[3] Samuel P. Huntington, *The Clash of Civilizations*, New York, Simon & Schuster, 1996.

[4] Elazar Barkan, *The Guilt of Nations: Restitution and Negotiating Historical Injustices*, Baltimore, Johns Hopkins UP, 2000. The United States has its own special guilt as written about by Samantha Powers, *A Problem from Hell: America and the Age of Genocide*, New York, Basic Books, 2002.

[5] Chester A. Crocker and Fen Osler Hampson with Pamela Aall, *Managing Global Chaos: Sources of and Responses to International Conflict*, Washington DC, United States Institute of Peace Press, 1996.

[6] Richard Falk looks to the bonding of the positive and inclusive aspects of secular and religious tendencies for a "humane globalization", in *Religion and Humane Global Governance*, New York, Palgrave, 2001, pp.1-4, 25-33, and his aim as stated on pp.9-10.

[7] The influential book and PBS series, *A Force More Powerful: A Century of Nonviolent Conflict*, New York, St Martin's, 2000, draws attention to tactics more than to theology but in such a way as to mark out paths for forgiveness and reconciliation in civil society.

[8] Notable also is the work of Coventry Cathedral in this respect. See Colin Holtum, *Reconciliation: The History and Purpose of Coventry*, City Vision, 1998.

[9] Books written while Bonhoeffer was in charge of the Confessing Church seminary at Finkenwalde after 1935. I am following L. Gregory Jones, "The Cost of Forgiveness: Grace, Christian Community and the Politics of Worldly Discipleship", *Union Theological Seminary Quarterly Review*, 46, 1992, pp.149-69. The biographical details of Bonhoeffer's life are best traced in Eberhard Bethge's biography, *Dietrich Bonhoeffer*, trans. E.H. Robertson *et al.*, London, Collins, 1970. Issues of forgiveness and remembrance continue to shape the Jewish community. The significance of this continuing discussion is made particular in Simon Wiesenthal, *The Sunflower: On the Possibilities and Limits of Forgiveness*, New York, Shocken, 1969 and later edns. The 1997 edition carries a symposium with responses from fifty-three persons of note engaged with the topic of forgiveness and whether or not it is possible with respect to the Holocaust.

[10] Corrie ten Boom with John and Elizabeth Sherrill, *The Hiding Place*, New York, Bantam, 1982.

[11] Simone Weil, *Gravity and Grace*, introduction by Gustave Thibon, trans. Arthur Wills, New York, Putnam, 1952.

[12] Todor Sabev, *The Orthodox Churches in the World Council of Churches: Towards the Future*, WCC Publications, 1996, pp.9-13. The publications of Thomas Fitzerald, George Limouris and Georges Tsetsis are among those of importance here. See also Ruth Rouse and Stephen C. Neill eds, *A History of the Ecumenical Movement*, Vol. I, 1517-1948, WCC Publications, 3rd edn, 1986, pp.193-211, 217-18.

[13] Desmond Tutu, *No Future without Forgiveness*, New York, Doubleday, 1999; see also the case for restorative justice in South Africa made by Charles Villa-Vicencio, "Restoring Justice: Dealing with the Past Differently", and his fuller study on human rights in international perspective, *A Theology of Reconstruction*, Cambridge, Cambridge UP, 1992.

[14] Martha Minow, *Between Vengeance and Forgiveness: Facing History after Genocide and Mass Violence*, Boston, Beacon, 1998.

[15] Donald Shriver reflects on his own developing perspective, "Slowly, I have arrived at the belief that the concept of forgiveness, so customarily relegated to the realms of religion

and personal ethics, belongs to the heart of reflection about how groups of humans can move to repair the damages that they have suffered from their past conflicts with each other. Precisely because it attends at once to moral truth, history and the human benefits that flow from the conquest of enmity, forgiveness is a word for a multi-dimensional process that is eminently political" (Shriver, *An Ethic for Enemies: Forgiveness in Politics*, New York, Oxford UP, 1995).

[16] See the analysis and cyclical graphs prepared by Lewis Kriesberg, *Constructive Conflict: From Escalation to Resolution*, New York, Rowman & Littlefield, 1998.

[17] Olga Botcharova analyzes the failure to attend to healing and ways of promoting reconciliation in "Implementation of Track Two Diplomacy", in Raymond Helmick, SJ and Rodney Petersen, *Forgiveness and Reconciliation: Religion, Public Policy and Conflict Transformation*, Philadelphia, Templeton, 2001, pp.269-94.

[18] Bessel van der Kolk, MD, *Traumatic Stress: The Effects of Overwhelming Experience on Mind, Body, and Society*, New York, Guilford, 1996.

[19] Richard Fitzgibbons, "Anger and the Healing Power of Forgiveness: A Psychiatrist's View", in Robert D. Enright and Joanna North eds, *Exploring Forgiveness*, Madison, Univ. of Wisconsin Press, 1998, pp.63-74. He endorses a definition of forgiveness given by philosopher Joanna North and psychologist Robert Enright who define forgiveness as "a matter of *willed* change of heart, the successful result of an active endeavour to replace bad thoughts with good, bitterness and anger with compassion and affection". See North, "Wrongdoing and Forgiveness", *Philosophy*, 42, 1987, pp.499-508. Brian Frost reminds us that forgiveness in politics, as in personal life, is a process "rather than something to be applied temporarily, like a poultice". Cited in Michael Henderson, *Forgiveness: Breaking the Chain of Hate*, Wilsonville OR, BookPartners, 1999, p.4.

[20] Thomas J. Sheff, *Emotions, the Social Bond, and Human Reality*, Cambridge, Cambridge UP, 1997. For further information on forgiveness and health, see the Campaign for Forgiveness Research: www.forgiving.org; and the International Forgiveness Institute: www.intl-forgive-inst.org.

[21] Andrew P. Morrison, MD, *The Culture of Shame*, Northvale NJ, Jason Aronson, 1996. See similarly, Donald Capps, *The Depleted Self: Sin in a Narcissistic Age*, Minneapolis, Fortress, 1993.

[22] It is paradoxical to see how during suffering one learns to forgive. A very famous case in Romania was Father Nicolae Steinhardt, who after being marginalized and threatened by the nationalistic government was arrested by the communists in 1959 for failing to betray his Romanian friends. He was accused of "crime of espionage against social order", and sentenced to 13 years of *muncă silnică* (heavy labour). It was in the dreadful Jilava Prison that he discovered the most intimate aspects of forgiveness. On 15 March 1960 he was baptized Christian by an Orthodox priest Mina Dobzeu, thereafter finding his experience in prison as something that he calls "a journey towards happiness". After being released from prison, he joined the monastic community from Rohia Monastery, where he lived until 29 March 1989, when he died in the hospital at Baia Mare, Romania. His memories had been recorded by him and kept secret until after the collapse of communism in 1989 when they became available to the public. His writings include *Jurnalul Fericirii* [The Journey of Happiness], Dacia, Cluj-Napoca, 1994. I owe this reference to Marian Simion of Holy Cross Greek Orthodox School of Theology and the Boston Theological Institute.

[23] See Michael Lerner's book of this title *The Politics of Meaning*, Boulder CO, Perseus, 1997. The complexities of this religious resurgence are sketched by Falk, *Religion and Humane Global Governance*, pp.63-70.

[24] *The Living God: A Catechism for the Christian Faith*, vol. I, trans. from the French by Olga Dunlop, Crestwood NY, St Vladimir's Seminary Press, 1989, p.191. See Stanley S. Harakas, "Forgiveness and Reconciliation: An Orthodox Perspective", in Helmick and Petersen, *Forgiveness and Reconciliation*, pp.51-78.

[25] Henderson, *Forgiveness*.

[26] L. Gregory Jones, *Embodying Forgiveness: A Theological Analysis*, Grand Rapids MI, Eerdmans, 1995.

[27] Marjorie Suchoki, *The Fall to Violence: Original Sin in Relational Theology*, New York, Continuum, 1995.

[28] Geiko Müller-Fahrenholz, *The Art of Forgiveness: Theological Reflections on Healing and Reconciliation*, WCC Publications, 1996.

[29] Shriver, Jr, *An Ethic for Enemies*.

[30] Everett L. Worthington, Jr, *Dimensions of Forgiveness: Psychological Research and Theological Perspectives*, Philadelphia, Templeton, 1998.

[31] In Enright and North eds, *Exploring Forgiveness*, p.20.

[32] Hannah Arendt, *The Human Condition*, second ed. with introduction by Margaret Canovan, Chicago, Univ. of Chicago Press, 1998, pp.238-39.

[33] Müller-Fahrenholz, *The Art of Forgiveness*, p.24. Recalling the work of Toni Morrison, he adds that in *Song of Solomon* she writes, "'If you take a life, you own it. You are responsible for it. You can't get rid of nobody by killing them. They are still there, and they are yours now.' This is a forceful way of saying that every act of transgression constitutes a bondage that keeps the perpetrator and victim locked together. The more violent the transgression, the deeper the bondage."

[34] Of special importance is the work of Patriarch Pavle of Serbia following the break-up of the former Yugoslavia. The Palestinian–Israeli conflict offers special challenges. See *In Communion*, winter 2000, pp.22-23.

[35] Stanley S. Harakas, "Forgiveness and Reconciliation. An Orthodox Perspective", in Helmick and Petersen, *Forgiveness and Reconciliation*, p.59. See also Sergei Hackel, "Paths to Reconciliation: Some Ways and By-ways from the Orthodox Past", *Sobornost*, 2.1, 1980, p.9.

[36] See in C. W. du Toit, *Confession and Reconciliation*, Pretoria, UNISA, 1998; also related is Wilhelm Verwoerd, *My Winds of Change*, Cape Town, Ravan Press, 1997; and Walter Wink, *Violence and Nonviolence in South Africa: Jesus' Third Way*, Philadelphia, New Society, 1989.

[37] The problem of impunity, gross and systematic human-rights violations that are not dealt with, is raised in Charles Harper ed., *Impunity: An Ethical Perspective: Six Case Studies from Latin America*, WCC Publications, 1996.

[38] Everett Worthington, Jr, *Dimensions of Forgiveness*, Philadelphia, Templeton, 1998, p.129.

[39] Miroslav Volf, *Exclusion and Embrace: A Theological Exploration of Identity, Otherness, and Reconciliation*, Nashville, Abingdon, 1996.

[40] Müller-Fahrenholz, *The Art of Forgiveness*, p.3.

[41] John Paul Lederach, *Building Peace*, Washington DC, United States Institute of Peace Press, 1997, p.30.

[42] See the review by Charles Villa-Vicencio of *Forgiveness and Reconciliation: Religion, Public Policy, and Conflict Transformation*, Philadelphia, Templeton, 2001. He writes that Anthony da Silva addresses the sequence question quite explicitly, drawing on Robert Schreiter's suggestion that a more appropriate sequence may be: "reconciliation, forgiveness, repentance", in Helmick and Petersen, *Forgiveness and Reconciliation*, p.304.

[43] Lederach, *Building Peace*, p.30.

[44] Michael L. Hadley ed., *The Spiritual Roots of Restorative Justice*, Albany NY, SUNY, 2001.

[45] Martha Minow, *Between Vengeance and Forgiveness*, Boston, Beacon, 1999, p.92.

[46] Howard Zehr, *Changing Lenses: A New Focus for Crime and Justice*, Scottdale PA, Herald, 1995, pp.181-86.

[47] Martin Wright, *Justice for Victims and Offenders*, New York, Open UP, 1991, pp.114-17.

[48] Daniel Van Ness and Karen Strong, *Restoring Justice*, Cincinnati OH, Anderson, 1997, p.31. Carolyn Boys-Watson, director of the Center for Restorative Justice, Suffolk University, defines our term in the following way: "Restorative justice is a broad term that encompasses a growing social movement to institutionalize peaceful resolutions to criminal and human-rights violations. These range from international peace-making tribunals such as the Truth and Reconciliation Commission of South Africa to innovations within our courts, jails, and prisons, such as victim-offender dialogue, community justice committees and victim impact panels. Rather than privileging the law and the state, restorative justice engages the victim, offender and the affected community in search of solutions that promote repair and reconciliation. Restorative justice seeks to build partnerships to re-

establish mutual responsibility for constructive responses to crime and wrongdoing within our communities." Paper delivered in 1999, on file at the Boston Theological Institute. See similar ideas in Barry Stuart, *Building Community Justice Partnerships: Community Peacemaking Circles*, Yukon, Community Peacemaking Circles, 1996. See also Shay Bilchik, *Guide for Implementing the Balanced and Restorative Justice Model: Report*, US Dept. of Justice Office of Justice Programs, 1998.

[49] See David A. Steele, "Conflict Resolution Among Religious People in Bosnia and Croatia", in Paul Mojzes ed., *Religion and the War in Bosnia*, Atlanta, Scholars, 1998, pp.246-53. Such local work towards reconciliation constitutes what Joseph Montville has referred to as Track Two diplomacy as opposed to Track One diplomacy, the official work of statecraft. See his article, "Religion and Peacemaking", in Helmick and Petersen, *Forgiveness and Reconciliation*, pp.97-116.

[50] Shriver, *An Ethic for Enemies*, 1995. A philosophical interest in forgiveness can be traced to Alasdair MacIntyre's work, *After Virtue*, Notre Dame IN, Univ. of Notre Dame Press, 1981, with few precursors. The field is not so bleak when we turn to literature. Themes of forgiveness run through the works of such authors as Fyodor Doestoevsky, Flannery O'Conner and Toni Morrison to name a few. Notable individuals like Simone Weil and Dietrich Bonhoeffer stand out as well. This privatization of forgiveness and reconciliation should not necessarily be seen as pejorative. As forgiveness and reconciliation became defined as a sacrament or rite of the Church it offered an opportunity for religious meaning and sincerity. See, for Orthodox churches, Metropolitan Emilianos Timiadis, ed. George K. Duval, *Priest and Renewal: Concepts for Pastoral Effectiveness*, Brookline MA, Holy Cross Orthodox Press, 1994, p.160.

[51] Paul Lehmann, *Forgiveness: Decisive Issue in Protestant Thought*, New York, Harpers, 1940, p.4 *et passim*. The local history of schools of theology in the Boston area, and particularly that of Andover Seminary at the close of the 19th century, reflect this theological turmoil.

[52] *Ibid.*, p.97.

[53] Walter Lowrie, *Our Concern with the Theology of Crisis*, Boston, Meador, 1932, pp.43-44.

[54] See Andrew N. Woznicki, *A Christian Humanism: Karol Wojtyla's Existential Personalism*, New Britain CN, Mariel, 1980, p.ix.

[55] The contribution of religion to global human rights is explored by John Witte ed., *Religious Human Rights in Global Perspective: Religious Perspectives*, Grand Rapids MI, Eerdmans, 2000. See also Falk, *Religion and Humane Global Governance*, *passim* and his *Human Rights Horizons: The Pursuit of Justice in a Globalizing World*, New York, Routledge, 2000. Jimmy Carter traces the recent history of a human rights policy in the United States in "The American Road to a Human Rights Policy", in Samantha Power and Graham Allison eds, *Realizing Human Rights: Moving from Inspiration to Impact*, New York, St Martin's, 2000, pp.49-61.

[56] It is of note that Western, or Latin, theology is finding a new *rapprochement* between Roman Catholics and Protestants on the doctrine of justification, an important step towards the healing of the division in the Western Church, a part of the journey along the way towards greater ecumenical understanding between East and West. See *The Joint Declaration on the Doctrine of Justification* (prepared between 1995 and 1997 by Roman Catholic and Lutheran theologians under the auspices of the Vatican and the Lutheran World Federation).

[57] Mark Heim develops a Christian theology of religious ends that builds on Alan Race's typology of exclusivist, inclusivist and pluralist by suggesting a fourfold grammar that allows integrity for different religious fulfillments, in *The Depth of the Riches: A Trinitarian Theology of Religious Ends*, Grand Rapids MI, Eerdmans, 2001, p.7.

[58] Arendt, *The Human Condition*, pp.238-39.

[59] Stephen N. Williams, *Revelation and Reconciliation: A Window on Modernity*, Cambridge, Cambridge UP, 1995, p.104.

[60] Williams draws attention to a recovery of the doctrine of the atonement in such authors as Thomas F. Torrance, *The Mediation of Christ*, Edinburgh, T. & T. Clark, 1992, p.103: "Reconciliation constitutes the inner dynamic content of revelation and revelation becomes effective precisely as reconciliation for thereby it achieves its end." Also in Colin

Gunton, *The Actuality of Atonement*, Edinburgh, T. & T. Clark, 1988; and Lesslie Newbigin, "Truth and Authority in Modernity", in P. Sampson, V. Samuel and C. Sugden eds, *Faith and Modernity*, Oxford, Regnum, 1994; in Williams, *Revelation and Reconciliation*, p.143.

[61] Dietrich Bonhoeffer, *Ethics*, New York, Macmillan, 1965; *idem, Christology*, London, Collins, 1960, pp.71-7.

[62] Williams, *Revelation and Reconciliation*, p.154, n.16. The question of why and in what way we may require a mediator for an adequate foundation for forgiveness and reconciliation is a topic that cannot be taken up in this chapter. The work of René Girard has become central here. For Girard, the sacrifice of the scapegoat becomes, in his understanding, the origin and description of religion. Biblical religion is unique, argues Girard, in that it does not side with the powerful who benefit from the violence of scapegoating, but aligns itself with victims. A point of special interest for Girard is that he finds in Jesus one who refuses to enter the spiral of violence, one who breaks this spiral by yielding to it despite his evident guiltlessness, and so through forgiveness opens the way to reconciliation. René Girard, *Things Hidden since the Foundation of the World*, Stanford, Stanford UP, 1987, p.154.

[63] Katerina Clark and Michael Holquist, *Mikhail Bakhtin*, Cambridge MA, Harvard UP, 1984, pp.347-48. In many ways the move towards dialogism and away from monologism is that which characterizes the work of Emmanuel Clapsis, *Orthodoxy in Conversation: Orthodox Ecumenical Engagements*, WCC Publications and Brookline MA, Holy Cross Orthodox Press, 2001. Addressing the critical issues of the day from an Orthodox perspective, the author takes seriously the value of ecumenical engagement.

[64] Jacques Derrida, *On Cosmopolitanism and Forgiveness*, London, Routledge, 2001, pp.27-60. Derrida's point that to the extent forgiveness is extended through "globalization" the Church is diminished in need is eschatological at best, but intriguing. For political reality as we know it, churches can be the first place of instruction in democratic principle and platform for entry into political dialogue. A politics of meaning, as epitomized in faith communities, can contribute to "deliberative democracy" as defined by Amy Gutmann and Dennis Thompson, *Democracy and Disagreement*, Cambridge MA, Harvard UP, 1996.

[65] Michael Lerner, Roger Gottlieb and others from humanist as well as more traditional religious rootage are often heard to make this point, e.g., Lerner's *The Politics of Meaning*, 1997; and Gottlieb's *Joining Hands: Politics and Religion Together for Social Change*, Boulder CO, Westview, 2002.

[66] Tutu, *No Future without Forgiveness*.

[67] See the review by Charles Villa-Vicencio of Helmick and Petersen, *Forgiveness and Reconciliation*.

[68] See various reports of the United Nations High Commissioner for Refugees (UNHCR); Judy Mayotte, *Disposable People? The Plight of Refugees*, Maryknoll NY, Orbis, 1992; and Gil Loescher, *Beyond Charity: International Cooperation and the Global Refugee Crisis*, New York, Oxford UP, 1993. The impact of this global movement of population upon life in North America is sketched by Harold J. Recinos, *Jesus Weeps: Global Encounters on Our Doorstep*, Nashville, Abingdon, 1992.

[69] Philip Jenkins, "The Next Christianity", *The Atlantic Monthly*, Oct. 2002, pp.53-68. Jenkins writes that we stand at a historical turning point as epochal today as the Reformation was almost 500 years ago. De-centralized, privatized Northern Christianity is being replaced by forms of Southern Christianity that are more traditional and communal in nature. Lester Kurtz, *Gods in the Global Village*, London, Pine Forge, 1995 offers a sociological approach to the contemporary morphing of religion; Aída Besançon Spencer and William David Spencer, *The Global God: Multicultural Evangelical Views of God*, Grand Rapids MI, Baker, 1998, offer insight into how Christianity itself is taking on a cultural framework shaped more by its patterns of growth in the global South.

[70] Raymond Brown, *The Churches the Apostles Left Behind*, New York, Paulist, 1984.

[71] Timothy (Kallistos) Ware, *The Orthodox Church*, Harmondsworth, Penguin, 1963. That the ministry of the bishop in the celebration of the eucharist constitutes and ensures the unity of the Church is the contention of John D. Zizioulas, *Eucharist, Bishop, Church*, Brookline MA, Holy Cross Orthodox Press, 2001.

[72] Avery Dulles, *Models of the Church*, New York, Doubleday/Image, 1978.

[73] See Vatican II, Decree on Ecumenism, *Unitatis Redintegratio*, nr. 11; Karl Rahner, *Foundations of Christian Faith*, New York, Crossroad, 1978. Different models of the Church through time and social experience are sketched by Hans Küng, *Christianity: Essence, History, and Future*, New York, Continuum, 1995.

[74] Frans Josef van Beeck, SJ, *Catholic Identity after Vatican II*, Chicago, Loyola, 1985.

[75] Francis A. Sullivan, SJ, *Magisterium: Teachng Authority in the Catholic Church*, New York, Paulist, 1983.

[76] Karl Barth, *Dogmatics in Outline*, New York, Harper Torchbooks, 1959.

[77] Hans Küng, *The Church*, New York, Sheed & Ward, 1968.

[78] *The Nature and Purpose of the Church*, WCC, 1998, p.9.

[79] Dietrich Bonhoeffer, *Sanctorum Communio: A Theological Study of the Sociology of the Church*, New York, Harper & Row, 1963.

[80] Yves Congar, *Laity, Church and World*, trans. Donald Atwater, Baltimore, Helicon, 1960; and George H. Williams, "Translatio Studii: The Puritans' Conception of their First University in New England, 1636", in *Festschrift für Heinrich Bornkamm. Archiv für Reformationsgeschichte* LVII. 1.2, 1966, pp.152-81.

[81] Alkiviadis Calivas, *Essays in Theology and Liturgy*, vol. I, *The Conscience of the Church*, Brookline MA, Holy Cross Orthodox Press, 2002, p.11 *et passim*. Falk lists the contributions of religion as including an appreciation for suffering, civilizational resonance, an ethos of solidarity, normative horizons, the connection of faith and power, a recognition of limits, a pilgrim identity and reconciliation: *Religion and Humane Global Governance*, pp.30-32.

[82] I am following Falk here, adopting his term and areas of potential "inhumane governance", *Religion and Humane Global Governance*, pp.21-25.

[83] A faltering hope in humanitarian effort is expressed by David Rieff in *A Bed for the Night: Humanitarianism in Crisis*, New York, Simon & Schuster, 2002, in distinction from the still optimistic views of Michael Ignatieff ed., with Amy Gutmann, of *Human Rights as Politics and Idolatry*, Princeton, Princeton UP, 2001. Akira Iriye contends that a global civil society has been fashioned by international organizations through the 20th century. See *Global Community: The Role of International Organizations in the Making of the Contemporary World*, Berkeley, Univ. of California Press, 2002. See his helpful references regarding religion and the role of the churches, a topic that requires much further work.

[84] Hans Küng, *A Global Ethic for Global Politics and Economics*, New York, Oxford UP, 1998; and see Richard Falk, "The Making of Global Citizenship", in Bart van Steenbergen ed., *The Condition of Citizenship*, London, Sage, 1994, pp.127-40. This can be seen implemented in Track Two diplomacy. See Joseph Montville, "Religion and Peacemaking", in Helmick and Petersen, *Forgiveness and Reconciliation*, pp.97-116.

Orthodox Spirituality and Social Activism
Reclaiming Our Vocabulary – Refocusing Our Vision

JOHN CHRYSSAVGIS

The word "spirituality" is as dangerous as the word "activism", if only because both words are so vulnerable to misunderstanding and misuse. When we speak of a spiritual person, we generally understand it as a signpost – here is someone whose head is in heaven, always in some "other" state, who can only see the mystical dimensions of the world. But we would rarely identify ourselves fully with such a person. By analogy, when we speak of an activist, we sometimes intend it as a warning – here is a person who is always involved, forever in the forefront, inevitably causing problems for someone or another. But we never would want our child to marry one, let alone become one. Meaning almost anything, the terms "spirituality" and "activism" mean almost nothing unless they are nuanced and clarified.

So what is it about language? An alert human infant early begins to build a vocabulary, to make sense of the chaos of sounds through articulation. A child recognizes that there are some noises we share with others, certain sounds that are deserving of response. This is precisely how – and, at the same time, probably how early – our theological vocabulary also begins to develop. Unfortunately, many years later, and after so many well-meaning adults who taught us Sunday school or theological courses, we are intent on fitting the vastness of the world and of God into small boxes of our own devising. We are, I think, called to reclaim our theological vocabulary. And, if we have any guides in this endeavour, at least as Orthodox Christians, it is the saints of the Church who teach us the process of learning and re-learning what it is consciously to know and to reflect God's love in the world.

Such words, then, as "spirituality" carry an enormous weight of baggage throughout history and our own life. "Spirituality" is a term that can project wrong cues; it can even cause a great deal of harm. I find that the long struggle to sort out a genuine theological vocabulary has made me more aware of ways in which religious language can often strike a false note – the narcissistic babble that transforms itself into spirituality, the conventional "language of a land with no known inhabitants".[1] The Church of the fathers has, of course, many inhabitants. And, in living with the saints, in realigning a genuine relationship with them, we find that vocabulary comes to life and forces us to question and even to shed inadequate definitions that we have received from our childhood or our culture, which we have formed – actually, we have deformed – as "spiritual" means in order to justify our "secular" ends, whatever these may be. We can often learn to refuse convenient codes, the "sacred lingo" of glassy-eyed piety, by grounding them in the world where we live as mortal beings in expectation of the eternal age that is to come.

The aim, ultimately, in any discussion about "spirituality" and "activism" is to bring about some form of reconciliation between the ways in which we understand our world and God. The goal is to bring healing to a world that has grown accustomed to an unholy dissociation between spirituality and morality, and to a disciplinary divorce within academia itself of Christian ethics (in Protestant confessions), moral theology (in Roman Catholic circles) and Christian spirituality (in Orthodox theology). We are called – somehow – to close the gap, to hold in tension the stress on fleeing from the world and the anxiety to change the world; to bring together the struggle towards personal holiness and the struggle towards social justice; to reconnect our need for personal salvation and the need for cosmic transformation. The problem is not that spirituality is "privatized" and internalized, or that activism is "globalized" and externalized, but that the two are distinguished from one another in the first place.[2]

In his book, *Unequal Protection: The Rise of Corporate Dominance and the Theft of Human Rights*, Thom Hartman refers to "the values we choose to live by" in a corporate and globalized world.[3] It is true that whenever we speak – whether about things in heaven or on earth – we are drawing upon established, indeed presumed values of ourselves and of our world. In fact, this may be the reason why some contemporary writers prefer to speak not only of a "global utility"[4] but also of "the art of profitability".[5]

Therefore, as I contemplated the topic on which I was asked to speak, I considered three fundamental terms in light of another art, namely "the art of prayer",[6] particularly as this is reflected in the early ascetic literature of the Christian East. These three concepts will serve as my basis for drawing connections between spirituality and activism, between contemplation and action, as well as for reclaiming basic theological vocabulary and refocusing our spiritual vision. I hope to approach these terms

with a proper sense of humility before the great mystery of language –
that human venture which begins with the ear and tongue of an infant,
proceeds through the tensions that eventually define the relationship
between our words and those of others, and finally reaches for the very
mystery of God's Word. Such language has the power to bless... as well
as to curse, the grace to heal... as well as to wound. It has the creative
force of a "word made flesh and dwelling among us in the world" (John
1:14). We are obliged to pay closer attention to it.

Eschatology: "Dying, yet behold we live"

I was in my early teens when I discovered the word "eschatology"
(from the Greek word *eschaton*, meaning "the last"). Right away, I knew
something was different about this word. It had a breadth and spacious-
ness far greater than any dictionary definition could allow. Many students of Orthodox theology encounter this word in a writer such as
Vladimir Lossky. I still recall my tattered copy of his *Mystical Theology
of the Eastern Church*.[7]

Now, most of us assume that the last times and the last things imply
some apocalyptic or escapist attitude towards the world.[8] It took a long
time for theologians to realize that eschatology is not the last, perhaps
unnecessary, chapter in some course or manual of dogmatics. Eschatology is not the teaching about what follows everything else in this world
and in these times. It is the teaching about our relationship to those last
things and last times. In essence, it is about the last-ness and the lasting-
ness of all things. The Omega gives meaning to the Alpha; this world is
interpreted in light of the age to come. The entire creation is a burning
bush of God's energies – to recall Gregory Palamas in the 14th century;
the beyond is discovered in the midst of life – to recall Dietrich Bonhoeffer in the 20th century.

However, it was my friends in the early desert of Egypt and Palestine
who would later plunge me all unwitting into the realm of eschatology.
That dry desert, from the middle of the 3rd century until around the end
of the 6th century, became the laboratory for exploring hidden truths
about heaven and earth, as well as a forging ground for drawing connections between the two. The hermits who lived in that desert tested and
studied what it means to be human – with all the tensions and temptations, all of the struggle beyond survival, all of the contact with good and
the conflict with evil. And on their course, some of them made many
mistakes; others made fewer mistakes. Whoever said that there is a clear
and simple answer to the questions of life? Yet, these men and women
dared to push the limits; they challenged and defied the norms of what
was acceptable in their age and society.

I think I received further insights into some of the deeper dimensions of eschatology when I faced my own mortality in the brokenness of my son's cerebral palsy. The word "eschatology" no longer seemed other-worldly to me; it did not focus exclusively on future events. I was intensely faced with the vulnerability of an infant – so intricately caught up in the last things. The lie about heaven being elsewhere split wide open when I admitted that I was really broken.

What is far more difficult and far more important than learning to live is learning to die. Once we sense that we are in the shadow of God, then we discover light, so much light that our vision of the world improves dramatically. Then, we know that holiness is near. Dying and loss are lessons in how to live and love. They are the stuff from which eschatology is made.

So our spiritual reflection on globalization is fatally flawed if it does not begin with the reality of the cross, with the suffering and cries of those deeply affected and directly threatened by its legacy. An eschatological interpretation of globalization introduces a raw criticism of power dynamics and human domination. It recognizes that what is personal and private is also political and public.

An eschatological vision of reality and the world offers a way out of the impasse of provincialism and the evil of confessionalism. It allows us the possibility to question and reject modern "market myths", such as the theory that growth benefits all, that freedom is market freedom, that our purpose is consumption and domination, or that corporate- and commercial-driven globalization are inevitable.[9] It reflects our refusal to acquiesce, whether out of innocence or intimidation, whether by choice or by force.

Finally, eschatology is our hope against all hopelessness. It is our conviction that our efforts on this planet are not ours alone, but that the Source and End of all life is working in us and through us, indeed above and beyond us for the wellbeing of all creation, including our tiny part in it.[10]

Silence: listening to the world

As a father of two teenagers, I know that silence (the Greek term is *hesychia*, which also signifies stillness) is not the absence of noise but the ability to tell the difference between the two. Children who are barked at all day by burned-out parents ultimately stop listening. Yet, listening is surely the prerequisite for silence. Such silence is active, alive and affectionate. It resembles a spider spinning its web, a silk-worm creating its silk. It reminds us to take our soul with us wherever we go.

What is far more difficult and far more important than learning to speak is learning to be silent. In the desert, silence is the daughter of patience, the mother of watchfulness. When all words are abandoned, a new awareness arrives. Silence awakens us from numbness to the world around us, from our dullness of vision: Abba Poemen said, "Be watchful inwardly; but be watchful also outwardly."[11]

For the early desert dwellers, silence is a requirement of life, the first duty of love. Silence is a way of waiting, a way of watching, and a way of listening to – and not ignoring – what is going on in our heart and in our world. It is the glue that binds our attitudes and our actions. Silence reflects our surrender to God and to new patterns of learning and living. Through being silent, we learn by suffering and undergoing, not just by speculating and understanding. Silence confirms our readiness to lead a counter-cultural way of life, to choose rather than to be led, to admit our limited perspective as consumers and to appreciate another, the unlimited perspective of "life in abundance" (John 10:10).

And what we learn in silence is that we are all intimately interconnected, all mutually interdependent. Dorotheus of Gaza said in the 6th century:

> Suppose we were to take a compass and insert the point and draw the outline of a circle. The centre point is the same distance from any point on the circumference... Let us suppose that this circle is the world and that God is the centre of this world; the straight lines drawn from the circumference to the centre are the lives of human beings... the closer these are to God, the closer they come to each other and to the centre of the world; and the closer they come to each other and to the centre of the world, the closer they become to God.[12]

The truth is that all things are so intimately inter-related, cohering in each other beyond our imagination. Nothing living is self-contained. There is no autonomy – only a distinction between a sense of responsibility and a lack thereof.

The result of any bifurcation between spirituality and activism is catastrophic. The way we pray is mirrored in the way that we treat our brother and sister. Moreover, we are also invited to respond to nature with the same delicacy and sensitivity with which we respond to people. All of us are co-celebrants in what Maximus the Confessor in the 7th century called "cosmic liturgy" – he might well have spoken of "cosmic economy" or "cosmic ecology".

Detachment: the value of action

Finally, the early ascetics also valued the term "detachment". For us, detachment is a concept that has lost its positive connotation.

Nowadays, it is used in a negative sense, to mean the opposite of a healthy engagement with the world and with other people. It conveys a sense of aloofness, a studied remoteness that implies lack of concern. Yet the monastic interpretation of detachment could not be more different. In the desert, detachment meant not allowing either worldly values or self-centredness to distract us from what is most essential in our relationship with God and with our world. Dorotheus of Gaza describes detachment as being free from forcing certain things to happen (the literal meaning of the Greek term *aprospatheia*). It is faith sufficiently strong as to be thoroughly realistic in its encounter with the world. It is paying close attention to details, even to the intake of food and the acquisition of possessions. Not in order to punish ourselves, but in order to discern the value of sharing, the presence of suffering, and the intrinsic honour of good things in life. This sort of detachment is neither passive nor remote; paradoxically, it is fully engaged with the world. It is a prayer that can absorb all manner of pain and transform it into hope.

For the desert elders, detachment from everything and everyone only underlined the dignity of everything and everyone. Detachment was the first step of monastic renunciation or of the flight to the desert. Yet, detachment was more than merely spatial or material: Abba Zosimas always liked to say,

> It is not possessing something that is harmful, but being attached to it.[13]

Detachment is not the inability to focus on things, material or other; it is the spiritual capacity to focus on all things, material and other, without attachment. It is primarily something spiritual; it is an attitude of life.

In this respect, detachment is ongoing, requiring continual refinement over years of practice. The desert elders speak of stages in the way of detachment, just as there are steps in "the ladder of divine ascent".[14] Detachment resembles the shedding of a number of coats of skin, until our senses are sharpened, or until – as one desert father put it – "our inner vision becomes keen".[15] When we learn what to let go of, we also learn what is worth holding on to. Think of it in this way: it is simply not possible to share something precious or even to hold a lover's hand, when we keep our fists clenched, holding tightly onto something. The purpose of monastic detachment was not to live apart from the social world, but to inspire about how to live in the world as a part of society. Detachment is love, a positive energy that must be incarnated into action.

The same attitude extends beyond one's connection with other people to one's relationship to material things:

Abba Agathon was once walking with his disciples. One of them, on finding a small green pea on the road, said to the old man, "Father, may I take it?" The old man, looking at him with astonishment, replied, "Was it you that put it there?" "No," said the brother. "How then", continued the old man, "can you take up something, which you did not put down?"[16]

The detachment recommended here is a form of letting go. We are to let go of our actions, of our words, and finally of our life. The aim of letting go is the learning of true prayer, the starting-point and ending-point of all action. By letting go, we learn to pray spontaneously, a gift that children seem to have innately, but which takes a life-time for us to recover as adults. And in this prayer, the way of silence and the way of service coincide. Abba Poemen said,

If three people meet, of whom the first fully preserves interior peace, the second gives thanks to God in illness, and the third serves with a pure mind, these three are doing the same work.[17]

Work is not separated from prayer. Instead, prayer frees us for carefree service of others, where we are no longer conditioned by the burden of necessity but always prepared for the novelty of grace. Just as silence conditions our words, so prayer conditions our works. Detachment signifies humility, and humility looks to shift the focus from oneself as the centre of the world and to place oneself in the service of others. The humble person is always satisfied, always shares, always gives, always gives thanks.

A truly detached person cannot tolerate creating miserable poverty for the sake of accumulating exorbitant wealth. The moral crisis of our global economic injustice is integrally spiritual; it signals something terribly amiss in our relationship with God, with people, and with things. Yet, insulated as we are by privilege and by the sin of attachment, so many of us remain blind to the ecological devastation created by current global trade and investment regimes.[18] The humble person is able to say "no" – or "enough" – when it comes to food and possessions. Detachment is a way of liberation. And the detached person is free, uncontrolled by attitudes that abuse the world, uncompelled by ways that use the world.

This implies that we are not tyrannical overlords – with a licence to dominate the earth and to control creation – but servants and ministers called to restore harmony with the rest of the world, to bring a sense of at-one-ment with the environment. Detachment is the worshipful acknowledgment that this world, "the earth... is the Lord's, and all the fullness thereof" (Ps. 23:1). It is an affirmation that the material creation is not to be exploited selfishly but to be returned in thanks to God, restored in communion with God.

When I recognize detachment as this powerful source of community and life, then I begin to break down barriers with my neighbour and my world, to recognize in others faces, icons; and in the earth the very face of God. Detachment implies loving; it is restoring the primal vision of creation, the original beauty of the world. It signifies moving away from what I want, to what the world needs. It is liberation from greed, control and compulsion. It is freeing creation itself from fear and destruction.

Conclusion

Walking the way of the heavenly kingdom, assuming the power of silence and recognizing the value of detachment is to regain a sense of wonder, to be filled with a sense of goodness, of God-liness. It is to recognize all things in God and to remember God in all things. Understanding the spiritual root of our economic globalization of consumption is the necessary corrective for our culture of wasting and wounding. Letting go and letting God – in a renewed eschatological attitude – is the crucial balance for our patterns of control. Keeping silence is a critical alternative to noticing the impact and effect of our actions. And detachment is an essential way of learning that fasting is the only corrective for our wasting, that communion is the only substitute for our consumption.

Sharing is the healing of the scarring that we have left on the body of our world, and on our neighbour as the body of God. When through silence and detachment we learn to share, our spirituality is anything but disconnected from our actions. Then, we no longer lead lives disengaged from the injustice in the world. Then, our vision becomes enlarged, forgiving, able to contain the Uncontainable. Whenever we embrace this cosmic vision, we cease to narrow life to our concerns, our desires and ourselves; attending in the process to our vocation to transform the entire creation of God. Then, the confession of Augustine of Hippo becomes our deeper longing:

> I no longer desire a better world because I am thinking of the present creation as a whole. And, in the light of this more balanced discernment, I come to see that higher things are better than the lower, but that *the sum of all creation is better than the higher things alone*.[19]

NOTES

[1] Cf. Kathleen Norris, *Amazing Grace: A Vocabulary of Faith*, New York, Riverhead Books, 1998, p.8.
[2] See the discussion on "methodological fault lines" in Cynthia Moe-Lobeda, *Healing a Broken World: Globalization and God*, Minneapolis, Fortress, 2002, pp.152-56. Fr

Dumitru Staniloae described the contemporary tendency to identify spirituality with disengagement from the world as "premature eschatologism". See his *Ascetica si mistica orthodoxa*, Alba Iulia, Editura Deisis, 1993, p.28.

[3] Thom Hartman, *Unequal Protection: The Rise of Corporate Dominance and the Theft of Human Rights*, Kutztown PA, Rodale Publications, 2002, pp.11-23.

[4] Cf. Michael Mandelbaum, *The Ideas that Conquered the World: Peace, Democracy and Free Markets in the 21st Century*, New York, Public Affairs, 2002, pp.328-52.

[5] Adrian Slywotzky, *The Art of Profitability*, New York, Warner, 2002.

[6] See Igumen Chariton of Valamo, *The Art of Prayer: An Orthodox Anthology*, London, Faber & Faber, 1966.

[7] Vladimir Lossky, The *Mystical Theology of the Eastern Church*, London, James Clarke, 1957; repr. New York, St Vladimir's Seminary Press, 1976.

[8] Even more enlightened and eloquent Orthodox theologians are guilty of narrowing the scope of eschatology: see Sergius Bulgakov, *The Orthodox Church*, New York, St Vladimir's Seminary Press, 1988, especially pp.176-86. An important and influential exception may be found in John Meyendorff, *Byzantine Theology: Historical Trends and Doctrinal Themes*, New York, Fordham UP, 1974, pp.118-223; and *idem*, "Does Christian Tradition have a Future?" *St Vladimir's Theological Quarterly*, 26, 3, 1982, pp.139-54.

[9] See Moe-Lobeda, *Healing a Broken World*, pp.48-65.

[10] See Sallie McFague, *The Body of God: An Ecological Theology*, Minneapolis MN, Fortress, 1993.

[11] Poemen 137; cf. Benedicta Ward ed., *The Sayings of the Desert Fathers*, Kalamazoo MI, Cistercian, 1985.

[12] See Eric Wheeler trans., *Dorotheus of Gaza: Discourses and Sayings*, Kalamazoo MI, Cistercian, 1977, pp.138-39.

[13] *Reflections* Ib and XVd, trans. J. Chryssavgis, *In the Heart of the Desert*, Bloomington IN, World Wisdom, 2003.

[14] Title of a 7th-century text by John Climacus; English trans. in *The Ladder of Divine Ascent*, Classics of Western Spirituality, New York, Paulist, 1982.

[15] Doulas 1.

[16] Agathon 11. See also Agathon 12.

[17] Poemen 29.

[18] Cf. Daniel Maguire, *The Moral Code of Judaism and Christianity: Reclaiming the Revolution*, Minneapolis, Fortress, 1993. See p.13, "One thing is clear: if current trends continue, we will not... We are an endangered species."

[19] *Confessions*, VII, xiii, 19.

Ethnic Conflicts and the Orthodox Churches
An Introduction

THOMAS FITZGERALD

The witness of the saints

There is an ancient Christian custom that each day of the year many saints are commemorated. In commemorating the saints, we are first of all remembering that Christ the Lord continues to act through his faithful followers. We are also celebrating the fact that specific persons have become collaborators with the Lord for the salvation of the world. Human persons matter. And human persons are called to be embodiments of God's presence, love, mercy, and reconciliation in this life.

Through the regular commemoration of the saints, we are vividly reminded not only of the rich history of Christianity but also of the catholicity and diversity of the Church. The saints come from different places, different cultures and different times. They speak different languages. On 5 October, in the Orthodox calendar, for example, we remember Charitine, the 4th-century Roman martyr, and Dionysius, the 3rd-century bishop of Alexandria. On the day before, 4 October, we remember Hierotheus, the 1st-century bishop of Athens, and Vladimir, the 11th-century prince of Novgorod. On the day after, 6 October, we remember Thomas, the 1st-century Palestinian apostle who travelled to India to preach the gospel. In a span of only three days, the commemoration of the saints reminds us of some of the places where the message of Christ has been preached through his followers who themselves were of different cultures.

The iconography of the saints also helps us to appreciate the universality of the gospel and the catholicity of the Church. The saints are not depicted in their icons in a bland and impersonal way. For the most part, they are portrayed in their context. They are dressed in the clothing of their world, of their culture. The icon helps us to appreciate the fact that the saints lived in a particular place and in a particular time in this world. And, at the same time, the icon helps to remind us that the living God was at work in their lives, in particular cultures and places. The men and women we see in the icons became God's friends and servants in the midst of the daily relationships and circumstances of this life.

The commemoration of the saints helps us to appreciate the fact that the Christian gospel is meant to be preached in every place and every language. The commemoration also helps us to sense that the Church is wider and deeper than our local parish or regional church. The witness of the saints helps to open us up to the reality of the gospel message and witness of the Church to its Lord which can be found in a wide variety of cultural contexts from the time of the apostles.

The Church is a community of faith which brings together persons of diverse cultures, nations, races and languages. There is a profound pluralism in the life of the Church which is truly a global body. Yet, the Church is not to be seen as an ethnic club or a multinational business. It is "God's own people" (1 Pet. 2:9). It is the "body of Christ" (1 Cor. 12:27). It is the "household of God in the Spirit" (Eph. 2:22). These and other images from the scriptures remind us of the unique and distinctive character of the Church as a community of believers who are in communion with the Holy Trinity. The unifying bond within the Church is not language or culture, or race or nation. Rather, the unifying bond is Jesus Christ. He is the One who is the head of the body, which is the Church (1 Cor. 12:27; Eph. 5:23). He is the one who leads us to the Father through the Spirit.

Personal identity

Each of us is a person with a unique and complex identity. Indeed, we might go so far as to say that our personal identity reflects a number of particular factors which are not always obvious. Among these factors are our relationships to others. We are members of a family, an extended family, a neighbourhood and a nation. Among these factors are also our gender and our race, our cultural inheritance and our primary language. In addition to this, our religious beliefs and moral convictions shape our personal identity. Yes, our personal identity ultimately reflects a number of factors which inter-relate to make us "who we are", which make our own personhood deeply personal. We are persons in and through the matrix of factors which are part our relationships among the person.

Orthodox Christians affirm something even more. Firstly, we affirm that there is a fundamental theocentric identity of every person who is created in the "image and likeness" of God (Gen. 1:26). We are most fundamentally sons and daughters of God. We are intimately related to the one God and Father of all. This identity is foundational because it is rooted in the very fact of creation. It is not dependent upon our beliefs, our convictions or our actions. It is a gift! Secondly, we would also affirm that every Christian shares a particular bond with Christ and with his people. This bond is established through the mysterious call of the Lord and expressed in a public manner through baptism. As baptized believers, we have been united with Christ in a deeply personal way which highlights our theocentric identity and which affects our relationship with others as well as the entire creation. The various other factors which are part of our particular human identity, such as our human relationships as well as race, nationality and gender, are not destroyed through our relationship with Christ. As part of our identity, they too are meant to express our deepest relationship with Christ. They can be transfigured through Christ and contribute to our salvation.

The creation of idols

We also know that the many factors which contribute to our personal identity can become disfigured, if we are not careful. In the language of spirituality, these factors can become distorted and can become "idols". An idol is anything which detracts our attention away from God, or which replaces God in our life. A created idol can, therefore, damage our relationship with the true God. It can damage our deepest identity as God's sons and daughters, and as followers of Christ. The idol can also damage our relationship with others. We can create idols of race, of gender, of language, of culture and of ethnicity. Indeed, religion can even become an idol.

Jesus' sharpest criticism was directed against the self-righteous Pharisees, who were among the religious leaders of the day. They loved to have "the place of honour at banquets and the place of honour at the synagogue" (Matt. 23:6). He referred to them as hypocrites (Matt. 23:15), blind guides (Matt. 23:16) and whitewashed tombs (Matt. 23:27) who "lock people out of the kingdom of heaven" (Matt. 23:13). They spoke about the religious laws, but they neglected "justice, mercy and faith" (Matt. 23:23).

Jesus' sharp criticism reflects the fact that the self-righteous Pharisees had come to idolize the religious laws and pure ethnic identity. At the same time, they had come to depersonalize those who did not or could not strictly follow the religious laws, as they interpreted them. They shunned those who were considered impure, and not part of their religious party and ethnic group, such as the Samaritans.

Undoubtedly, Jesus had this in mind when he said to the self-righteous Pharisees, "The sabbath was made for man, not man for the sabbath. The Son of man is Lord even of the sabbath" (Mark 2:27). In other words, religious laws and practices are not ends in themselves. Jesus was not criticizing the importance of the sabbath and its proper observance.

He was criticizing those who neglected or abused others in the name of the sabbath observance. The story of the healing of the paralytic shows this clearly (see John 5:1-16). Sabbath observance was important but it was not of ultimate importance. Jesus affirmed that the human person, the true icon of God, has a dignity and value which was not dependent upon ethnic identity, moral purity, physical attributes or the fulfilment of religious law. The law of sabbath observance was important, but it could be distorted and this could lead to tragic consequences.

When we create idols, our deepest identity as sons and daughters of God is distorted. The idolization of race, gender, ethnicity, nation, language, culture status, money or religion can lead to disastrous consequences, not only for our own personal identity but also for those around us. The creation of idols can easily lead to racism, sexism, chauvinism, discrimination and the violation of human rights. The creation of idols by persons can lead to violence, war and death.

Divisions among the churches

The creation of idols can lead to church divisions. Those of us who study issues of church division can find a correlation between ethnic and cultural differences on the one hand, and breaks of communion on the other. The major divisions in the early Church reflected serious theological or doctrinal concerns. But these breaks in communion also reflect ethnic, cultural and political differences. This is certainly the case in the division after the council of Ephesus in 431 and after the council of Chalcedon in 451. Moreover, let us also remember that persecution and violence accompanied these divisions.

The division between the Church of Rome and the Church of Constantinople during the Middle Ages also reflected underlying cultural and ethnic antagonism. Certainly, there were serious theological and ecclesiological issues at the heart of the alienation. At the same time, there were also serious differences in political and cultural relationships. There were ethnic and tribal animosities between the Romans (Byzantines) of the East, and the Franks and later the Normans and Venetians of the West. The tragedy of the fourth crusade is but one of many examples which could be noted.

In recent centuries, the development of the Orthodox Church in the United States has been hampered by de facto divisions at the parish and diocesan levels which also reflect ethnic and cultural loyalties from the Old World. A number of parishes have been able to treasure their ethnic roots while at the same time placing primary importance upon the centrality of the gospel and the catholicity of the Church. Yet, some other parishes continue to see themselves as enclaves whose primary purpose is to maintain a particular ethnic identity. Thus, some often see Orthodox Christianity in America as a complex compilation of "ethnic churches" which are at odds with each other and whose long-term future looks doubtful.[1]

Yet the council of Constantinople in 1872 condemned ethnophylitism as heresy.[2] Ethnophylitism was seen as a perversion of a positive understanding of nationalism. It was an "idolization of nationalism". Therefore, the council opposed the organization of the Church along nationalistic or ethnic lines. The Church was not meant to serve as a prop for nationalistic movements or sentiments. With this in mind, the council forcefully condemned "racism, ethnic feuds, hatreds, and dissensions within the Church of Christ as contrary to the teaching of the gospel and the holy canons of our blessed fathers".[3]

The heart of the matter and the matters of the heart

Theologians certainly need to take seriously the insights of social scientists and political scientists into the more obvious causes and effects of ethnic conflicts, of racial discrimination and of human-rights abuses. Their thoughtful investigations and observations cannot be ignored in our efforts to speak about the reality of the living God today and our obligations as believers. Already, we have been enriched by the many presentations in this conference.

At the same time, we theologians cannot forget that we have much to say about the heart – both the heart of God, and our own human heart. The passage from St Augustine comes readily to mind: "You have made us for your self, O God, and our hearts are restless until they rest in you."[4] These simple words remind us that our deepest identity is found in our relationship with God. At the same time, the words remind us that our lives can become restless when we are not in touch with the living God, the centre of our existence.

The words of St Augustine also remind us of the more ancient words of the psalm: "Set a guard over my mouth, O Lord, keep watch over the doors of my lips. Do not turn my heart to any evil, to busy myself with wicked deeds, in company with those who work iniquity; and do not let me eat of their delicacies" (Ps. 141:3-4).

Ethnic conflicts and all forms of racial discrimination have their root in the human heart. As the ancient fathers and mothers of the desert tradition tell us, "hardness of heart" is the tragedy of our inner life which manifests itself in our external life. When we live our lives apart from the living God, our identity is distorted and our hearts become restless. We seek self-satisfaction and self-glorification rather than the opportunity to praise and glorify God. We use others for our own ends rather than honouring the other and loving the other as our own self (Mark 12:31).

Christ and the Samaritan woman

The Church has had to face many challenges throughout its history. Each time the Church encounters a challenge, it is necessary for it to reflect prayerfully upon its scriptures and Tradition. In our present discussion on the tragedy of ethnic conflicts, I would draw attention to two important references.

The first comes from the gospel of St John. It is the story of the Samaritan woman, the woman at the well, found in chapter 4 (1-42). I am sure the story is familiar; so let me highlight a few relevant points.

At Jacob's well, Jesus asks the woman for a drink of water. The woman, whom the tradition calls Photini, is surprised that Jesus, the noted rabbi, would speak with her. She is a woman, a Samaritan, and we learn she has been married a number of times. According to religious laws of the day, she had three strikes against her! She was a woman, she was a Samaritan and she was an adulteress.

Since we are concerned with ethnic conflicts, let us simply focus upon the fact that she was a Samaritan. In pluralistic 1st-century Palestine, the Pharisees viewed Samaritans as half-breeds, as unclean and as outcasts. They were seen as the heretics! According to the proper Pharisees, Jesus should have avoided her at all costs. But he did not. He encountered her as a person. He disregarded the ethnic hatred and the religious fanaticism. He set historical animosities aside. He entered into a dialogue with her about worship and about life itself. As the story shows, Photini's life was changed forever by the encounter and by her profession of faith! Indeed, she accepted Christ as the Messiah and became a missionary, leading other Samaritans to the Lord.

When the apostles returned to meet Jesus, we are told that they were surprised that Jesus was speaking to the Samaritan woman. Their surprise must indicate that the reconciling message of the Lord had not yet penetrated their "hard hearts". Perhaps they were still living according to the old values and the old stereotypes. Yes, at that moment, even the apostles who had been travelling with the Lord had a difficult time in receiving the message of Christ and in putting aside their ethnic pride and prejudices. Fortunately, the message of the Lord eventually changed them as well!

The catholicity of the Church

My second reference comes from the catechetical homilies of St Cyril of Jerusalem. Through these homilies, Cyril was preparing catechumens for their baptism. Their baptism was a deeply personal event which could not be underestimated. It marked their union with Christ. But, at the same time, their baptism was a cosmic event which united them to Christ's Church, and truly placed them in a new relationship with all of creation.

With this in mind, Cyril speaks to the catechumens about the Church. He tells them that the Church is the *ekklesia*, the assembly, because through it and in it the living God calls forth and assembles all peoples. And within this cosmic context, St Cyril describes the catholicity of the Church in bold terms. These are terms which immediately prevent the catechumens from seeing this body of Christ simply as another voluntary man-made association. Rather, it is a community of faith rooted in the very being of the triune God. It is a community centred upon the will of the Father revealed through Christ and perfected by the Spirit. It is a community of faith which exists for the glory of God and for the life of the world.

The Church is called catholic, says Cyril, for five reasons:

> The Church is called catholic because it is spread throughout the world, from one end of the earth to the other; and because it teaches universally and completely all the doctrines people need to know concerning things visible and invisible, heavenly and earthly; and because it brings to holiness all of humanity, governors and governed, learned and unlearned; and because it universally treats and heals every form of sins, which are committed by soul or body; and because it possesses in itself every expression of virtue which is known, both in deeds and words, and every kind of spiritual gifts.[5]

Each of these five points deserves much reflection. But I would simply make three observations. Firstly, Cyril reminds us that the Church is catholic in the sense of being universal. It is not bound to one race or people; it extends all over the world, from one end of the earth to the other. Secondly, at the same time, the Church is truly local because it has a direct relationship to real persons in their given situation. It brings all to holiness and it treats all sin. And, finally, this means that the catholicity or fullness of faith cannot be separated from the reality of holiness, of healing, of reconciliation and of virtue.

Here, we Orthodox today need to be especially mindful. We have a tendency triumphantly to declare that we profess the true faith! Yet, at the same time, we tend to forget the intimate connection between professing the true faith, worshipping in spirit and truth, and living a virtuous life. Cyril reminds us of this intimate and necessary connection. Indeed, it is no accident that in the midst of every eucharist we are challenged with the words: "Let us love one another so that with one mind we may confess, the Father, Son, the Holy Spirit: the Trinity one in essence and undivided." There is an intimate relationship between faith and love, between the manner in which we approach the living God and the manner in which we treat one another.

During the years my wife and I had the honour to serve the Patriarchate and the World Council of Churches, we had many valuable opportunities to visit churches and faithful in many parts of the world. These visits were always a blessing. Yet, not all of them were without difficulties. The most painful moments came when we met those who were the victims of violence inflicted by Christians, and when we prayed with those who had been hurt by wars undertaken by Christians, and when we would walk in those places where racism and ethnic conflict led to pain, destruction and death.

We cannot ignore the sad fact that in various places Christians have abused their faith by using it as a justification for evil deeds. The Christian faith has been abused and used to demonize and to harm others. Moreover, we cannot ignore the sad fact that divisions among Christians have contributed to discrimination, to racial and ethnic hatred, and to ethnic cleansing. In many places the blood of tribal relations has been more powerful than the waters of baptism. We have seen tragic examples in such places as Lebanon, Northern Ireland, Rwanda and the Balkans.

Conclusion

The apostles were surprised by Jesus' concern for the Samaritan woman. Their surprise reflected the fact that Jesus was not bound to the patterns of ethnic pride, racism and sexism which were part of the culture of the day. The gospel challenged the idols. The gospel which the Lord preached was meant for all peoples. But it was also a challenge to those who received the message and took it to heart. The gospel was a challenge to overcome the stereotypes and prejudices which were enmeshed in cultures.

The gospel of Christ continues to challenge us to live in full accordance with its message.

So, let us view the Church as truly the Church of Christ: the people of God, the body of Christ, the temple of the Spirit.

Let us view the Church not only as a community which proclaims the gospel but also as a community which lives out that message in the midst of the world.

Let us view the Church not only as a community which honours God in worship but also as a community which honours in service the "least of the brethren" (Matt. 25:40).

Let us view the Church not only as the sign and servant of God's salvation but also as the sign and servant of God's reconciliation in society.

Allow me to conclude with the words of St Gregory of Nyssa from his commentary on the Beatitudes. St Gregory says,

> Blessed are the peace-makers for they shall be called the children of God. Who are these persons? They are those who imitate the love of God for humankind. Who reveal in their own lives the characteristics of God's activity. The Lord and giver of life completely does away with anything that is without affinity and foreign to goodness. This work, he also directs for you. Namely, to cast out hatred and abolish war, to exterminate envy and to banish strife, to get rid of hypocrisy and to extinguish from within resent of injuries which linger in the heart.[6]

NOTES

[1] See Martin E. Marty, *Modern American Religion*, Volume 1, Chicago: Univ. of Chicago Press, 1986, pp.125-30.
[2] See pp.155-56 of this volume.
[3] Cited in Metropolitan Maximos of Sardis, *The Oecumenical Patriarchate in the Orthodox Church*, Thessaloniki, Patriarchal Institute, 1976, pp.308-309.
[4] St Augustine, *The Confessions*, 1.
[5] St Cyril of Jerusalem, *Catechesis*, 18.
[6] St Gregory of Nyssa, *Homilies on the Beatitudes*, 7.

Ethnicity, Nationalism and Religion

GEORGES TSETSIS

> Any form of national egotism whereby the love of one's own people leads to
> the suppression of other nationalities or national minorities, or to the failure to
> respect and appreciate the gifts of other people, is a sin and rebellion against
> God, who is the Creator and Lord of all peoples.[1]

If I start by quoting this aphorism of the 1937 Life and Work conference in Oxford, it is to recall that the subject of ethnicity, nationalism
and religion did not appear only recently in the ecumenical agenda, following the eruption of ethnic conflicts in several parts of the world in the
last two or three decades. Churches involved in the Life and Work and
Faith and Order movements in the 1920s and 1930s and, after their amalgamation in 1938, in the World Council of Churches, have dealt extensively with these crucial issues, prompted by alarming developments in
Europe during the interwar years, and later in the aftermath of the second world war. But even before that, in the late 19th century the Orthodox Church was compelled to deal with the issue of ethnicity, when
nationalistic disputes in the Balkans started to threaten Orthodox unity.

However, the proliferation in the last few years of ethnic conflicts
and regional wars, stimulated by nationalistic aspirations almost in every
continent, has encouraged the churches to deepen reflection on these
issues, in order to be able to contribute to the resolution of conflicts. The
study initiated by Faith and Order in 1990, on the topic "Ethnic Identity,
National Identity and the Search for the Unity of the Church", is an evidence of the churches' will to reflect deeply on these burning issues. It
was therefore quite timely to include this issue in the agenda of the present conference, and I thank its conveners for asking me to present the
subject.

If for a Greek-speaking person it is relatively easy to deliver a conference address in English or French about the meaning of religion, it is
not so simple to do the same as far as ethnicity and nationalism are concerned. Simply because in the Greek language these two notions, both
originating from the word *ethnos* – that literally means "nation" – very

often overlap and lead to confusion. For example, "nationality" corresponds to *ethnikotēs* in Greek, "nationalism" to *ethnikismos* and "ethnicity" to *ethnismos*. Therefore before speaking about the relation of ethnicity and nationalism to religion and to the Church in particular, it will be helpful first to clarify the meaning of these two terms as they are currently used.

Definitions – some examples

Ethnologists, anthropologists, historians and politicians have made many attempts to define the meaning of the terms "ethnicity", "ethnic group" and "nation". Let me give some examples.

According to Richard Schermerhorn, a pioneer of the study of ethnic relations, an "ethnic group" is a collectivity within a larger society, having real or putative common ancestry, common memory of a historical past, and a cultural focus on one or more symbolic elements defined as the epitome of their peoplehood: for example, kinship patterns, physical continuity, religious affiliation, language, nationality and a consciousness of kin among members of the group. For Joshua Fishman, "ethnicity" was always experienced as a kinship phenomenon, as a continuity within the self and within those who share an intergenerational link to common ancestors. In this sense ethnicity is a tangible, living reality that makes every human a link in an eternal bond from generation to generation, from past ancestors to those in the future. For anthropologist Fredrik Barth, the term "ethnic group" designates a population that is largely biologically self-perpetuating, that shares fundamental cultural values, and has a membership which identifies itself as constituting a category distinguishable from other categories of people.[2] For Steve Fenton, ethnicity is a social phenomenon embedded in social, political and economic structures that form an important element of both the way ethnicity is expressed and the social importance it assumes.[3]

As to "nation" and "nationalism", an interesting definition of the term "nation" is given by *The International Relations Dictionary*, which asserts that a nation is a social group that shares a common ideology, common institutions and customs, a sense of homogeneity, as well as a sense of being associated with a particular territory, considered to be peculiarly its own.[4] From his perspective, Ernest Renan believes that a nation is grounded in common history, language and culture. It is a soul, a spiritual principle, and the end-product of a long period of work, sacrifice and devotion. It presupposes a past, but it resumes itself in the present by a tangible fact: the clearly expressed desire to continue life in common. On the other hand, according to Joseph Stalin, a nation is a historically constituted community of people and not a tribal or racial entity.

It is not a casual or ephemeral conglomeration, but a stable community of people, formed on the basis of a common language, territory, economic life and psychological make-up, manifested in a common culture. For anthropologist Clifford Geertz, in addition to common history, language, culture and territory, the basic components that make up a nation include religion and custom.[5]

From the point of view of the consultation on "Ethnicity and Nationalism" held in Colombo, Sri Lanka, in November 1994 which was jointly sponsored by the World Council of Churches, the Lutheran World Federation and the World Alliance of Reformed Churches, "ethnicity" is a collective group consciousness defined by reference to a configuration of elements, such as language, homeland, descent, religion and values; while "nationalism" is a collective group consciousness built around the boundaries of an actual or perceived nationhood. As to "religion", it constitutes a key factor that shapes the identity and character of a community on the basis of doctrines, rituals and a code of behaviour and ethical values.[6]

Beside these definitions, however, one should add that "ethnicity", in its meaning as *ethnismos* is also identical to love of and dedication to one's homeland, as well as to national consciousness and patriotism. On the other hand, nationalism, in the sense of *ethnismos*, could certainly mean attachment to national ideals, but it could also be synonymous with chauvinism or phyletism, when it fails to acknowledge, or deliberately ignores, the distinctiveness of the others. The crucial issue is how to discern healthy and legitimate nationalism in the sense of *philopatria* (love of the country) aiming at the prosperity of a people and the preservation of its national and cultural identity, from those corrosive and divisive forms of chauvinistic ethno-nationalisms that result in wars and endless conflicts.

This is the challenge that we all face today, following the socio-political developments in the second half of the 20th century in many parts of the world, and particularly in Eastern Europe and the Caucasus since 1990.

In the preface to a collective volume they edited in 1996, John Hutchinson and Anthony D. Smith pointed out that after the surfacing of ethnic movements in the 1950s in Asia and Africa, and later on in the 1960s and 1970s in Europe and the Americas, and more particularly after the disintegration in 1990 of the Soviet Union, in the territory of which emerged within a few years some twenty new nations and countries "based largely upon dominant ethnic communities,... ethnicity has become a central issue in the social and political life of every continent".[7]

It is worth noting that this assertion was almost identical with the view formulated two years earlier by the Ecumenical Patriarch Bartholomew in an address he delivered at the opening session of the conference on peace and tolerance, convened by the Ecumenical Patriarchate, in cooperation with the Appeal of Conscience Foundation (Istanbul, 7-9 February 1994). Referring to the fratricidal war which was then devastating Yugoslavia, as well as to ethnic conflicts affecting at that time Central Asia and the Caucasus, Patriarch Bartholomew remarked that "nationalism remains one of the central problems of the Church", which ought to be answered "in a deep and uncompromising ecumenical spirit". And after having urged those in power "to overcome divisions and disputes brought about by excessive nationalism", the Patriarch reiterated the appeal made by the Orthodox Primates at the conclusion of their first, in modern times, summit meeting *(synaxis)* at the Phanar in March 1992, calling on all religious leaders to offer "particular attention, pastoral responsibility and wisdom inspired by God, in order to avoid the exploitation of sentiments for political and nationalistic reasons".[8]

This was a legitimate pastoral concern of paramount importance, for the simple reason that, following the rapid and quasi-cosmogonical socio-political changes which occurred in Central and Eastern Europe in the early 1990s, after the abrupt collapse of the "Eastern bloc" and the marginalization of its totalitarian ideology, the spectre that started haunting Western societies was, according to Ali Rattansi, "no longer communism, but a series of racisms and ethno-nationalisms".[9]

Nationalism and its consequences

One has to admit, however, that the ethno-nationalism to which Rattansi refers is not a new phenomenon which sprang up in the aftermath of the dislocation of the Soviet Union and of the Federal Republic of Yugoslavia. The concept of ethno-nationalism emerged in the 19th century, as a consequence of the Enlightenment, and when nation-states began to replace multinational empires, thus becoming the political model *par excellence*. And to be more accurate one could say that in fact "since the French revolution nationalism has been the main spiritual and emotional force cementing all the elements of statehood into nation-states".[10]

In July 1966, at a crucial moment of modern history, when the world was undergoing a revolutionary social change after the end of colonialism and the creation of new states particularly in the southern hemisphere, the WCC convened in Geneva a world conference on Church and Society, in order to discuss the role of Christians in face of the technical and social revolutions of our time. Referring to these newly created, or to be created, states, this highly important conference, unique in the ecumenical chronicles, admitted that "a sense of nationalism is essential for the building of a new nation". After having asserted this, however, the conference added that this nationalism ought not to be confused with any kind of aggressive nationalism that leads to wars and conflicts, but on the contrary it "must be based on the equality of nations and on mutual cooperation. It should be a means of achieving integration and not become an instrument for emphasizing the divisions which in the past were ethnic, religious or frontier issues."[11]

Yet, political developments in Africa, Asia and the Middle East in the course of the second half of the 20th century, or the changes that occurred in the former Eastern Europe in the early 1990s, demonstrated that in many cases national emancipation had disastrous consequences. The armed conflict between India and Pakistan, continuing even today over the issue of Kashmir; the Arab-Israeli wars over the still-unresolved question of Palestine; the civil war in Lebanon; the deadlock created after the occupation and division of Cyprus; the clash between Tamils and Sinhalese in Sri Lanka; the bloody confrontation of Hutus and Tutsis in Rwanda; the war between Ethiopia and Eritrea; and more recently the tragic fratricidal wars in the territory of Former Yugoslavia; the conflict between Armenians and Azeris over the issue of Nagorno-Karabakh; the armed confrontation of Russians and Chechens or of Georgians and Abkhasians in the Caucasus – these are only a few flagrant examples of the fact that conflicts created by the aspirations and apprehensions of ethno-nationalism have become a source of instability and threat to world peace.

The question that preoccupied the wider public opinion all these years was whether religion constituted a key factor in the resurgence of ethnic conflicts. This very question was insistently raised and commented in different ways, particularly after the break-out of the civil war in Yugoslavia, when the belligerents were depicted not so much on the basis of their nationalistic, ideological and geopolitical aspirations, but rather on the basis of their religious affiliation. That is to say, "Serbian Orthodox against Croatian Roman Catholics", "Bosnian Muslims against Serbian Orthodox", "Christian Croats and Serbs against Muslims of Bosnia", "Roman Catholic Croats and Bosnian Muslims against Orthodox Bosno-Serbians"! The same religious character was attributed earlier to the Lebanese civil war, although the root cause of this conflict was not any theological dispute between Shiite Islam and Maronite Christianity, but the misery and the subsequent revolt of the populations of the Beka'a-Valley and of the Palestinian refugee camps, who could no longer stand the provocative life-style of a Lebanese elite, formed both by Christians and Sunnite Muslims. And, in fact, as Tarek Mitri once remarked, "on both sides of the barricades there were people who never went to the church or to the mosque, who have never read the Qu'ran or the gospel".[12]

It is worth mentioning also that at the height of the war in Croatia and Bosnia-Herzegovina, and later during the NATO raids in Serbia and Montenegro following the Kosovo crisis, there were attempts to qualify these events as nothing else but a new crusade of the "Catholico-Protestant West" against the "Orthodox East". Some (e.g. the French psychoanalyst Julia Kristeva), even invoked the theological controversy of Orthodox and Roman Catholics over the *filioque* clause, in order to explain NATO's attitude vis-a-vis Serbia. Whether it was Clinton and Blair, Chirac and Schroeder, Milosevic, Putin or Simitis, in listening to talk about the term *filioque*, they would ask in astonishment, "What are you talking about?"! [13]

During these tragic years, churches and ecumenical organizations repeatedly tried to dissociate the religious element from the various ethnic conflicts and confrontations that shook the Balkans and the Caucasus and attempted to mediate for peace and reconciliation. For example, the assembly of bishops of the Orthodox Church of Serbia in its encyclical of May 1993 indicated that the chief causes and actors of the misfortune of the peoples of Yugoslavia were not the religious communities of this country, but the power-holders "no matter which side they belong to, who by spirit, mentality and methods were all trained in the same school of a totalitarian, godless communist system".[14] This point was reiterated explicitly and unambiguously later by Metropolitan Amfilohije of Montenegro during a conference organized in Brussels by Pax Christi, namely that the war in Yugoslavia was not a religious war encouraged by religious leaders, but a civil war "to which politicians and former communists gave religious coloration in order to exploit the religious factor in this conflict".[15]

Similarly, and always on the situation in Yugoslavia, the aforementioned conference on peace and tolerance was quite explicit when it stated that the war in former Yugoslavia is not a "religious war and that the appeals and exploitation of religious symbols to further the cause of aggressive nationalism are a betrayal of the universality of religious faith".[16] The same clear position was taken also over the issue of Nagorno-Karabakh by Armenian Catholicos Vasken I and the Azeri Sheikh ul Islam Pacha-Zadeh, who in a peace-making effort declared, "We firmly refuse the attempts to present this conflict as inter-religious. Those who preach hate among religions commit a heavy sin before the all-Highest."[17]

From its side, the World Council of Churches as early as 1991 was describing the armed confrontation in Yugoslavia as "civil war",[18] and was challenging those involved in the hostilities "to resist every attempt to use religious sentiment and loyalty in the service of aggressive nationalism".[19] At the same time, the Conference of European Churches, inspired by the theme of the Second European Ecumenical Assembly (Graz 1997) "Reconciliation – Gift of God and Source of New Life", and conscious of the fact that the ethnic conflicts in South Eastern Europe were jeopardizing European integration, was calling on the churches to undertake an "active role in peaceful resolution of the conflicts... and participate in the peace and reconciliation processes".[20]

Yet, one has to admit that although ethnic conflicts are not religious in essence, they nevertheless take on a religious character in cases where the belligerents belong to two different faiths. And most particularly when religious symbols are used in order to boost the fighting spirit of the combatants, or the nationalistic feelings of the masses. Flagrant examples of such exploitation of religious sentiments were given in many recent ethnic conflicts such as the war in Bosnia involving Christians and Muslims; the confrontation of Sinhalese Buddhists and Hindu Tamils in Sri Lanka; the territorial dispute of Kashmir involving Muslims and Hindus; and the socio-political upheaval in Fiji involving indigenous Christians (Methodists) and Indian Hindu settlers. In all these conflicts the religious component was quite obvious. But, "a crime committed in the name of religion is a crime against religion" as the above-mentioned Bosphorus declaration stated.[21]

Here lies precisely the responsibility of the Church, or of any other religious body. Namely, to act prophetically, and to be an agent of peace and reconciliation.

The effect of nationalism on the Orthodox Church

An immediate victim of the ethno-nationalism following the gradual dismantlement of the Ottoman empire in the 19th century and the subsequent creation of new nation-states in the Balkans was, undoubtedly, the Orthodox Church. Indeed, political aspirations, ethnic rivalries and the use of the religious factor in order to promote nationalistic ideas in the newly emerging states severely hit Orthodoxy and profoundly affected the very essence of the one, holy, catholic and apostolic (Orthodox) Church.

In the Ottoman empire, the Orthodox Church existed and gave its witness as a supranational entity, in spite of the ethnic origins and the cultural particularities of the peoples that formed the entire "Orthodox nation" (*to genos tōn Orthodoxōn*) living in this vast empire. The emergence, however, of "national churches" within these newly formed nation-states "caused rivalry and hostility between neighbours, brought discord over jurisdictions, and created enemy images at the expense of the unity and the mission of the Church".[22] And interestingly enough, the nationalism that erupted among the Orthodox of all ethnic backgrounds of the empire was not directed only against the Muslim ruler, but also against fellow Orthodox.

For example, the Church of the newly independent Greek state broke its ties with the mother church of Constantinople, because, according to the theoretician of Greek nationalism Adamantios Korais, it was unthinkable for the clergy of free Greece to obey the instructions of a patriarch, captive in the Ottoman capital. In fact this was the argument used by the Orthodox Church of Romania when it submitted to Constantinople the request for autocephaly. On the other hand, Bulgarians could not tolerate any more Greek hierarchs on their soil, and Romanians could not accept the canonical rights of the Serbian Patriarchate in some areas of the Balkans. As a consequence of the gradual nationalization of the local Orthodox churches and the ecclesiastical disputes that followed, "the unity of the 'Orthodox commonwealth', which for almost ten centuries had extended over the whole of Eastern Europe and the Middle East, was irrevocably broken".[23] We are today the powerless witnesses of the end result of this fragmentation, when the Orthodox Church not only cannot speak and act as a single body, but even worse, is unable to convoke its great council that has been in preparation for 41 years (in fact 72 years, if we take into account the 1930 inter-Orthodox pre-synodical meeting of Mount Athos!).

If, however, the term "catholicity" denotes, according to John Karmiris, "the fullness of the one, true and perfect Church through which the salvation of the whole world is sought", one can easily detect the incompatibility between this ethno-nationalism, developed in the whole "Orthodox space" during the 19th century, and the Orthodox ecclesiological understanding of the catholicity of the Church. For Orthodoxy, it was a tragedy indeed to "reduce the universal and eternal Church, by identifying it with local 'national' churches, restricted geographically and unduly influenced by civilization, language, idiosyncrasy... and serving political purposes, dictated by nationalism, racism and chauvinism of peoples and states".[24]

It is precisely this narrow concept of ethno-nationalism, qualified as phyletism, that was condemned as heresy by the 1872 great council of Constantinople, attended also by the patriarchs of Alexandria and Antioch, as well as by the archbishop of Cyprus.

According to this council, nationalism or ethno-phyletism was a perversion of normal patriotic sentiment and constituted the worst enemy of

Orthodox unity. "In the Christian Church", the Council said, "which is a spiritual communion, predestined by its Lord to contain all nations in one brotherhood in Christ, phyletism is alien and unthinkable... All Christian churches founded in the early years were local and they were named after the town or the country of their residence and not after the ethnic origin of their people." The biblical terms "'Church of the Thessalonians', 'Church of Laodiceans' etc., do not indicate an ethnic group, for there has never been either a Thessalonian or Laodicean nation. They refer to the faithful living in the cities of Thessalonica and Laodicea, regardless of their ethnic origins." After having observed that the creation of churches on ethnic grounds alone constituted a "mortal blow" against the faith in one, holy, catholic and apostolic Church, the council of Constantinople censured and vigorously condemned "racism, ethnic feuds, hatreds and dissentions within the Church of Christ, as contrary to the teaching of the gospel and the holy canons of our blessed fathers".[25] According to Vladimir Lossky, the decision of this great council ought to be the basis governing Orthodox relations. Lossky firmly believed that "every special conscience linking us with one national or political or cultural group must disappear, giving place to a 'catholic' conscience which is greater than that conscience, that links us to the whole humanity".[26]

* * *

Like it or not, the present system of Orthodox governance is a reality today, and one has to accept this historical evolution. But if Orthodoxy is expected to give a convincing concerted and united Orthodox witness in today's pluralistic world, then the rediscovery of an Orthodox conscience, to which Lossky refers, that goes beyond ethnic and national cleavages is, I believe, an urgent matter. Orthodoxy will be credible only when all local autocephalous and autonomous Orthodox churches are able to speak and act *as one single body and not as separate ethnic or national entities.*

Before concluding, I wish to remark that in dealing with the issues of ethnicity, nationalism and religion we must not lose sight of the fact that all nations exist under God's sovereignty and that no religion or ideology can replace the God-given unity of humankind, since God himself "from one blood [one ancestor] made all nations to inhabit the whole earth, and he allotted the times of their existence and the boundaries of the places where they would live" (Acts 17:26). We must remember that "there is no longer Jew or Greek, there is no longer slave or free, there is no longer male and female; for all of [us] are one in Christ Jesus" (Gal.

3:28). And we should also meditate on what the author of the epistle to Diognetus was saying to his correspondent. Namely that Christians certainly "dwell in their own countries, but only as aliens; as citizens they take part in everything, but endure all hardships as strangers; every foreign land is a fatherland to them, end every fatherland is foreign. They inhabit the earth, but they hold citizenship in heaven".[27]

This fundamental Christian understanding must be the basis of our behaviour towards our neighbours, in times of both peace and of conflict.

NOTES

[1] Report of section I of the Oxford conference on "Church, Community and State", in M. Kinnamon and B. Cope eds, *The Ecumenical Movement: An Anthology of Key Texts and Voices*, Geneva, WCC / Grand Rapids MI, Eerdmans, 1997, p.271.

[2] These definitions are taken from J. Hutchinson and A.D. Smith eds, *Ethnicity*, Oxford, Oxford UP, 1996, pp.16, 63 and 75.

[3] S. Fenton, *Ethnicity, Racism, Class and Culture*, London, Macmillan, 1999, p.21.

[4] J. Plano and R. Olton, *The International Relations Dictionary*, New York, Abc-Clio, 1969, p.119.

[5] Definitions taken from J. Hutchinson and A.D. Smith eds, *Nationalism*, Oxford, Oxford UP, 1994, pp.16, 18 and 29-30.

[6] See consultation report in T. Tschuy, *Ethnic Conflict and Religion: Challenge to the Churches*, Geneva, WCC Publications, 1997, p.156.

[7] Hutchinson and Smith eds, *Ethnicity*, preface, p.v.

[8] See patriarchal address in *Orthodoxia*, 131, 1994, pp.335-41.

[9] A. Rattansi, "'Western' Racisms, Ethnicity and Identities in a 'Post-Modern Frame'", in A. Rattansi and S. Westwood eds, *Racism, Modernity and Identity on the Western Front*, Cambridge, Polity, 1994, p.1.

[10] N. Koshy, *Churches in the World of Nations*, Geneva, WCC Publications, 1994, p.46.

[11] *World Conference on Church and Society, Official Report*, Geneva, WCC, 1967, p.106.

[12] *The Role of the Church in Conflict Situations*, Uppsala, Life and Peace Institute, 1991, p.122.

[13] It was bizarre, to say the least, to speak about a "holy alliance" of European and American Christians against the "Orthodox East" as it was frequently done in the secular and church press of Greece during the Yugoslav crisis. After all, Greece joined NATO not because of any fear of the Roman Catholic or the Protestant West, but of the countries of the North, including Tito's Yugoslavia, namely countries of the traditional Orthodox space, that for centuries now dream to have direct access to the Mediterranean!

[14] See "The Tragedy of Bosnia", in *Background Information*, CCIA/WCC, 1994, 1, p.117.

[15] See Metropolitan Amfilohije's interview in *Service Orthodoxe de Presse*, no. 187, April 1994, p.18.

[16] See *The Bosphorus Declaration*, in H. Bos and J. Forest eds, *"For Peace from Above" – An Orthodox Resource Book on War, Peace and Nationalism*, Bialystok, Poland, Syndesmos, 1999, p.133.

[17] *Ibid.*, p.135.

[18] See *Minutes of the 43rd Central Committee meeting of the World Council of Churches 1991*, Geneva, WCC Publications, 1991, p.37.

[19] "Message to the Churches in the Countries of Former Yugoslavia", in *Minutes of the 45th Central Committee meeting of the World Council of Churches 1994*, Geneva, WCC Publications, 1994, p.78.

[20] *Report on the 11th Assembly of the Conference of European Churches, Graz, Austria, 30 June – 4 July 1997*, Geneva, Conference of European Churches, p.165.

[21] Bos and Forest, *"For Peace from Above"*, p.133.

[22] T. Sabev, "Church, Nation and Nationalism", *Etudes Theologiques* 12, "Religion et Société", Chambésy, Les Editions du Centre Orthodoxe, 1998, p.263.

[23] P. Kitromilidis, "Orthodoxy and Nationalism", in Hutchinson and Smith, *Ethnicity*, p.208.

[24] J. Karmiris, "Catholicity of the Church and Nationalism", in S. Agouridis ed., *Procès-Verbaux du Deuxième Congrès de Théologie Orthodoxe à Athènes, 19-29 août 1976*, Athens, no publ., 1978, p.470.

[25] See "Patriarchal and Synodical Documents on the Bulgarian Schism", p.429, cited in Maximos of Sardes, *The Oecumenical Patriarchate in the Orthodox Church*, Thessaloniki, Patriarchal Institute of Patristic Studies, 1976, pp.303-309.

[26] V. Lossky, *In the Image and Likeness of God* (Greek translation), Thessaloniki, no publ., 1974, p.176, cited by Karmiris, *op. cit.*, p.479. No doubt the instrumentalization of Orthodoxy by politicians, and sometimes even by church leaders, in order to foster political and nationalistic aspirations could have detrimental consequences for the Church itself. The Church of Greece still suffers from the consequences of the "Greece for Greek Christians" policy, applied during the dictatorship years. And yet the colonels, some of whom came from the bosom of pietistic movements, claimed to be Orthodox! But what about Gennady Zyuganov, who prior to the 1996 presidential elections, although affirming that he did not believe in God, nevertheless was stating that his communist party of Russia would assist the Orthodox Church of Russia "acknowledging its role in the formation of Russian statehood, Russian national identity, patriotism, and the cultural and spiritual traditions of the Russian people"? See "The Position of the Communist Party of the Russian Federation Regarding the Issue of Religion", in V. Fedorov, F. Stolz and H. Weder eds, *Religion and Nationalism in Russia*, St Petersburg, Apostolic-City-Nevskij Prospect Press, 2000, p.251.

[27] Justin the Confessor and Martyr, *Letter to Diognetus*, V 15, in *Bibliothiki Hellinon Pateron*, vol. 2, Athens, Apostoliki Diakonia, 1955, p.253.

Ethnicity, Nationalism and Identity

EMMANUEL CLAPSIS

Historians have noted with an alarming concern that more than half the world's civil conflicts after the dissolution of the British, French, Dutch, Belgian and Portuguese empires (1945-60) can be traced to ethno-religious causes. This proportion had increased to three-quarters in the period from 1960 to 1990 and accelerated again with the collapse of the Soviet Union in 1991.[1] The explosive resurgence of ethno-religious conflicts in different parts of the world inevitably affects the cause of ecumenism and the public witnesses of God's churches. But above all, it has caused an immeasurable suffering and loss of human life. The advances and the proliferation of weapons of mass destruction, the use of media and communication technologies to justify and exacerbate the use of excessive violence, and the human inclination to divide and fragment humanity into groups that may viciously oppose each other, all compel humanity to improve its understanding and respect of differences within and across national boundaries for the purpose of preventing, as much as possible, deadly conflicts. Such an endeavour is not alien to our ecumenical vocation since modern ecumenism is partly a response to ethno-religious conflicts of the immediate past, and it has conceived the unity of the churches as a presupposition for the unity and peace of humankind.[2]

Towards an understanding of ethno-religious conflicts

In ethno-religious conflicts religion has often been used as a force that intensifies cruelty and misanthropy instead of advancing the cause of peace. In the midst of violent conflicts, however, heroic voices for peace and reconciliation have also been heard, supported by acts of extraordinary human compassion rooted in God's love. Others in similar situations have opted to remain silent or even to pray "privately" and from a safe distance for peace and reconciliation or even for the demise of their enemies. The involvement of religion in ethnic conflicts is highlighted by the final report of the Carnegie Commission on Preventing Deadly Conflict, which sadly observes,

Despite the fact that a belief in peace and brotherhood is professed by a wide variety of faiths, religious leaders frequently support and even incite inter-group violence. Today, we note with deep concern a growing fringe in many religions that is characterized by self-glorification on the one hand, and a big-oted, often fanatical depreciation of "outsider" groups on the other.[3]

Does religion have the potential to generate hatred, violence and injustice against others? Social scientists continue to debate the actual origins and causes of religious violence and how it can be prevented.[4] The British sociologist David Martin believes that,

> The selection of religion as the source of evil needs itself to be analyzed as a cultural trope residually derived from the massive conflict in European culture, especially Latin European culture, over the role of religion during the past two centuries. The ideologies of secular establishment have promoted the idea so successfully that Christians have internalized it and asked forgiveness for it when, in terms of serious contribution to a debate, it is a vast oversimplification.[5]

Of course, Martin does not exonerate religion from any involvement in, or contribution to, violent ethnic conflicts in different parts of the world, but he invites us to be critical of the "picture-book world of television" that attributes to religion complex social conflicts simply because religious symbols accentuate or explain differences that different groups of people in conflict have. "It is the object of sociology, indeed of any serious knowledge, to question the obvious. Things are usually more complicated than they seem and the obvious is often the false."[6]

Ethno-religious conflicts cannot be adequately understood by attributing them to single causes. They are, rather, outbursts of many local, national and global social factors that need to be understood in all their complexity and interaction as they lead to situations of conflict. It is much more accurate to view the increasing resurgence of tribalism in different parts of the world as a response to the effects of globalization and the need of different communities of people to find their place and be recognized in the emerging new world. I agree with the Indian psychoanalyst Sudhir Kakar, who has studied the brutal outbursts of religious violence between Hindus and Muslims in his native land, when he concludes,

> What we are witnessing today is less the resurgence of religion than of communalism where a community of believers not only has religious affiliation but also social, economic, and political interests in common which may conflict with the corresponding interests of another community of believers who share the same geographical space.[7]

Based on this assumption, our study needs to turn its attention to how collective identities are formed and under what conditions they become the grounds for enmity, oppression and violent conflict. How does religion function in the context of social conflict, human hatred and oppression, if we accept the premise that in such situations religious communities cannot resort to privatism or use the pretext of neutrality?

Identity formation

Every human being has a personal and social identity whose formation begins at the early stages of the human life-circle. The sense of subject, "I am", is complemented by the sense of belonging to a community, "We are." Human persons in the present world are social events containing in their personhood differentiation and plurality. They are, as Sudhir Kakar states, systems of "reverberating representational worlds, each enriching, constraining, and shaping the others, as they jointly evolve through the life-cycle".[8] None of these inter-related worlds that constitute human subjectivity are "primary" or "deeper" than the others from a psychoanalytic perspective, although at different times human subjectivity may be predominantly experienced in one or another mode. The self-assertion of "We are" has the potential for confrontation with the "We are" of other groups and, therefore, collective identities are inherently carriers of aggression. This aggressive element of collective identities, together with fears that reflect human vulnerability and the will to secure our survival, has the potential to generate violence. Yet, in some instances, people of the same collective identity, as they experience imaginary or real threats to their personal and/or collective identities, do not resort to violence. They opt instead to resolve their differences or secure their personal and/or collective identities through peaceful means. For our purpose of preventing the deadly conflicts that often occur in the name of religion, it would be helpful to understand the motives that lead other people who respond to the precepts of their religious faith to choose violence over nonviolence, or death over life.

Ethnicity – a significant factor

The resurgence of ethnicity in different parts of the world, and the recognition that contemporary states are almost universally multi-ethnic in composition, reflect the fact that ethnicity remains a strong factor in modern societies. Social scientists, guided by different assumptions, premises and ideologies, have applauded the current resurgence of ethnicity and/or its continuing strength as a specific way to: preserve a precious cultural heritage; soften class lines; protect to win economic and political advantages for disadvantaged groups; furnish a more intimate and flavourful connection with large impersonal societies; and retard the shift of overwhelming power to the state. Others would point out that the current stress on ethnicity is divisive and inegalitarian in its effects. Stephen Steinberg, from an African-American perspective, argues that current attention to ethnicity tends to blind us to the structures of discrimination:

> Indeed, black intellectuals and leaders have had good reasons to balk at the pluralist doctrine. As a group, blacks have always experienced the bitter side of pluralism, and ideological justifications for maintaining ethnic boundaries carried insidious overtones of racial segregation... Just as ethnic groups have class reasons for tearing down ethnic barriers ahead of them, they also have class reasons for raising ethnic barriers behind them. Thus, it is not uncommon for ethnic groups to invoke democratic principles to combat ethnic exclusivity of more privileged groups, but to turn around and cite pluralistic principles in defence of their own discriminatory practice.[9]

Steinberg and others who address similar criticism against ethnic resurgence attack the vice of ethnic separatism and implore us not to forget that assimilation enables ethnic groups to expand the boundaries of their communities and participate equitably in societal structures of power distribution.

Why does ethnicity continue to be a significant factor in most societies despite the predictions of developmental social theories that modernity and more specifically the effects of urbanization will contribute to the significantly sharp decline of ethnic attachment? Social scientists note that ethnicity in modern mobile societies has changed significantly:

> To think of oneself as an Oglala Sioux or Chippewa is quite different from thinking of oneself as a Native American resident of Chicago or Los Angeles. We lose explanatory power if we equate contemporary urban ethnicity – with its large symbolic, affective qualities – with the more deeply rooted attachments and firmer boundaries of less mobile times and places. The latter may decline in some settings even while the former grows in influence.[10]

Ethnicity engenders sentiments of likeness that create an ethnic group with emotional bonds that generate solidarity among its members. However, the emotional bonds and solidarity among members of an ethnic group must not be exclusively attributed to primordial sentiments because, as Daniel Bell has argued, such feeling served material interests well. He notes that material interests are well-served by ethnically based movements precisely because they "combine an interest with an effective tie".[11] Ethnicity is not only a primordial sentiment, an emotional attachment to "my people", or a valuable tool for the protection or enhancement of states. It is a way of trying to deal with the experience of anomie and the feeling of alienation. It can be seen as a "mode of reintegration of population elements into structures which are less anomic and alienative than their members might otherwise be exposed to".[12] In situations of social conflict, ethnic identity becomes more salient as a way for people to make firm their solidarity with others who have similar interests and imaginary or real origins and feel alienated from the larger society.

Assimilation is a highly complex social process of "boundary reduction" that occurs either voluntarily or by force in some multi-ethnic societies. It is an effective process of social integration in societies where power and value conflicts are not predominant and different ethnic groups have developed positive attitudes towards each other. As a result of this, discrimination and prejudice are considered in these societies to be social vices and efforts are made to move beyond them. If such presuppositions do not exist, however, the assimilation process is forcefully imposed by the state and can lead to eruptions of ethnic discontentment, violence and, ultimately, to ethnic cleansing.

Learning to live together

The presuppositions for an effective assimilation mentioned above also become the consequences of the assimilation process as they contribute to a more equitable distribution of power and social integration. Social integration which may be seen as a sub-process of assimilation occurs when the members of an ethnic group are distributed across the full range of associations, institutions and regions of a society in a pattern similar to that of the population as a whole.[13] As different ethnic groups learn to live together they develop, or rather recast, their values and norms of living to reflect the transformation of their ethos from the way that it existed in isolation to what it becomes as it relates to other ethnic groups. This process transforms at different degrees all the ethnic groups of a given society. However, smaller, less compact, and resource-poor ethnic groups are more likely to be affected by this process of acculturation than those dominant ethnic groups which may significantly define the values and norms of the society at large without consciously recognizing their cultural influence upon those whom they dominate. Finally, assimilation leads to amalgamation when no socially visible genetic differences separate the members of different ethnic groups. The socially visible genetic differences, however, are not as rapidly reduced in a race-conscious society.

The formation of collective identities and, more specifically, of ethnic and national identities, is a complex issue. In the past, ethno-religious identities were positively assessed as necessary (whether divinely or naturally given) to regulate human life, personally and collectively. Religion sacralized social structures by attributing to them a sacred and consequently inviolate nature. Schleiermacher referred to the nation as "a natural division of the human race, endowed by God with its own character". He asserted that every nationality is destined through its peculiar organization and its place in the world to represent a certain side of the divine image, for it is God who directly assigns to each nationality its definite task on earth and inspires it with a definite spirit in order to glorify himself through each one in a peculiar manner.[14] The dark side of nationalism was noted as a deviation or a source of conflict and fragmentation, but generally the trend was to affirm positively national identities. Now we approach ethnic and national identities as potential sources of violent conflict, as we seek ways to affirm those pro-social elements in them that advance peaceful coexistence in our irreversibly pluralistic modern world. As the Carnegie Commission noted:

> To diminish the likelihood of violence, it is important to identify elements of government, social structure, institutions, leadership, and public attitudes that can be used to enhance orientation of caring, concern, social responsibility, and mutual aid within and between groups. Such ends are facilitated by cross-cutting relations that bring members of different groups together under favourable conditions on a regular basis, whether within or across national boundaries. It is important that groups develop positive reciprocity in their relationships, that there be perceived elements of mutual benefit from their interaction.[15]

The ecumenical vision for the unity of God's churches in life, faith and witness contributes to the advancement of peace because it unites people across ethnic, national and denominational boundaries as it invites them to recognize the greater unity that God has bestowed on them despite their historical differences. This quest for unity is currently threatened by the increased use of religion and, more particularly, of Christianity in ethnic conflicts. Thus it is within the purview of Faith and Order in cooperation with other units of the WCC to study the impact of ethnicity and religion upon ecumenism. The nature of this study demands the enrichment of our theological reflection by the insights of social science, since ethnicity and nationalism regulate the lives of people in modern society in a highly contested and conflicted manner. They are highly contested, complex and conflictual social forces because, at least from a sociological perspective, they mediate the participation of the people in structures and distributions of power in society that regulate people's collective lives. Ethnicity, nationalism and religion ingrained in societal power structures are ambivalent social forces that people or groups of people can use either for altruistic and communal advances or for self-serving purposes. These forces have the potential to construct collective identities that contribute to the advancement of peace or they can be forces of violence, depending on imaginary or real social conditions and challenges. Montserrat Guibernau states,

> The extreme complexity of nationalism springs from the radically different interpretations to which it can be subject. In certain cases nationalism is employed in association with xenophobia, racism, fascism and all sorts of violent behaviour against "the others". On other occasions, it refers to the legitimate aspiration of peoples willing to sustain and develop their culture and vindicate their right of self-determination.[16]

R. Scott Appleby, in his exhaustive historical survey of ethno-religious conflicts, comes to the conclusion that,

> Most religious societies, in fact, have interpreted their experience of the sacred in such a way as to give religion a paradoxical role in human affairs – as the bearer of peace *and* the sword. These apparently contradictory orientations reflect a continuing struggle within religions – and within the heart of each believer – over the meaning and character of the power encountered in the sacred and its relationship to coercive force and violence.[17]

The ambivalent character of nationalism is something that the ecumenical movement recognized very early on as it attempted to understand and interpret theologically the politics of nationalism and nation-building in Asia, Africa, Latin America and the Middle East. The Salonika report (1958)[18] exhorted the churches to recognize the moral and spiritual justification of nation-building movements in these regions as a means for the emancipation of dependent people. It recognized also other oppressive forms of nationalism and the fact that even liberating nationalism carries in itself "the seeds of perversion".[19] Once we recognize the ambivalent nature of ethnicity, nationalism and religion, we are painfully aware of the limited and fragile scope of our ecumenical reflection on these important matters, as well as the inadequacy of such a theological reflection without an active commitment to, and participation in, acts that promote a culture of peace, justice and tolerance.

Collective identities

The recognition of the ambivalent nature of social reality and its configurations allows us to approach issues of personal and collective identities from an always critical perspective grounded in Christian anthropology, learning from the insights of social scientists and the experiences of others who may not think, believe and act as we do. What it means to be a human person, and how society should be constructed and function, must reflect the sensitivities that we have gained from such conversations. Our reflections on these important matters must never be considered as final and absolute since these categories are reserved only for eschatological realities. The task of trying to find the presence of God in personal or collective human identities, regardless of whether they are religiously inspired or not, challenges us to reflect on God's providential presence and action in the ambivalent domain of history.[20] In what ways is God actively present in the world and how can Christian communities identify with and participate in God's actions in history, while remembering always the corruptibility of our human responses and efforts?

In pre-modern times people sustained and developed their communal identity within the perimeters of defined spatial and timely boundaries. Their collective identity gave to their lives a sense of belonging and direction and built into them the solidarity necessary for their communal survival. Ethnicity in this context referred to the condition of belonging to a social group that claimed or was accorded special status on the basis of complex, often-variable traits including religious, linguistic, ancestral or physical characteristics. Ethnicity was rather understood as an extended kinship and as such it was divinely bestowed upon particular people. In the Old Testament, the Israelites, by virtue of God's special election, constitute "a holy nation" (Ex. 19:6), "a people holy to the Lord... chosen... out of all the peoples on earth" (Deut. 7:6). The early Christian Church in the New Testament is called "a holy nation, God's own people" (1 Pet. 2:9). Ethnic differentiations are transcended in the Church, however, for as St Paul indicates: "there is neither Jew nor Greek... for you are all one in Christ Jesus" (Gal. 3:28). Ethnic diversity and differentiation are not denied, but nations become relational. It is through the descent of the Holy Spirit on them that they begin to communicate with each other (Acts 2:3-11) and, transformed by Christ's salvific work, that they will enter God's kingdom as nations in all their variety and with their distinctive gifts (Rev. 21:24). Personal and collective identities are not differentiated in scripture, since it would be then, as it is now, inconceivable for human persons to function or understand the world apart from their communal identities which bind them to others. In the Church, ethnic identities become relational and gain a universal horizon that relativizes their differences because of their unity with God.[21] The unity of the nations is derived from the fact that all of them are creations of God destined by their existence to move towards God in praise. St Paul preached to the Athenians,

> From one ancestor [God] made all nations to inhabit the whole earth, and he allotted the times of their existence and the boundaries of the places where they would live, so that they would search for God and perhaps grope for him and find him – though indeed he is not far from each one of us (Acts 17:26-27).

While we continue to believe, together with St Paul, that human beings are prone to find their place in the world by God's providence and through their association with other people of similar beliefs, alleged origins, cultural orientations and socio-economic interests, we must recognize that the "allotted times of existence and the boundaries of the places where they would live" as nations have been transgressed through voluntary or involuntary migration and compressed by the process of globalization.[22] Thus, different nations, religions, Christian churches and other cultural, religious and racial communities must find ways to coexist in the same living space and time without domination, abuse or violent conflicts, while remaining open to the possibility that in the new social realities God is at work even as people experience the forces of death and domination.

I strongly believe that the churches need to continue, or rather begin, their conversation on what the new social reality of globalization means; how it affects human identities; what are the advantages and the disadvantages of such a new and unprecedented social reality (whose effects seem to be irreversible elements for our life in the world); and how globalization affects the life and the witness of the churches. Our ultimate objective in this kind of study is to maintain our unity and continuity with the apostolic faith and at the same time actively work for social arrangements that advance justice, peace and respect for each other's gifts of life.

The opportunities and dangers of ethnic differentiation

In the history of humanity and of the Church, ethnic differentiation provided opportunities for peaceful coexistence but also for ethnic antagonism and conflicts. Yet the ethno-religious conflicts of the 20th century are distinctly modern, derived from the interaction of ethnicity with modern individualism, state structures and the global aspects of capitalism. In the past, different ethnic and religious communities co-existed in harmony in many cosmopolitan capitals of empires and great merchant cities such as Constantinople, Beirut and even Sarajevo. The harmonious coexistence was primarily attributed to the fact that they were not called to join together in democratic self-government. Problems and conflicts of personal and collective identities emerged once it was recognized that governments get their legitimacy from the people and not from divine right, ancient inheritance or sheer power. Different ethnic, religious, racial and cultural communities have to move out of their isolation and interact with each other, participate in a public discourse for the common good, formulate policies and consent to the distribution of power that safeguard their public interests and define their obligations.

When ethnicity gains political aspirations it gives birth to nationalism. Nationalism as a political notion emerged in the late 18th century and it is closely related with the ideas of popular sovereignty, democracy, and the notion that state and nation should be congruent. The movement from empires to democratic and sovereign states is known as a complex history of liberation from oppressive structures and the emergence of new forms of domination. Late modernity, through the process of globalization (as we have already noted), has compressed irreversibly the time and space that defined the boundaries necessary for the formation of communities. This has exacerbated the encounter between different ethnic, religious, racial and cultural communities by forcing them to cohabit in the same living space and, regardless of their dispositions, to experience the presence of others who demand to participate in the power structures that regulate the common public space. In the modern globalized world, people, cultures, societies, religions and civilizations which were previously more or less isolated from one another are now in regular and almost unavoidable contact.

Sociologists have observed that in late modernity personal and collective identities are corroded, while at the same time particular identities are revitalized or encouraged to emerge as a way of gaining control over systemic power.[23] Thus, globalization challenges the power of the state in many respects and, rather than spelling the end of nationalism, encourages its renewal and continuous production because, as Graig Calhoon states,

> Nationalism is the rhetoric of identity and solidarity in which citizens of the modern world most readily deal with the problematic nature of state power and with problems of inclusion and exclusion.[24]

National identity is the most potent collective identity in the modern world because it is understood to provide a basic foundation for social cohesiveness and participation in the distribution of power that regulates life in society. Whenever a person or group feels that their interests, culture or socio-economic concerns are threatened by actual or imaginary forces, their collective identity is heightened, and they look to their cultural, religious and ethnic identity for ways to combat their feelings of helplessness and to serve as vehicles for the redress of injuries to their self-esteem.

Some of the fears which bring latent group identity alive include the following: dangers to the material existence of the individual; feelings of loss and helplessness that accompany dislocation and migration from rural areas to the shanty towns of the urban megalopolis; the disappearance of crafts skills which underlay traditional work identities; the humiliation caused by the homogenizing and hegemonizing impact of the modern world which pronounces ancestral cultural ideals and values outmoded and irrelevant; the perceived or actual disregard by the state of a group's interest or disrespect for its cultural symbols; and changing political constellations such as those which accompany the end of empires. This situation becomes alarming because globalization has brought the world to a great, complex and contradictory stage of on-going transformation with great potential for a better future for some and immense suffering and dislocation for the majority of people who inhabit this planet. Many people feel a heightened sense of uncertainty and insecurity as they experience the strain and the breakdown of fami-lies, social support networks, old ways of forming group solidarity, and other traditional patterns of living. Thus, it is my contention that religion does not by itself mediate violence but rather, together with other social factors, contributes to the generation of violence as people within a group react to internal or external threats against the viability of the group's identity and its participation in local, national and global struc-tures of power.[25] Thus, if religion is not the primary or the only cause of violent conflicts in the world, we must recognize that neither peace nor reconciliation can be established simply through the contributions of religion.

Such an undertaking demands that the churches recognize the impor-tance of witnessing to the love of God for the world as a community of God's churches, in cooperation with other people and communities of other living faiths and ideologies who have the same aspiration for life in the world. Furthermore, as the Carnegie report says,

> working for the prevention of deadly conflict is, over the long term, too hard – intellectually, technically and politically – to be the sole responsibility of any single church, institution or government, no matter how powerful or willing it may be. Strengths must be pooled, burdens shared, and labour divided among actors. This is a practical necessity.[26]

All religions, including Christianity, have been contributing factors to violent conflicts at some points and at other points have contributed significantly to the advancement of peace and reconciliation by embrac-ing other groups with compassion rooted in faith. In the distribution of blame for the deadly use of religion, or of praise for the advancement of peace by religious communities, we must be courageous enough to rec-ognize the failures of all religions (including ours) and gracious enough to acknowledge the extraordinary acts of peace and human compassion that people of different faiths and ideologies have exemplified in situa-tions of deadly conflicts. The awareness of the great complexity of the issues that this study will address should not lead to paralysis or to surrender to the passive acceptance of a violent world. On the contrary, this fragile and vulnerable world can become the focus of our love and we can respond to its needs by uniting the life-giving resources that God has given to his Church with similar gifts that exist in other living faiths, ideologies, and in the world, for the purpose of becoming heralds of peace, working for justice, and recognizing the dignity and the rights of others across national, religious, cultural or social boundaries. The real challenge that we face as churches is not whether we will work for peace, justice and tolerance in the present world, but rather how the voice of God for peace, reconciliation, justice can become stronger, louder and translatable in our actions as we desire to participate in God's continuous work for the salvation of the world.

Pluralism – a positive challenge

The multiplicity of collective and personal identities in modern society, and the freedom that people have to choose what they will be and with whom they will associate, lead to the belief that personal or collective identities are not naturally or divinely given, but are instead social constructs and, therefore, are revisable and subject to reconfiguration, growth or corruption. Rather than dreaming about the demise of nationalism and ethnicity in the globalized world, it is rather more realistic and accurate, for the sake of advancing peace and unity, to seek the redefinition of personal and collective identities by recognizing the already inherently existing plurality in every personal and collective identity. The pluralism of existing identities in the modern world informed by the assumption that collective identities are revisable, subject to growth and to enhancement, challenges us to explore the possibilities to reconfigure the concept of nationhood by recognizing, respecting and engaging with its unavoidable internal pluralism as it tries to find its place in the modern world. As the Carnegie Commission noted,

> Citizens from different nationalities, as from different regions, religions or occupations, need to be able and willing to engage each other in discourse about the social arrangements which hold them together and order their lives – in brief, about their common good. Moreover, the same is crucial within nationalities. There is no reason to accept monolithic conformity within any one nation or people (insurgent or in power). Not only may states be multinational or multicultural, nations themselves must – if they are to be allies of liberty – admit and encourage internal diversity whether they are coterminous with states or exist as subsidiary identities within states. It is necessary, in other words, that the nation be open to democracy and diversity, whether or not the close link between the nation and state is severed. In power, extreme

nationalists do not just repress other peoples; they repress the diversity and creativity of people within the very nation they cherish.[27]

This context will force us to reflect theologically on the plurality of personal and collective identities in the modern world and in what ways religion and more particularly Christianity contribute to the specificity of personal and collective identities through the exclusion or the inclusion of the other/s and differences.[28] Reflecting on how personal or collective identities are passionately defended on religious grounds, it will be important to clarify whether identities are social constructs or are given by God or nature to particular people in specific territories. The challenge that we face as Christians is whether we will recognize others in their irreducible differences as God's children and respect them as such or mis-recognize them and contribute to their oppression as undesirable transgressors of our living space. How can we develop a culture of peace and tolerance based on the gospel of Jesus Christ and the tradition of God's Church? The Carnegie Commission on Preventing Deadly Conflicts recognizes in its final report that religious leaders and institutions not only find themselves in a privileged position to address situations of conflict, but their contribution towards building a culture of peace is very much needed and required:

> The Commission believes that religious leaders and institutions should be called upon to undertake a worldwide effort to foster respect for diversity and to promote ways to avoid violence. During any interfaith and intrafaith gathering, they should discuss as a priority matter, ways to play constructive and mutually supporting roles to help prevent the emergence of violence. They should also take more assertive measures to censure coreligionists who promote violence or give religious justification for violence. They can do so, in part, through worldwide promulgation of norms for tolerance to guide their faithful.[29]

The Declaration towards a Global Ethic of the Parliament of the World's Religions is a notable example of such an undertaking. It calls Christians and people of other living faiths to recognize the irreversible pluralism of the modern world that invites them to rethink their ethical responsibility and commitment to a culture of nonviolence and respect for life, of solidarity and a just economic order, of tolerance and a life of truthfulness, of equal rights and partnership between men and women. Situating our quest for the unity of the Church in the context of the conflict and waste of human lives and resources that plague our modern world reveals the importance of our ecumenical dialogue, fellowship and witness for the life of the world. Furthermore, it challenges us to develop a theology that attempts not only to interpret ethnic conflicts from a theological perspective but also to challenge the Christian churches to commit themselves to a culture of peace and to work actively for its realization.

NOTES

[1] R. Scott Appleby, *The Ambivalence of the Sacred: Religion, Violence and Reconciliation*, Latham MD, Rowman & Littlefield, 2000, p.58.

[2] N. Lossky et al. eds, *Dictionary of the Ecumenical Movement*, WCC, 2002, p.709.

[3] Carnegie Commission on Preventing Deadly Conflict *Final Report with Executive Summary*, New York, 1997, p.153.

[4] For revisionary interpretations of ostensibly religious conflicts of the past see Philippe Wolff, "The 1391 Pogrom in Spain: Social Crisis or Not?", *Past and Present*, 50, 1971, pp.4-18; George Rude, *The Crowd in History: A Study of Popular Disturbance in France and England, 1730-1848*, New York, 1964; Janine Estebe, *Tocsin pour un massacre*, Paris, Centurion 1968; *idem, Mirrors of Violence*, Delhi, Oxford UP, 1990. For an interesting discussion of whether religion should be blamed as the source of dogmatism, fanaticism, prejudice, repression and persecution see David Martin, *Does Christianity Cause War?*, Oxford, Clarendon, 1997.

[5] Martin, *Does Christianity Cause War?*, p.20.

[6] *Ibid.*, p.6.

[7] Sudhir Kakar, *The Colours of Violence; Cultural Identities, Religion, and Conflict*, Chicago, Univ. of Chicago Press, 1996, p.186.

[8] *Ibid.*, p.188.

[9] Stephen Steinberg, *The Ethnic Myth: Race, Ethnicity and Class in America*, New York, Athenium, 1981, pp.255, 258.

[10] J. Milton Yinger, "Ethnicity", in *Annual Review of Sociology*, 11, 1985, p.161.

[11] N. Glazer and P.D. Moynihan eds, *Ethnicity: Theory and Experience*, Cambridge MA, Harvard UP, 1975, p.169.

[12] Yinger, "Ethnicity", p.161.

[13] *Ibid.*, p.154.

[14] E. Kedourie, *Nationalism*, London, Hutchinson Univ. Library, 1986, p.58.

[15] Carnegie Commission, *Final Report*, p.xv.

[16] Montserrat Guibernau, *Nationalisms: The Nation-State and Nationalism in the Twentieth Century*, Cambridge, Polity, 1996, p.4.

[17] Appleby, *The Ambivalence of the Sacred*, p.27.

[18] *Dilemmas and Opportunities for Christian Action in Rapid Social Change*, WCC, 1959.

[19] *Ibid.*, p.57. This quotation is taken from M.M. Thomas, "Nation", *Dictionary of the Ecumenical Movement*, p.710b.

[20] D. J. Hall and Rosemary Radford Ruether, *God and the Nations*, Minneapolis, Fortress, 1995, pp.17-24.

[21] Damaskinos Papandreou, "Ekklesia kai Ethnotita", in *Orthodoxia kai Kosmos*, Katerini, Tertios, 1993, pp.75-85. Orthodox theologians debated the issue of nationalism and the Church at the second conference of Orthodox theological schools held in Athens in 1978. From the perspective of the Church's catholicity, they renounced nationalism and emphasized the inclusive universality of God's Church. At the same time, it was recognized that the Orthodox churches have voluntarily or involuntarily, but always against their faith, subscribed to national and racial chauvinism. Savas Agourides ed., *Deuxième Congrès de théologie orthodoxe*, Athens, 1978, pp.458-518. John Karmires in particular, in his article on the catholicity of the Church and nationalism published in the proceedings of this conference (pp.458-81), stated: "It is not permissible that the universal and eternal Church should be restricted and reduced, by identifying with small local 'national' churches, restricted geographically and unduly influenced by civilization, language, idiosyncrasy and the nations of the different peoples and races of the earth, serving at times small and temporary political and state purposes, dictated by nationalism, racialism and chauvinism

of peoples and states" (p.470). The same author, reflecting on the historical performance of Orthodoxy, noted: "In recent times certain local Orthodox churches, for mainly historical reasons and not for dogmatic and organizational reasons, sometimes allowed themselves to be led away by excessive nationalism and racism, clinging for a short time unduly to their own nations and becoming unwilling instruments of chauvinistic pursuits of the national states in violation of the catholicity of Orthodoxy" (p.470). See also on the same topic: Demetrios J. Constantelos, "Ethnic Particularities and the Universality of Orthodoxy Today", and John Meyendorff, "Ethnic Particularities and the Universality of Orthodoxy Today", in Nomikos M. Vaporis ed., *Rightly Teaching The Word of Your Truth: Studies in Honour of His Eminence Archbishop Iakovos*, Brookline MA, Holy Cross Orthodox Press, 1995, pp.75-87 and 89-98; Todor Sabev, "Church, Nation and Nationalism", in Editor??, *Religion et société*, Chambesy, Les Éditions du Centre orthodoxe, 1998, pp.259-67. Orthodox theologians, while they denounce ethnicity and nationalism and affirm the universality of God's Church, have not adequately reflected on what ways God is actively present in the diversity of collective identities that characterize the life of the modern world, or on what the public role of the Orthodox Church in an increasingly pluralistic world should be.

[22] For the human consequences of this transgression of time and space see Zygmunt Bauman, *Globalization: The Human Consquences*, New York, Columbia UP, 1998, pp.6-76.

[23] Peter Beyer, *Religion and Globalization*, London, Sage, 1994, p.2.

[24] Graig Calhoon, "Nationalism and Civil Society: Democracy, Diversity and Self-Determination", in *idem* ed., *Social Theory and the Politics of Identity*, Oxford, Blackwell, 1994, p.305.

[25] D. Horowitz, in *Ethnic Groups in Conflict*, Berkeley and Los Angeles, Univ. of California Press, 1985, expresses the theory that the international environment, especially the ending of colonial rule, is responsible for ethnic conflict.

[26] Carnegie Commission, *Final Report*, p.xiv.

[27] *Ibid.*, p.327.

[28] Metropolitan John Zizioulas, "Communion and Otherness", *St Vladimir's Theological Quarterly, 38*, 1994, pp. 347-61; Miroslav Volf, *Exclusion and Embrace: A Theological Exploration of Identity, Otherness, and Reconciliation*, Nashville, Abingdon, 1996; Paul R. Sponheim, *Faith and the Other: A Relational Theology*, Minneapolis, Fortress, 1993; *idem*, "The Other is Given: Religion, War and Peace", *Word and World*, 15, 1995, pp.428-42; Francis Jacques, *Difference and Subjectivity: Dialogue and Personal Identity*, New Haven, Yale UP, 1991.

[29] Carnegie Corporation, *Preventing*, p.118.

Ethnic Conflicts and the Orthodox Church

METROPOLITAN JOHN OF KORCE

The 21st century, with its globalization, new technology, loss of traditional values, and cultural and religious pluralism, presents a variety of challenges for the whole human community. Undoubtedly, the Orthodox Church cannot exclude herself from these challenges. She must confront them, not merely to defend herself from them, as has been the case so often, but in order to find original and creative solutions as part of her global responsibility. In this, she must be rooted in her doctrine, history, and rich tradition without ceasing to be a creative, living organism, invigorated, moved and enlightened by the Holy Spirit, who has inspired and continues to inspire her life.

Generally speaking, the Orthodox Church is often viewed, measured, judged and evaluated – unfortunately often also by her own members – primarily on the basis of her history over the last two centuries, that is, as a church closely tied to a single culture in a specific geographic location and interested only in the past. Viewing the Orthodox Church from that perspective alone has done a great injustice to her rich tradition.

In fact, historically, the Orthodox Church was born, developed and lived in an ecumenical and pluralistic milieu. In the Roman empire and later in the Byzantine empire (including with this period the Ottoman empire), ecumenism and globalization were common. The Orthodox Church had a global mission, not only in the doctrinal sense, but also as a member of a global and ecumenical community. The people of the Balkans, where a large portion of the Orthodox were concentrated, lived in a commonwealth with close ties to each other. In addition, they had cultural and commercial connections with other parts of Europe, Africa and Asia. Up until the time that St Kosma was preaching and carrying out his apostolic ministry in the Balkans, the self-understanding of the population was global and ecumenical. What is more, at an even later period, if someone was asked what he was, he would first answer that he was a Christian. Only after the third or fourth question would he give his ethnic identity. People identified themselves from the perspective of faith. The words *elinas* and *turk* were understood to refer to one's faith, not one's ethnicity.

Nationalism and a narrow ethnic understanding are something new to the Orthodox people of the Balkans and are closely tied to the emergence of the nationalistic ideas of the 19th-century secular intelligentsia which saw the Church merely as a means of achieving their nationalistic goals. Unfortunately, this continues today. As these movements emerged, the Church was not enthusiastic about them because she felt that they were not in accord with the universal nature of Orthodoxy, but she, as Fr John Meyendorff said,

> obviously lacked the intellectual strength, the theological discernment and the institutional structures which could have exorcised the demons of the nationalistic revolution... So patriarchs, bishops and indeed parish clergy – sometimes enthusiastically, at other times wearily – joined the sweeping nationalistic movement, becoming directly involved in its political success but also – more dangerously – accepting its ideological positions.[1]

In the beginning, these new ideas – the awakening of the national consciousness – helped the struggle of the Orthodox people of the Balkans to rid themselves of the Turkish yoke. The Church, by supporting her people in this struggle, started to have more and more of an ethnic character. Because all members shared a single religion, faith and nation were tied closely together and began to be indistinguishable, creating a confusion of categories. Later, this nationalism, that in the beginning was seen as a liberating force, became an impetus for division and hatred: everyone against everyone else. Moreover, this nationalism was not directed solely against peoples of another religion, but against people of the same faith as well, because a particular nationalism is deaf to other forms of nationalism. The national rights claimed by each nation are mutually exclusive, resulting in ongoing ethnic conflict. In the Balkans, as well as in all parts of Europe, nationalism that began as a liberating force, in the end, in the words of Patriarch Bartholomew,

> turned out to be a double-edged sword; in the hands of tyrants, it has been destructive – indeed, the most destructive force in human history, killing 75 million human beings between 1914 and 1945 alone. We must ask ourselves boldly and honestly: Is it not time to rein in the excesses of nationalism?[2]

After the fall of communism, in the institutional, economic and political collapse, and the moral and spiritual vacuum that resulted from it, extreme nationalism found fertile ground. Different political groups attempted to use national and religious feelings to achieve their political goals, thus creating an immense whirlpool of hatred, confusion and suffering. The great hatred that characterized the struggle of the classes was replaced by another hatred: ethnic hatred. It is interesting to note that the ranks of extreme nationalists were filled in large measure by the same people that previously had instigated class hatred. Also, at times they attempted to give to their wars a religious character, wanting to exploit the powerful emotions that are triggered when people believe that their religion is in danger. Many in the Balkans ironically have dubbed these wars "the religious wars of the atheists".

So, one of the most difficult challenges that has confronted and continues to confront the Orthodox Church is her position regarding ethnic conflicts. In the past decade the need to find a solution to this challenge has become more and more urgent because some of the most bloody ethnic conflicts have occurred in Balkan and Eastern European countries where the Orthodox population is in the majority. During this time of crisis, the Orthodox Church, as a result of the long persecution, was found to be weak and unprepared. In some cases, the Church herself was drawn into the conflict. She was found in a more-or-less similar situation when the nationalistic movements of the 19th century began. Now, however, the situation is more sinister because the enthusiasm of national liberation, which first motivated the Church's involvement in that movement, has been replaced by extreme nationalist hatred.

We have to keep in mind that this is a complex issue that cannot be judged simplistically and superficially, because when we speak about the Church we have to remember that she consists not only of the ecclesiastical hierarchy and believing members with different levels of faith and experience, but also of many purely nominal Orthodox.

Orthodox understanding of Church, nation and war

The relationship between Church and nation is complex and the two are inseparable because the members of the Church are also part of the nation. This becomes even more complicated when all members of the nation are members of one Church. Although much has been said about this issue, there are many unanswered questions about the relationship between national identity and the Church:

> From a dogmatic and mystical point of view, the issue of Church and national identity is only a part of the great question of the relation of the Church with human history and cultural creation. However strange this may seem, after two thousand years of Christian history this question, notwithstanding its greatness and its actuality, has not yet found a conciliar answer within the Church. It has not found it, because it has not been raised in the Church. It has not been raised, because it has not been envisaged.[3]

Therefore, in the great challenge of ethnic conflict, the Orthodox Church must speak openly and clearly, unfolding her precious teaching to all her believers. She must make them conscious of the Orthodox understanding of Church, nation and war in order that these issues do not remain within the closed circles of academics and theologians. Let us pause to consider the Orthodox understanding of nation and war because ethnic conflicts are a corrupt compound of the two.

Church and nation

Christian anthropology is based upon divine revelation which says that "God created man in his own image and likeness" (Gen. 1:26,27, 5:1). The incarnation of the Lord and his soteriological work demonstrate that God is not the God of the Jews alone, but also of the Gentiles (Rom. 3:29). The Church which is built upon this foundation does not divide people on either national or class grounds: in her "there is neither Greek, nor Jew, circumcision nor uncircumcision, Barbarian, Scythian, bond nor free: but Christ is all, and in all" (Col. 3:11). Hence, the Church by her very nature is universal and, therefore, supranational. In the Church "there is no difference between the Jew and the Greek" (Rom. 10:12). This is the basis for the Christian understanding of nation and race. The witness of holy scripture as well as various apostolic and post-apostolic texts are evidence of the self-understanding of the early Church. The epistle to Diognetus is not only one of the oldest witnesses of this self-understanding but also one of the clearest.[4]

An over-emphasis on the nation, sometimes even above the Church, not only is a new phenomenon but is a flagrant violation of the ethos of Orthodoxy and a denial of it. This over-emphasis of nationalism has caused much damage to church life and to the internal unity of the Orthodox churches because it has often caused these churches to be more focused on their national interests than on the Orthodox Church as a whole. Schmemann writes,

> Admitting the positive value of nationalism in Christianity, we must not fall into the trap of idealizing history, fixing our eyes on the light, and shutting out what is dark. The progress and earthly life of the Church is not an idyll. On the contrary, it requires struggles and a vigilant ecclesiastical conscience... The danger of nationalism lies in its subconsciously altering the hierarchy of values, so that the nation no longer serves Christian justice, truth or itself, and no longer evaluates its life in accordance with these qualities. Instead, Christianity itself and the Church begin to be assessed and evaluated by the extent to which they serve the state, the nation, etc.[5]

The Orthodox Church has officially condemned nationalistic rivalries within the Church of Christ. In 1872 a synod held in Constantinople condemned the sin of phyletism, saying, "We renounce, censure, and condemn racism, that is, racial discrimination, ethnic feuds, hatreds, and dissensions within the Church of Christ." Today we must do this repeatedly because this has been one of the main problems of the "one, holy, catholic and apostolic Church".

We can say without exaggeration that the Church of the New Testament was built upon the blood shed in the conflict between nation and universality. The pan-human, universal and messianic mission of Christ was not understood by the leadership of Israel. Caiaphas prophesied and said, "You know nothing at all, nor do you consider that it is expedient for us that one man should die for the people, and not that the whole nation should perish" (John 11:49-50). "Then, from that day," the Evangelist tells us, "they plotted to put him to death" (John 11:53). And so, in order to save the nation, they crucified the Lord himself. The pretext of saving the nation put the Church of the Old Testament and her high priest in confrontation with God. This event tells us much: We must take care to say to our people that many of the things alleged to be for the good of the nation can make us the enemies of justice, and perhaps even of the Lord himself. It is not uncommon that certain means used to defend the nation, and, in the short run, to benefit her, have caused crimes and injustices to be done towards other individuals and nations. Any crime and injustice is a re-crucifixion of the Lord of justice. All those that crucified the Lord found good reasons to do so: Caiaphas for the nation; Pilate for the state; the people for piety; the soldiers for military discipline. And so together they all murdered a man in whom there "was found no fault". But no reason, no motive, no goal can justify the killing of innocents, and oppression and injustices done to others.

In contrast, the apostle and evangelist of the Church of the New Testament answered to the prophecy of Caiaphas that Christ did not die "for that nation only, but also that he would gather together in one the children of God who were scattered abroad" (John 11:52). The members of the human race were seen as children of God, and no specific nation could have a monopoly on virtue and holiness. The taking-on of human nature by God called all nations to participate in the mystical body of Christ, in "one, holy, catholic and apostolic church". Christ has taken into himself all of humanity, not only that which exists today, but those that were and those that will come after. He is not a tribal leader whose authority should facilitate national unification, but God who saves us from sin and death. A Christ limited to one ethnic group or several ethnic groups, or to one period or several periods of history would be a mutilated Christ. Those that limit Christ so crucify him again.

To love one's nation does not mean to hate and exclude the others. You cannot serve one nation at the expense of another. The interests of a country cannot be above justice, otherwise that nation becomes an idol. "What are the interests of our country", asked Lactantius in his *Divines Institutes*, "but the inconveniences of another state or nation?"[6] Not only is the nation not helped by this, but on the contrary this will turn to its disadvantage. The pastoral letter of Patriarch Tikon addressed to the Orthodox faithful of Russia[7] shows that the position of the Church regarding the relation between the nation and justice has not changed, despite all the atrocities that have occurred.

Church and war

From the Orthodox point of view, war and the understanding of it is wide, complex and multi-faceted. Although in all times the Church has called upon her children to love their homeland on earth and not to spare their lives to protect it if it was threatened, and although the Church has honoured warrior-saints whose icons were carried into battle by soldiers chanting "grant victory to the Orthodox Christians over their adversaries", nonetheless, in the Orthodox Church the idea of a "holy war" has never been accepted – not even a "just war". In the Fathers of the Eastern Church and in the canonical tradition of the Orthodox Church, you cannot find any ethical explanation for a "just war". From an Orthodox point of view, war is a sin and an evil, and the Church should fight against it. In the best of cases, war can be a "necessary evil", although this term is not precise and can be misleading. Let us remember that even in the Old Testament, which was full of war and bloodshed, God did not allow David to build his temple because he had shed so much blood, thus revealing that in bloodshed there is nothing "holy" or "just".[8]

In the canons that regulate the life of the clergy, the Church held to an ideal standard that often was difficult for laypeople, due to human weakness. Hence, the canonical exclusion of the clergy from all military duty, which was permitted to laypeople, demonstrates the ethical position of the early Church towards war.[9] Early Christianity did not condone any use of violence. In the writings of Tertullian, Origen and the apologists in general, the non-use of violence is clearly stated. St Basil imposed an ecclesiastical penance on military personnel who had taken part in war.[10] And although killing in war was not considered a murder, as we see from the canon of St Basil, war was not seen as something "holy" or "just", and those who participated in it were not allowed to take communion for three years to show that there was still a need for purification before they could meet the Lord. Christianity preached that one ought to conquer evil with good, and in the place of war to draw on prayer and the power of

God. In the Christian empire, although the army was kept to protect the state and to fight against the barbarians, war was seen as a "necessary evil" and the doctrine of a "just war" was never developed.

After the fall of the Byzantine empire, and later of the Ottoman empire, when the national autocephalous churches were formed, under the influence of nationalistic feelings, war was seen in a more positive light. Although the Orthodox Church did not hold to any doctrine of "holy" or "just war", she did not have a strong voice against war because there was confusion about the categories of nation and religion. In recent years many voices have been raised against the use of religion in the ethnic conflicts of the Balkans. One of the strongest voices is that of Archbishop Anastasios of Albania, whose motto that "the oil of religion must never be used to flame the conflicts, but to soothe hearts and heal wounds", has become a classic statement, not only in the Orthodox Church worldwide, but in wider circles as well.

The Church transcends ethnicity

In this time of globalization (and, unfortunately, of uniformity as well), many traditional values are seen to be at risk. One of these is the feeling that national identity is being lost, and this often breeds a fear of outsiders and increases nationalistic feelings, and can cause such sinful phenomena as xenophobia and inter-ethnic enmity, leading often to the restriction of the rights of individuals and nations, persecutions, wars and other manifestations of violence. The opposition to this can be found within the Christian message. The mission of Christianity and its values is a global mission, and should not fear any type of globalization. The cure for the sickness of secular globalization and the loss of values is found not by withdrawing into an ethnic and national refuge, but through administering the medicine of its universal mission. The true Christian cannot feel threatened ethnically because a Christian globalization does not deny ethnicity. The global mission of Christianity is not uniformity, but unity.

The Church does not deny ethnicity, because to deny it would be to deny the mystery of personhood and the particularity of each individual; instead, the Church transcends ethnicity. The Church must consider the nation and war according to her absolute and eternal values: all other values, whatever they may be and no matter how worthy their motives may be, are lesser and relative. Divine revelation and life in Christ through the sacraments of the Church are absolute; therefore, any other relative value that impinges upon these absolute values cannot be accepted by the Church – the heavenly homeland is above any earthly one. The holy righteous John of Kronstadt wrote this about love of one's earthly homeland:

Love the earthly homeland... it has raised, distinguished, honoured and equipped you with everything; but have special love for the heavenly homeland... that homeland is incomparably more precious than this one.[11]

In ethnic conflicts, the Church should have a strong prophetic voice, and, when she observes that among her people or others sick nationalistic movements, motivated and fed by hatred, are taking place, she should diagnose the illness with discernment and love. The Church must not tolerate ethnic hatred, out of which are born racism and fascism. She must fight unswervingly against this demon of hatred. A true love for the nation means a desire to cure its sickness. As a devoted doctor seeks to cure sicknesses without worrying about what the sick will think of him, so also the Church, motivated by a true love for the nation and its people, and with the prophetic power of the Holy Spirit, must give the diagnosis and administer the appropriate medicine without regard to what people will think. The prophetic role of the Church is to say what God is saying. We know from the holy scriptures how costly the phrase "thus says the Lord" was for the prophets. All of them were persecuted and killed because they said "thus says the Lord" and proclaimed the words of God. Kings, rulers, priests and people wanted the prophets to say only what they wanted to hear, but the prophets said what the Lord was saying. The truth can be persecuted, but it will live. Its words are eternal, because "thus says the Lord". By not telling the truth to others, we show that we do not love them.

On the basis of a Christian anthropology that believes that God "has made from one blood every nation of men" (Acts 17:26), the Church sees that human unity is deeper, and ethnic divisions superficial and non-essential. The only legitimate division will occur when "all the nations will be gathered before [the Son of man], and he will separate them one from another, as a shepherd divides his sheep from goats" (Matt. 25:32).

I would like to conclude with words of N. Berdayev:

There have always been two races in the world; they exist today, and this division is more important than all other divisions. There are those who crucify and those who are crucified, those that oppress and those who are oppressed, those who hate and those who are hated, those who inflict suffering and those who suffer, those who persecute and those who are persecuted. It needs no explanation on whose side Christians should be.[12]

NOTES

[1] John Meyendorff, *The Byzantine Legacy in the Orthodox Church*, Crestwood NY, St Vladimir's Seminary Press, 1982, pp. 226-27.

[2] Patriarch Bartholomeos of Constantinople, from an address delivered in Istanbul, 8 Feb. 1994. Reprinted in Hildo Bos and Jim Forest eds, *For the Peace from Above: An Orthodox Resource Book on War, Peace and Nationalism*, Syndesmos, 1999.

[3] A. Kartachov, *The Church and National Identity*, Paris, 1934 (in French).

[4] "For Christians are not distinguished from the rest of mankind either in locality or in speech or in customs. For they dwell not somewhere in cities of their own, neither do they use some different language, nor practise an extraordinary kind of life. Nor again do they possess any invention discovered by any intelligence or study of ingenious men, nor are they masters of any human dogma as some are. But while they dwell in cities of Greeks and barbarians as the lot of each is cast, and follow the native customs in dress and food and the other arrangements of life, yet the constitution of their own citizenship, which they set forth, is marvellous, and confessedly contradicts expectation. They dwell in their own countries, but only as sojourners; they bear their share in all things as citizens, and they endure all hardships as strangers. Every foreign country is a fatherland to them, and every fatherland is foreign. Their existence is on earth, but their citizenship is in heaven."

[5] A. Schmemann, "Tserkov' i tserkovnoye ustroistro", in *Messager de l'Exarchat du Patriarche russe en Europe occidentale*, March 1949.

[6] "What are the interests of our country but the inconveniences of another state or nation, that is, to extend the boundaries which are violently taken from others, to increase the power of the state, to improve the revenues, – all which things are not virtues, but the overthrowing of virtues: for, in the first place, the union of human society is taken away, innocence is taken away, the abstaining from the property of another is taken away; lastly, justice itself is taken away, which is unable to bear the tearing asunder of the human race, and wherever arms have glittered, must be banished and exterminated from thence. (...) How can a man be just who injures, who hates, who despoils, who puts to death? And they who strive to be serviceable to their country do all these things: for they are ignorant of what this being serviceable is, who think nothing useful, nothing advantageous, but that which can be held by the hand; and this alone cannot be held, because it may be snatched away."

[7] "What a difficult, but yet elevated task it is for a Christian, to retain within himself the great joy of non-anger and love even when his enemy has been overthrown, when the persecuted martyr prepares himself to judge his recent persecutor and oppressor. The providence of God has already placed certain children of the Russian Orthodox Church in front of this temptation. Passions arise (...) Orthodox Russia, let this shame pass by you! Let this curse not touch upon you. May your hand not be reddened by blood, which cries out to heaven. Do not let the enemy of Christ, the devil, carry you away by the passion of vengeance and to besmirch the endeavour of your martyrdom from the hands of the violators and persecutors of Christ. Remember: pogroms are the victory of your enemies. Remember: pogroms are a dishonour for yourself, a dishonour to the Church! For the Christian, the ideal is Christ, who used no sword to defend himself, who brought the sons of thunder to peace, having prayed for his enemies on the cross. For the Christian, the guiding light is the command of the holy apostle, who suffered much for his Saviour and who sealed his dedication to him by his death: 'Beloved, never avenge yourselves, but leave it to the wrath of God: for it is written: "Vengeance is mine, I will repay, says the Lord." No, "if your enemy is hungry, feed him; if he is thirsty, give him drink; for by so doing you will heap burning coals upon his head"' (Rom. 12:19-20).

[8] "David said to Solomon, 'My son, I planned to build a house to the name of the Lord my God. But the word of the Lord came to me, saying, "You have shed much blood and have waged great wars; you shall not build a house to my name, because you have shed so much blood in my sight on the earth"'" (1 Chron. 22:7-8).

[9] Canon LXXXIII of the 85 Canons of the Holy and Altogether August Apostles says, "If a bishop, presbyter, or deacon, shall serve in the army, and wish to retain both the Roman magistracy and the priestly office, let him be deposed; for the things of Caesar belong to Caesar, and those of God to God."

[10] Canon XIII: "Our fathers did not think that killing in war was murder; yet I think it advisable for such as have been guilty of it to forbear communion three years."

[11] Quoted from *Bases of the Social Concept of the Russian Orthodox Church*, II, 2.

[12] N. Berdyayev, *Christianity and Anti-Semitism* (the religious destiny of Judaism), Paris, 1935, p.30 (in French).

Orthodoxy, Nationalism and Ethnic Conflict

PASCHALIS M. KITROMILIDES

Developments in Eastern and South-eastern Europe during the last decade of the 20th century, following the collapse of the communist regimes in 1989-91, appeared to confirm a long tradition of prejudicial thinking about the eastern half of the European continent, and especially about the Orthodox Balkans as a region of extremes, recurring confrontations and endemic violence. This impression has prevailed for a long time in Western perceptions. Important works of Western scholarship, instead of moderating it or correcting it, have often contributed decisively to it. A characteristic expression of this attitude in epigrammatic concision came in the observation of a pioneer early 20th-century British anthropologist of the Balkans, Mary Edith Duhram, who characterized Balkan history and politics as "an opera buffa written in blood".[1]

Although a long history has unfolded in the region since Miss Duhram's peregrinations in the highlands of Montenegro and Albania, little has happened to mitigate or change mental habits in thinking and defining the character of the politics and culture of the region. Recent events, especially the civil wars that tore apart the Yugoslav federation in the 1990s, have confirmed and sharpened negative perceptions and stereotypes.[2] Among the protagonists in the "opera buffa" and one of the main contributors to multi-faceted conflict and disorder in the Balkans has been considered to be the Orthodox Church, which represents the majority religious confession in the area. It would have been pointless to even attempt to sample the pertinent writing, mostly works of journalists and partisan observers who extrapolate from current practices, forms of behaviour and ideological statements to general and all-encompassing theories and interpretations concerning the bellicosity of Orthodoxy and the propensity of the Orthodox Church towards authoritarianism, intolerance, fanaticism and chauvinism. Furthermore, such criticism attributes these tendencies and characteristics not to human failure and to the workings of evil in the world or to the historical circumstances that often determine the praxis and the discourse of the Church, but to the fundamental doctrines, principles and traditions of Orthodoxy and of the local churches that compose it.

I would like to challenge this view, not from a religious perspective, but from the perspective of cultural history and from the vantage point of the historical study of the Orthodox regions of Europe. I do not think that it would be profitable or edifying to attempt to refute such views and arguments by trying to show how hollow, misinformed and often not entirely disinterested they may be. It would be more constructive, in my judgment, to reflect on the historical condition of Orthodoxy and on its involvement in the world. To this end I would like to put forward three propositions as objects of reflection and points of departure for a critical dialogue.

1. Orthodoxy on a social and political level equals ecumenicity in the authentic and original spirit of evangelical Christianity and of the Christian tradition

Any serious consideration of the doctrinal basis and of the moral teaching of the Orthodox Church will recognize that, despite the vicissitudes experienced by the Church in medieval and modern times and despite the temptations of history, the Orthodox Church in the East has retained in its theology and social philosophy the genuine Christian outlook, as codified in the New Testament and patristic thought. It is, therefore, rather paradoxical and certainly occasionally amusing to witness attempts by contemporary social scientists,[3] who try to work out the "theoretical" connection between what they understand as Orthodox teaching and attitudes and the militantly secular political philosophy of nationalism, which is mostly a product of 19th-century intellectual and political quests. I am referring here to the Orthodox view and understanding of social and political questions, which has remained firmly anchored in New Testament and Greek patristic theology and has added little to this body of ecumenical teaching since the seventh ecumenical council.[4]

What emerges from this heritage in connection with social and political questions, especially questions of human community and the relations between individuals and groups, is the ecumenical teaching of St Paul against all earthly distinctions of race, class and sex, of freedom and slavery, of wisdom and ignorance in the communion of the faithful. There is very little beyond this that can be found in Orthodox religious teaching. Statements and pronouncements by individual Orthodox clergy, or even by ecclesiastical bodies in particular localities and under particular circumstances, can be found to diverge from this overall ecumenical teaching, but these do not express the canonical attitude of the Orthodox Church as a whole and can represent either expressions of its decentralized structure and of the dynamics of local communities or obvious human submission of its members to the temptations of history.

2. The identification of Orthodoxy with nationalism is a product of anachronistic judgment and misunderstanding of the historical record

The multifold forms of submission to the temptations of history to which I referred above essentially make up the content of the ecclesiastical history of Eastern and South-eastern Europe in the early modern and contemporary periods. It is this historical context that explains the identification of the Orthodox Church with nationalism. This is apparent in the writings not only of casual or superficial observers, but also of serious historians who have written authoritatively on the history of Eastern and South-eastern Europe. The identification is drawn both for the Middle Ages and for the modern period. In the case of the Middle Ages, the religious behaviour of the Orthodox patriarchates of the Bulgarian and Serbian empires has been treated as one of the expressions of national or proto-national sentiment in these medieval states.[5] The same logic has guided the narrative and interpretation of the modern history of Orthodox societies in Eastern and South-eastern Europe: the Orthodox Church has been invariably treated as a repository of national identity and national culture, either in connection with phenomena marking the behaviour of imperial states such as Russia or in the case of subjugated societies such as the Christian communities of the Balkans. The standard argument in conventional historiography has been that the Orthodox Church has preserved national identity in captivity or under the onslaught of Westernizing reform from above and saved the authentic character of the national culture and identity of Orthodox peoples in the eastern half of Europe.[6]

This, I think, is a classic case of anachronistic historical logic. It represents a projection backwards of frameworks of thought elaborated in order to sustain the ideology of national churches in the 19th century. If the necessary distinctions and abstractions are made and the historical record is read in the light of the historicity of sources and of the forms of behaviour they reflect, what will emerge is the rather simple fact that whenever we can locate phenomena akin to nationalism, ethnic affirmation and ethnic conflict, the critical factor is the presence not of the Church, but of the state, either in the form of medieval empires or of modern nation-states –projected or actual – trying to establish and aggrandize themselves.

Indeed part of the process of empire- or nation-building has been the creation of independent churches connected with regional state projects. It was this tendency that produced the national Orthodox churches in the 19th and 20th centuries as an integral part of the articulation and affirmation of the national identity of the newly independent states that sought to consolidate their social cohesion and to affirm their presence against the multi-ethnic empires from which they had seceded. And it was the powerful and captivating rhetoric of national historiography that was cultivated as part of the affirmation of the national culture of these new states that coloured the whole earlier historical record and recast the interpretation of the past in order to fit the new ideology of nationalism. Again it must be pointed out, especially to those who see a propensity towards nationalism as germane to Orthodoxy, that the involvement of Christian churches in projects of national affirmation cannot by any stretch of the imagination be considered an idiosyncrasy of the Orthodox world in view of the role of Catholicism in Ireland and in Poland, of Protestantism in Germany and Scandinavia, to say nothing of the role of Anglicanism as a state religion and of imperial Catholicism in Spain and Portugal and in their overseas empires.

It is true that the churches, both in Russia and Ukraine and especially in the Balkans under Ottoman rule, did provide protection and solace to the Christian people and a refuge to local cultural traditions, but this was a pastoral, not a political, project of the Church in order to preserve the faith.[7] Nationality and ethnic claims were not on the Church's cultural agenda before the 19th century.[8]

3. The local national Orthodox churches on account of their discourse and action in the world are not free of responsibility for misjudgments and anachronisms concerning their involvement with nationalism and ethnic conflict

Everything that I have said so far appears to be in glaring contradiction to recent forms of behaviour and to earlier, especially 19th-century, phenomena in the Orthodox world. Among recent forms of behaviour, the involvement of members of Orthodox clergy and laity invoking their Orthodox identity in ethnic and civil conflicts in Yugoslavia, the fiery rhetoric in the Church of Greece over a range of political issues, the involvement of the Church of Cyprus in nationalist struggles in the island, represent but a few examples. Among 19th-century historical phenomena, the role of the Greek Orthodox Church in the promotion of Greek irredentist projects and especially the involvement of Greek and Bulgarian clergy in the violent struggles in Macedonia constitute perhaps the weightiest evidence for the identification of Orthodoxy with

nationalism and might be cited as cases of the contribution of the Orthodox Church to the inception and escalation of ethnic conflict. Examples
could be multiplied. The role of the Orthodox Church in articulating
national identity among the Romanian-speaking population in 19th-
century Transylvania is a case in point.[9] Perhaps the epic role of the
Russian Orthodox Church in the great patriotic war against the Nazis
during the second world war represents the most prominent and heroic
expression of the supposed propensity of Orthodoxy towards nationalism – an expression which Western critics of Orthodoxy do not like to
mention when castigating the Orthodox Church for this propensity.

My argument would be that all these cases and examples, all this
mass of supposed evidence, essentially points to one thing: the way
modern state logic has manipulated and has been internalized by ecclesiastical institutions – to the point that one could legitimately suggest
that the national churches have undergone a considerable degree of de-
Christianization in their values.[10] This whole syndrome, nevertheless,
does not tell us anything about Orthodoxy, about the character and essen-
tials of Orthodox faith, about Orthodox social values, about Orthodoxy's
attitudes in the world and especially about the Orthodox conception of
human persons and of the community in which they ought to live.

Christian humility at the dawn of the new millennium invites the
churches, their hierarchies and their lay faithful to serious introspection
and soul searching over precisely this aspect of the Orthodox predica-
ment: the gradual, unconscious and unreflective substitution in the scale
of values of the official churches of faith in the nation in place of faith
in Christ. This should be a source of self-criticism, of a serious appraisal
of the historical trajectories of the Church and of a reawakening of a
Christian perspective on the Church's involvement in the world.

NOTES

[1] Maria Todorova, *Imagining the Balkans*, New York, Oxford UP, 1997, p.15.
[2] For effective historical criticism of the stereotype of the Balkan propensity to violence see
Mark Mazower, *The Balkans: A Short History*, New York, Modern Library, 2000, pp.145-
56.
[3] A good example of the confusion which derives from basic ignorance of the fundamentals
of the historical record is reflected characteristically in Julia Kristeva, "Le poids mys-
térieux de l'orthodoxie", in *Le Monde*, 18-19 April 1999. Similar confusions can easily
arise from Samuel Huntington, *The Clash of Civilisations and the Remaking of World
Order*, New York, Simon & Schuster, 1996, which is open to many misreadings. It has
elicited an interesting response by François Georges Thual, *Géopolitiques de l'orthodoxie*,
Paris, Dunod, 1994, a work, nevertheless, not entirely free of anachronistic thinking.
[4] For a learned and lucid synopsis of Orthodox teaching see Demetrios J. Constantelos,
"Ethnic Particularities and the Universality of Orthodox Christianity Today", in *Journal of
Modern Hellenism*, 7, 1990, pp.89-105.

[5] E.g. D. Obolensky, "Nationalism in Eastern Europe in the Middle Ages", in *idem, The Byzantine Inheritance of Eastern Europe*, London, Variorum, 1982, study no. XV.

[6] For a classic statement of this view see George G. Arnakis, "The Role of Religion in the Development of Balkan Nationalism", in Charles and Barbara Jelavich eds, *The Balkans in Transition*, Berkeley CA, Univ. of California Press, 1963, pp.115-44. Also Charles Jelavich, "Some Aspects of Serbian Religious Development in the Eighteenth Century", in *Church History*, 23, 1954, pp.144-52.

[7] For further elaboration on the character of pre-modern Orthodox society and on the content of the life of the faithful in it before the age of nationalism may I refer to P.M. Kitromilides, "Balkan Mentality: History, Legend, Imagination", in *Nations and Nationalism*, 2, 1996, esp. pp.176-79.

[8] On this transformation see P. M. Kitromilides, "'Imagined Communities' and the Origins of the National Question in the Balkans", in *European History Quarterly*, 19, 1989, pp.149-92, esp. pp.177-85 (= John Hutchinson and A.D. Smith eds, *Ethnicity*, Oxford, Oxford UP, 1996, pp.202-208).

[9] This episode in the history of nation-building in Central Europe has formed the object of a classic study by Keith Hitchins, *Orthodoxy and Nationality*, Cambridge MA, Harvard UP, 1977.

[10] Cf. Stevan K. Pavlowitch, "A propos de l'Eglise serbe. Considérations d'un historien orthodoxe sur le malheur d'être une agence, un monument ou un revêtement", in *Deltio Kentrou Mikrasiatikon Spoudon*, 13, 1999-2000, pp.353-62. This is a very important text that puts the whole question of the interplay of Orthodoxy with politics in its appropriate perspective. On the specific problem of the role of religion in the Yugoslav conflicts of the 1990s, see the testimonies by religious leaders in Paul Mojzes ed., *Religion and the War in Bosnia*, New York, Oxford UP, 1998, an important work whose significance is borne out in the commentary by Stevan Pavlowitch in *The Slavonic and East European Review*, 77, 1999, pp.576-79. The same historian's pertinent remarks in *Serbia: The History behind the Name*, London, Hurst, 2002, are fundamental for understanding the relevant issues.

Injustice and Prophetic Evangelism

KWAME JOSEPH LABI

There is neither Jew nor Greek, there is neither slave nor free, there is neither male nor female; but you are all one in Christ Jesus. (Gal. 3:28)

The collapse of communism, one of the most oppressive and anti-religious (not to say anti-Christian) ideological systems of governance in human history, affirmed the truth of the promise of Christ that not even the gates of hell shall prevail against his Church. It did, however, also reveal that the communist ideology was probably not the greatest threat or challenge to Christianity. For the collapse of communism also saw an upsurge in ethnic and nationalistic intolerance, fanning some of the worst conflicts in modern human history. I hasten to add that many of these had religion as their driving force.

Injustice and conflict

I believe that if one were to scratch a little deeper than the surface for the root causes of many of these and other conflicts around the world, one would discover injustice. Let me limit myself to Africa for some examples, since I am from Africa. It is rather easy to see the genocide in Rwanda or what happened in the Liberian civil war as inexplicable madness. Indeed it is. Nothing can justify the inhumanity of what occurred in either of these two situations; and the international community's efforts to bring the perpetrators of the genocide in Rwanda to justice is a step in the right direction. However, for a real and enduring solution to the conflict in Rwanda, these efforts need to go beyond the juridical to address the systemic injustice that has kept the Hutu majority oppressed and marginalized for so long.

Such systemic injustice, be it in Rwanda, Sudan, the Balkans or Western Europe, has often manifested itself as a "de-humanization" of one people by another. I use that term deliberately, because I believe that it is only when a people have been so totally de-humanized, even demonized, that one can justify the kind of injustice that the Jews, for instance, suffered at the hands of the Nazis, or that the Palestinians suffer today at the hands of the Israelis (with all of us looking on helplessly), or that the peoples of Africa have endured throughout history.

Ethnicity and the Church

Orthodox incarnational theology means that the Church is as much local as it is universal. It means that its particularity in this place and time is as important as its universality in space and time. This has resulted in the historical reality in which whole cultures can be said to have been shaped by a certain ethos that can only be described as Orthodox and in which whole peoples (*ethnē*) have identified themselves with the Church or the Church with them.

Unfortunately, one cannot say that the Orthodox "world" has been free of some of the worst forms of ethnicity, sometimes even resulting in conflict between peoples of the same faith. Again in Africa, I cannot but mention the case of the war between Ethiopia and Eritrea as an example. That conflict, it seems to me, has highlighted a fundamental dilemma faced by many of our churches, but by no means limited to the Orthodox – the dilemma of our primal allegiance. Putting it this way may be a bit unfair, but I cannot help but wonder sometimes how we as Christians are to interpret this verse of St Paul that I have placed at the beginning of my presentation. After 25 years as an Orthodox Christian, I cannot help but observe that many in our churches have not succeeded in transcending the ethnic boundaries in which they are placed. For many the Church is the extension of our ethnic identity, and faith is at the service of promoting that identity.

Even under the most normal of circumstances this, I believe, has serious implications for the witness of the Church. In situations of conflict it is the very credibility of that witness that may be called to question. Indeed many recent, as well as ongoing, situations of conflict have raised that very question of the credibility of our witness in today's world.

Prophetic evangelism

I believe that the churches, including the Orthodox Church, are faced with a crisis of evangelization. This is not to say that the gospel is no longer preached today. On the contrary, there is a surge in evangelical fervour and activity that is sweeping through the churches and that has left few churches untouched, even the Orthodox churches. What I do mean, however, is that evangelism has somehow lost its prophetic voice. Prophecy is no longer seen as an essential part of evangelism and the mission of the Church. The clergy of the Church are still kings and priests like Christ but unfortunately are no longer prophets. The discussion earlier on in this conference about a social gospel and the need for social engagement is, in my view, a symptom of this crisis. Slowly a false dichotomy that we Orthodox have happily bought into and perfected has been introduced between a "social gospel" as that which addresses social issues (such as justice) and "evangelization" as preaching the "good news". This has enabled us and other churches to return to a much narrower view of the missionary and evangelical calling of the Church that is deprived of the risk of prophecy.

By prophecy I do not mean "soothsaying", as prophecy is narrowly understood in my part of the world. By prophecy I mean "risking obedience" to confront the injustices of human society, in order that the broken-hearted might be healed, the blind might receive their sight, and the captives and oppressed might be set free (see Luke 4:18-21). It is this kind of prophecy that is at the cutting edge of mission and ensures the integrity of the "Good News" that we preach. Without it, evangelism often only serves to maintain the status quo and further alienates the people for whom the Good News is meant.

Prophetic mission means that the Church identifies herself with the concerns, anxieties, struggles, hopes and fears of those who are made poor and excluded by an unjust world. It means that the Church cannot but take sides with the weak, the suffering and the oppressed and against the forces that keep them so. Since I have been at the World Council of Churches I have encountered (or perhaps I should rather say I have been confronted by) an unfortunate perception of the "Church" among some of the poor and marginalized groups with whom I work. For many of these, the Church is somewhat outside of themselves (up there, if you want). At best the Church has an "outreach" for them and "helps" them. At worst the Church does not care. Prophetic mission means that the poor and down-trodden are enabled to reclaim the Church as their own, so that she can become truly again that Body of Christ in whom all are reconciled to each other and to God.

In other words, prophetic mission and evangelism is about proclaiming and living the values of the kingdom of God. It is about living our prayer, "Thy kingdom come; Thy will be done, on earth as in heaven." It alone convicts us of the necessity of seeking the reconciliation of all of humanity to itself and to God, and working, indeed laying down our lives, for a new human community based on God's justice and God's righteousness. In that new reality, in that kingdom reality, at least in the Church, there will be no place for ethnic conflicts, because indeed there will be "neither Jew nor Greek, ... slave nor free, ... male nor female"; but all will be "one in Christ Jesus".

The Universal Claims of Orthodoxy and the Particularity of its Witness in a Pluralistic World

PETROS VASSILIADIS

Orthodoxy as an ecclesial category, and its eschatological dimension
Orthodoxy is normally defined in confessional or denominational terms, that is, as the Eastern branch of Christianity, which was separated from the West around the beginning of the second millennium CE. This is at least how the *Oxford Dictionary of the Christian Church* describes the Orthodox Church, as "a family of churches, situated mainly in Eastern Europe: each member Church is independent in its internal administration, but all share the same faith and are in communion with one another, acknowledging the honorary primacy of the Patriarch of Constantinople". This definition no longer holds true. According to its most serious interpreters, Orthodoxy refers to the wholeness of the people of God who share the right conviction (*ορθή δόξα* = *orthē doxa*, right opinion) concerning the event of God's salvation in Christ and his Church, and the right expression (*orthopraxia*) of this faith. *Orthodoxia* leads to the maximum possible application in *orthopraxia* of charismatic life in the freedom of the Holy Spirit, in all aspects of daily public life, social and cosmic alike. Everybody is invited by Orthodoxy to transcend confessions and inflexible institutions without necessarily denying them. The late Nikos Nissiotis has reminded us that Orthodoxy is not to be identified only with us Orthodox in the historical sense and with all our limitations and shortcomings:

> We should never forget that this term is given to the one, (holy, catholic and) apostolic church as a whole over against the heretics who, of their own choice, split from the main body of the Church. The term (Orthodoxy) is exclusive for all those, who willingly fall away from the historical stream of life of the One Church but it is inclusive for those who profess their spiritual belonging to that stream.[1]

The term "Orthodoxy", therefore, has more or less ecclesial rather that confessional connotations.[2]

This ecclesial understanding of Orthodoxy was first put forward by the late George Florovsky who, speaking at an ecumenical meeting in the name of the one Church, declared, "The Church is first of all a worshipping community. Worship comes first, doctrine and discipline second. The *lex orandi* has a privileged priority in the life of the Christian Church. The *lex credendi* depends on the devotional experience and vision of the Church."[3]

Elsewhere,[4] I have argued that out of the three main characteristics that generally constitute Orthodox theology, namely its "eucharistic", "trinitarian" and "hesychastic" dimensions, only the first one can bear a universal and ecumenical significance. If the last dimension and important feature marks a decisive development in Eastern Christian theology and spirituality after the final schism between East and West, a development that has determined, together with other factors, the mission of the Orthodox Church in recent history; and if the trinitarian dimension constitutes the supreme expression of Christian theology ever produced by human thought in its attempt to grasp the mystery of God, after Christianity's dynamic encounter with the Greek culture; it was, nevertheless, only because of the eucharistic experience, the matrix of all theology and spirituality of Christianity, that all theological and spiritual climaxes in our Church have been actually achieved.

And the eucharist, heart and centre of Christian liturgy, is always understood in its authentic perception as a proleptic manifestation of the kingdom of God, as symbol and image of an alternative reality, which was conceived before all creation by God the Father in his mystical plan (the *mysterion* in the biblical sense), was inaugurated by our Lord, and is permanently sustained by the Holy Spirit. What is, nevertheless, of paramount and undisputed importance is that this kingdom is expected to culminate at the *eschata*. This, in fact, brings us to the eschatological dimension of the Church.[5] Eschatology constitutes the central and primary aspect of ecclesiology, the beginning of the Church, that which gives her identity, sustains and inspires her in her existence. Hence the priority of the kingdom of God in all ecclesiological considerations. Everything belongs to the kingdom. The Church in her institutional expression does not administer all reality; she only prepares the way to the kingdom, in the sense that she is an image if it. That is why, although to the eyes of the historian and the sociologist the Church is yet another human institution, to the theologian she is primarily a mystery, and we very often call her an icon of the kingdom to come.

Eschatology, however, constitutes also the starting-point of the Church's witness to the world. It is to the merits of modern Orthodox theologians,[6] who reaffirmed the paramount importance of eschatology for Christian theology, although very little has been written about the relationship between the Church's (eschatological) identity and her (historical) mission.[7] The mission of the Church is but a struggle to witness and to apply this eschatological vision of the Church to the historical realities and to the world at large. Christian theology, on the other hand, is about the right balance between history and eschatology. We should never forget that theology and the Church exist not for themselves, but for the world. The tension, therefore, between eschatology and history, or, to put it more sharply, the relationship between the ecclesial community and our pluralistic society, is one of the most important chapters in the Church's witness today.[8]

However, if for Christian theology the Church's ecumenicity and her universal claims are quite simple to establish,[9] it is not at all an easy task to determine her witness in today's pluralistic context, especially in view of her eschatological particularity. In the remaining space I will focus on three areas, in an effort to shed light on the issue we are discussing: (a) the Church's attitude towards modernism,[10] and the whole range of the achievements of the Enlightenment, especially within the framework of post-modernity; (b) the understanding of universalism in Christian mission theology; and (c) the present understanding and application of eschatology and the importance of the rediscovery of the Church's authentic eschatological identity.

Pluralism as a "modern" phenomenon and "post-modernity"

Pluralism is definitely related to, and for most scholars is the result of, "modernism", the most tangible outcome of the Enlightenment that prevailed in Europe and dominated all aspects of the public life of our Western civilization after the disastrous religious wars in the 17th century that ended with the famous peace of Westphalia in 1648. In my view, modernism has arisen from a certain perspective on the so-called external mission of Christianity. Having been deprived of privileged status and dominant and exclusive presence in the public domain, Christianity set out to conquer the world. In this way, the modernist revolution had a lasting and catalytic, though indirect, effect on the religious life of the Christian world on both sides of the Atlantic. The real consequence of modernism in Christian mission has not yet been given the attention it deserves, although pluralism has been focused upon and correctly assessed in ecumenical reflections by the missionary movement.[11]

In order to define properly the present context of the Church's witness, it is necessary to locate pluralism within the framework of modernism and dialectics between modernism and post-modernism. For this reason, I have chosen to tackle the issue through a reference to the contrast between pre-modernity, modernity and post-modernity.[12]

In the pre-modern world, the sacred cosmic stories of all religions provided, each for its own culture, the most public and certain knowledge human beings believed they had about reality. After the Enlightenment, that is, in modernity, secular science replaced religion as the most public and certain knowledge that human beings believed they had of their world, whereas religious stories were reduced to matters of personal belief and opinion. The ideal of modernism was the separation of the Church from the state (or religion from society), the relegation of religion to the private or personal realm, and the declaration of the public realm as secular, in other words free from all religious influence. Pluralism was, therefore, established as the necessary context for the welfare of a civilized society. During almost the entire period of modernity, Christianity was reserved, if not hostile, to both pluralism and the principles of modernism. This is more evident in Eastern Christianity, whereas in the West the opposite path was followed, that of an almost complete surrender, especially in Protestantism.

"Post-modernity" is an ambiguous term used to name an ambiguous time of transition in history. The post-modern period has its beginnings in the emergence of the social sciences, which at its earlier stages undermined the authority of religion and their public presence, and contributed to the secularization of society. When, however, the same techniques of sociological and historical criticism were finally applied to science itself, including the social sciences, it was discovered that scientific knowledge was also an imaginative interpretation of the world. For some, this discovery was more shocking than the discovery that the earth was not the centre of the universe.[13] Suddenly, all our world-views, including the so-called scientific ones, were relativized. This made people aware that their respective (modern) views of the world could not automatically be assumed to be objective descriptions. As a result, pluralism has been highlighted more in post-modernity than in modernity itself.[14] All these developments have brought religion, and the Church in particular, back into the public domain. This made theology adopt a new approach and articulate what is generally called "public theology".[15]

Having said all this, it is important to reaffirm what sociologists of knowledge very often point out, that is, that modernism, counter (alternative) modernism, post-modernism, and even de-modernism, are always simultaneous processes.[16] Otherwise post-modernism can easily end up and evaporate to a neo-traditionalism, and at the end to a neglect or even negation of the great achievements of the Enlightenment and the ensuing scholarly critical "paradigm". The rationalistic sterility of modern life has turned to the quest for something new, something radical, which nevertheless is not always new, but very often the old recycled: such as neo-romanticism, neo-mysticism or naturalism.[17]

I firmly believe that the Church cannot exercise her mission in today's pluralistic world in a meaningful and effective way without a reassessment of the present context, without a certain encounter with modernism.[18] By and large, there still exists an aloofness between Christianity and modernity[19] which is caused not only by the former's rejection of the latter, and the negative attitude towards the whole range of the achievements of the Enlightenment, but also by the obstinate persistence of the adherents of modernism – and of course the democratic institutions that come out of it – to allow historic and diachronic institutions, like the Church, to play a significant role in public life, without being either absorbed or alienated by it, with the simple argument that they derive their origin in the pre-modern era. If today this encounter is possible, and even desirable despite the tragic events of 11 September 2001, this is because of the undisputed transition of our culture to a new era, the post-modern era that brought with it the resurgence of religion.

Earlier we pointed out that post-modernity is inconceivable without some reference to modernism as such. In the past, Peter Berger tried to describe the attitude of the Church towards the modernist revolution, and the pluralistic condition that entailed, in terms of two opposite positions: accommodation and resistance.[20] In my view both these positions are inadequate from a theological point of view (more precisely, from an Orthodox theological point of view).

Resistance is no longer suggested as a practical solution, because of the progress made in the theology of mission, as we will see later.[21] As to accommodation, the impossibility of its application derives from a theological and ecclesiological ground.[22] For the Church and her theology are incompatible with at least three cornerstones of modernism: (1) secularism, (2) individualism and (3) privatization.

If the Church accommodates to modernism and accepts secularism, then automatically her role, her nature and mission are all exhausted in her institutional expression. The Church will become yet another institution of this world, which can of course be welcomed, and even become a desirable player, by the dominant modern paradigm in the public domain, but she will lose her prophetic, and above all her eschatological, character. The Church, drawing her *esse* and identity neither from what she is at the present, nor from what it was given to her in the past, but from what she will become in the *eschaton*, must not only avoid acting as an institution of this world, she must also critically respond to and prophetically challenge all institutional and unjust structures.

With regard to individualism, it is quite obvious that the Church as a communion of faith, a *koinonia* of free people (and not as an oppressive communitarian system that ignores individual human rights),[23] is incompatible with any system that has as a basic principle the individual being and not his or her relations with the "other", any other, and of course God, the "Ultimate Other".

Finally, the relegation and extrusion of the Church exclusively to the private domain contradicts her identity, and above all nullifies her responsibility and imperative duty to evangelize, to take the good news to the end of the world. This mission, of course, should not have an expansional character with imperialistic attitude and behaviour, as happened in the past,[24] nor should it aim "at the propagation or transmission of intellectual convictions, doctrines, moral commands etc., but at the transmission of the life of communion, that exists in God".[25]

If, nevertheless, neither resistance nor accommodation of the Church to the modern critical paradigm is legitimate on theological grounds, there is a third solution that has been applied by the Church on grounds of her missionary responsibility during the golden era of the 4th century CE, that of social integration, the famous Byzantine synthesis, when the Church took the risk to embrace the "empire" and practically reject the "desert".[26] At that critical moment in her history the Church had not only integrated with contemporary society of the Roman empire – one could *mutatis mutandis* call it "modern"; she had not only shown respect to what was earlier called "Whore Babylon" (Rev. 17:5); but she had even included the empire – certainly a "secular" institution – in her liturgical tablets. The only thing she preserved intact was her identity (and this not without difficulties and risks) and her prophetical voice over the historical process. In other words, she followed in this respect the example of St Paul and not the radical stance of the seer/prophet of the Apocalypse.[27]

The understanding of universalism in the theology of Christian mission

The essence of what has been briefly presented has been on the ecumenical agenda of world mission, the turning-point of which was the 1963 world mission conference in Mexico. It was there that ecumenical theology of mission replaced the negative assessment of modernism by a more positive one. Since then, most of the earlier models of evangelization of the whole world, as well as of mission as proclamation and conversion in their literal sense, were enriched by a new understanding of mission mostly represented by a variety of terms like "witness" or *martyria*, "public presence", "dialogue" and "liberation".[28]

This is not to say that churches no longer organize evangelical campaigns or revival meetings; in fact, many Christians are still asked to take up conversion as their top mission priority. What I mean is that all churches on the institutional level are coping in one way or the other with the questions of many contexts, many religions, many cultures and systems of values – what we call pluralism or the effects of globalization. Rather than proclamation alone, all churches are exploring in their own ways a different understanding of "Christian witness". In addition to the earlier models of evangelization of the whole world, as well as of mission as proclamation and conversion in their literal sense – that is, besides preaching Jesus as the "the way, the truth, and the life" (John 14:6), as the sole saviour of human sin – the Church began to address human sin in the structural complexities of our world, and started ministering to the socially poor and marginalized of our societies in their contexts, and above all entering into a constructive dialogue with pluralism, and at the end of the road with modernism or post-modernism, thus making her presence visible in society.

Of crucial importance at this stage was the reassessment of the concept of universalism which, according to some analysts, is the primary cause of all religious, social and even ethnic conflicts. It was then that we rediscovered that the early Church understood her mission in a broad variety of ways.[29] Following Martin Goodman's analysis,[30] I have argued elsewhere that following the steps of Judaism, Christianity, in fact, developed an informative, educational, apologetic and proselytizing mission to propagate its faith.[31] However, this pluralistic understanding has gradually given place more or less to a universalistic understanding, a universal proselytizing mission, which during the Constantinian period became dominant through its theological validation by the great ancient Christian historian Eusebius. However, it never became entirely dormant in the undivided Church,[32] with a very few exceptions of course.

Universal proselytizing mission was actually promoted in a systematic way only in the second millennium, during which the concept of universalism was developed. With the theological articulation of Christocentric universalism the old idea of "Christendom" has determined to a considerable degree the shaping of our understanding of mission.[33] Universal proselytizing mission was given fresh life by the discovery of the New World, and by the prospect of christianizing the entire inhabited earth. It reached its peak with the so-called African and Asian Christian missions during the last century.[34] This concept of "Christendom", however, carried with it other non-Christian elements to such an extent that eventually industrialized development of bourgeois society in Europe and America, as well as colonialism and expansionism of any sort, walked hand in hand with Christian mission.

It has been rightly argued that during that "old ecumenical paradigm" Christians felt that they were called "to convey to the rest of humanity the blessings of Western (i.e. bourgeois) Christian civilization... The slogan 'the evangelization of the world in this generation' emphasizes the missionary consciousness of this early movement, in which genuine missionary and evangelistic motives were inextricably combined with cultural and social motives."[35]

It was for these reasons that Christian theology on the world mission scene adopted a more holistic view, and with the contribution – among others – of Orthodox theology, suggested a radical shift to a "new paradigm", away from "Christocentric universalism", towards a "trinitarian" understanding of the divine reality and towards an *oikoumene* as the one household of life.[36] For mission theology, these meant abandoning the primary importance of proselytism, not only among Christians of other denominations, but even among peoples of other religions. "Dialogue" was suggested as a new term parallel to, and in some cases in place of, the old missiological terminology.[37] Nowadays, the problem of reconciliation in the religious field has become not simply a social necessity but a legitimate theological imperative.[38] In the *Guidelines on Dialogue with People of Living Faiths and Ideologies,* published some 25 years ago by the WCC, the people of the other faiths are for Christians "no longer the objects of (their) discussions but partners in (their) mission)".[39]

Thus, the Christian theology of mission no longer insists on the universal proselytizing mission, but on the authentic witness of the Church's eschatological experience. This was, in fact, made possible by the fundamental assumption of trinitarian theology, "that God in God's own self is a life of communion and that God's involvement in history aims at drawing humanity and creation in general into this communion with God's very life".[40] Taken a little further, this understanding of Christian witness suggests that the problem of ethics, that is, the problem of overcoming the evil in the world – at least for Christianity – is not only a moral and social issue; it is also – and for some even exclusively – an ecclesial one, in the sense that the moral and social responsibility of Christians, their mission in today's pluralistic world, is the logical consequence of their ecclesial (i.e. eschatological) self-consciousness.

Today in the field of world mission we speak for the "oikoumene which is to come" ("*τὴν οἰκουμένην τὴν μέλλουσαν*" – *tēn oikumenēn tēn mellousan*), according to the terminology of Hebrews (2:5; cf. 13:14ff.), as it is described in the book of Revelation (chs 21 and 22), as an open society, where an honest dialogue between existing living cultures can take place. The world pluralistic society can and must become a *household* (οἶκος – *oikos*), where everyone is open to the "other" (as they are open to the Ultimate Other, i.e. God), and where all can share a common life, despite the plurality and difference of their identity. In modern missiology the term οικουμένη (*oikoumenē*) and its derivatives (ecumenism, etc.) no longer describe a given situation. When we talk about the οικουμένη (*oikumenē*) we no longer exclusively refer to an abstract universality, such as the entire inhabited world, or the whole human race, or even a united universal Church. What we actually mean are substantial – and at the same time threatened – relations between churches, between cultures, between people and human societies, and at the same time between humanity and the rest of God's creation.

The importance of the rediscovery of the authentic prophetic eschatological vision of the Church

This eschatological perspective on the understanding of the Church's witness, and view of the Orthodox eschatological identity, makes a reassessment of the prophetic eschatological vision of the Church an absolute imperative. For the ineffectiveness of Christian witness in today's pluralist world is partly due to the distortion of the eschatological vision of the Church. And it is not only Western Christianity, but Eastern Orthodoxy as well, that gradually lost the proper and authentic understanding of eschatology.[41] Throughout the medieval and post-medieval periods the strong eschatological vision of the early Church was almost completely lost.[42] It was only in the liturgy, and more particularly in the eucharistic tradition of Christianity, and especially and much more clearly in Eastern Orthodoxy, that it never disappeared completely.

Of course, even the liturgy was not preserved intact, as was shown by social and cultural anthropological analysis. As we indicated earlier, it was through the social sciences, and especially through cultural anthropology,[43] that the importance of liturgy for the identity of all religious systems and societies was actually reinforced in academic discussions. I have argued elsewhere[44] that there are two major understandings of liturgy. According to the first one, the liturgy is understood as a private act, functioning as a means to meet some particular religious needs: i.e. both the need of the community to exercise its power and supervision on its members, and the need of the individual for personal "sanctification". I will call this understanding of the liturgical act juridical. According to a second understanding, however, the liturgy functions as a means for the up-building of the religious community, which is no longer viewed in institutional terms or as a cultic organization, but as a communion and as a way of living. And this is what I call "communal" understanding of liturgy.

The juridical understanding of liturgy encourages and in effect promotes a sharp distinction between the various segments of the religious society (clergy and laity, etc.), thus underlining the dimensions of super- and sub-ordination within the ritual, and contributing to the maintenance of social structure not only within the religious community itself, but also by extension within wider social life. This juridical understanding of liturgy, in addition, develops separation and certain barriers, sometimes even hostility, between members of different religious systems, thus intensifying phenomena of intolerance and fanaticism. With such an understanding of liturgy there is no real concern for history, social life and public presence of the Church, nor any acceptance of pluralism.

At the other end, the communal understanding of liturgy discourages all distinctions between the various segments, not only within the religious communities themselves but also, by extension, within wider social life. This understanding of liturgy dissolves barriers between members of different religious systems, thus promoting religious tolerance and peace, and accepts pluralism as a God-given context of mission. In modern Orthodox contexts both these attitudes have been experienced and expressed. And this phenomenon has puzzled Church historians, when they tried to evaluate the public presence of Orthodoxy.

However, even outside the liturgy of the Church – which as we pointed out is closely related to, and in fact determines, her eschatological dimension – in the course of history Christianity has reflected upon an "applied eschatology"; but articulated different, sometimes contradicting, in some cases even distorted, types of eschatology. John Meyendorff distinguishes three such types in the Church's life, which cover all aspects of Christian ethics, the application of which in a sense determines the variety of Christian attitudes towards pluralism and modernism.[45]

The first one is the apocalyptic version of eschatology. According to this version the kingdom of God is coming soon, and therefore there is not anything to expect from history. Christians can do nothing to improve human reality. No real mission or social responsibility or public presence or culture is possible or even desirable. God is seen alone as the Lord of history, acting without any cooperation or synergy (cf. 1 Cor. 3:9). The New Jerusalem is expected to come from heaven all prepared (Rev. 21:2), and we have nothing to contribute to it. This view, which was rejected by the ancient Church, allows only repentance and ascetic life to combat the passions.

The second type, which stands in opposition to the first, is humanistic eschatology. This eschatology has an optimistic understanding of history, and has been dominant in Western society since the time of the Enlightenment. In the Orthodox realm this kind of eschatology has taken the form of a revival of the old paradigm of the Byzantine synthesis, this time in the narrow limits of nationalistic religious entities: Holy Russia, Great Serbia, the chosen Greek Orthodoxy etc. are some expressions, which taken even further envisage a dangerous development of an Orthodox axis, which will conquer the faithless, or even heretic, West!

The third type of eschatology is prophetic eschatology. It is the only acceptable type of eschatology, and it is based on the biblical concept of prophecy, which in both the Old and the New Testaments does not simply forecast the future or announce the inevitable, but also places humans before an option, a choice between two types of personal or social behaviour. The people of God are free to choose, but the prophet has informed them of the consequences; and the consequences today are the realities of the pluralistic (post)modern world.

With the exception of some diaspora (or better "Western") and newly established missionary communities – modern Orthodoxy in its historical expression finds itself in a rather strange situation. Our metropolitan "mother" churches are in fact struggling between two poles, quite opposite or at least unrelated to each other: on the one hand, the ideal of the later hesychastic movement – of course wrongly interpreted and applied – has given rise to an individualistic understanding of salvation, which only partially takes history and pluralism seriously into account; on the other hand, a completely secularized approach is adopted in dealing with historical developments. As in the Old Testament, in later and even recent Judaism, the splendour of the Davidic kingdom usually overshadowed the more authentic desert and prophetic vision of a wandering people of God, so in contemporary Orthodoxy the famous "Byzantine synthesis" seems to be the only model – again unsuccessfully envisioned or applied – which almost all national autocephalic Orthodox churches constantly refer to.

It is not a surprise, therefore, that in contemporary Orthodoxy – and I would also add in the Church universal – the creative tension between history and the *eschaton* has almost disappeared. No one preaches about the reality of the kingdom drastically entering into our pluralistic reality. Even our modern church buildings have ceased to reflect the kingdom reality, having rather become imitations, and sometimes even caricatures, of traditional (but meaningful) edifices. Again, only in the eucharistic liturgy is there something to remind us, that when we offer our "reasonable worship" we offer it "for the life of the world", remembering not only past events, but also future realities, in fact the (eschatological) reality *par excellence:* Christ's "second and glorious Coming".[46] Naturally, then, only those Orthodox communities which have undergone liturgical and eucharistic renewal are able to experience or rediscover a proper understanding of eschatology. The rest are struggling to overcome today's real challenges of globalization by a retreat to the glorious past, despite their strong pneumatological and eschatological tradition. But thus they become vulnerable at best to a kind of traditionalism and at worst to an anti-ecumenical, nationalistic and intolerant fundamentalism, attitudes of course totally alien and unacceptable to the Orthodox ethos.

To sum up: Orthodoxy – like the Church Universal – in order to effectively witness to the gospel in today's pluralistic context, in addition to an affirmation of her ecclesial rather than confessional identity, desperately needs a new relation with modernism, a new and dynamic understanding of universalism and a rediscovery of the authentic perception of eschatology.

NOTES

[1] N. Nissiotis, "Interpreting Orthodoxy", *The Ecumenical Review*, 14, 1961, p.26. Cf. also the notion of *sobornicitatea* (open catholicity) advanced by D. Staniloae, *Theology and the Church*, p.7. More on this in N. Mosoiu, *Taina prezentei lui Dumnezeu în viata umană. Viziunea creatoare a Părintelui Profesor Dumitru Stăniloae*, Pitesti / Brasov / Cluj-Napoca 2000, pp.246ff.

[2] For this reason one can safely argue that the fundamental principles of Christian spirituality, of the Christian mission, are the same in the East and in the West. What I am going to say, therefore, applies to the entire Christian faith, to the one, holy, catholic and apostolic Church. In what follows, therefore, I will freely alternate the terms "Orthodoxy" and "Christianity", avoiding as much as possible any reference to the canonical boundaries of the term "Church".

[3] G. Florovsky, "The Elements of Liturgy", in G. Patelos ed., *The Orthodox Church in the Ecumenical Movement*, WCC, 1978, pp.172-82, 172.

[4] Cf. my "The Eucharistic Perspective of the Church's Mission", in P. Vassiliadis, *Eucharist and Witness: Orthodox Perspectives on the Unity and Mission of the Church*, WCC Publications/Holy Cross Orthodox Press, Geneva/Brookline MA, 1998, pp.49-66, 50.

[5] The early Christian tradition stresses, in one way or another, the eschatological and not the historical dimension of the Church. Even the episcopocentric structure of the Church was understood eschatologically. The bishop, e.g. as *primus inter pares* presiding in love over the eucharistic community, was never understood (except very late under the heavy influence of scholasticism) as a vicar, representative, or ambassador of Christ, but as an image of Christ. So with the rest of the ministries of the Church: they are not parallel to, or given by, but identical with those of, Christ. That is also why the whole of Orthodox theology and life, especially as this latter is expressed in Sunday's liturgical offices, are centred around the resurrection. The Church exists not because Christ died on the cross, but because he is risen from the dead, thus becoming the *aparche* of all humanity. See J. Zizioulas, *Being as Communion: Studies in Personhood and the Church*, New York, St Vladimir's Seminary Press, 1985; also *idem*, "The Mystery of the Church in Orthodox Tradition", in *One in Christ*, 24, 1988, pp.294-303.

[6] Almost all prominent Orthodox theologians of the recent past (G. Florovsky, S. Agouridis, J. Meyendorff, A. Schmemann, J. Zizioulas, to name just few) have underlined the escha-

tological dimension of Orthodoxy. Cf. also E. Clapsis' doctoral dissertation, *Eschatology and the Unity of the Church: The Impact of the Eschatology in Ecumenical Thought*, Ann Arbor MI, U.M.I., 1988; also his "Eschatology", in the *Dictionary of the Ecumenical Movement*, N. Lossky et al. eds, WCC, 2002, pp.361a-364a.

[7] Cf. my *Eucharist and Witness, passim*; also "L'eschatologie dans la vie de l'Eglise: Une perspective chrétienne orthodoxe et son impact sur la vie de la société", in *Irénikon*, 73, 2000, pp.316-34.

[8] Cf. Staniloae's strong criticism of the trend in contemporary Orthodoxy to identify Orthodox spirituality with a disregard for everyday life, a phenomenon described in his own words as "a premature eschatologism". D. Stǎniloae, *Ascetica si mistica orthodoxa*, Alba Iulia, 1993, p.28 (in Romanian).

[9] More on this in (Archbishop of Albania) Anastasios Yannoulatos, *Universality and Orthodoxy*, Athens, 2000 (in Greek); also in T. FitzGerald, "Orthodox Theology and Ecumenical Witness: An Introduction to Major Themes", in *St Vladimir's Theological Quarterly*, 42, 1998, pp.339-61, 360.

[10] In this essay I use the terms "modernism" (and "pre- or post-modernism") as an ideological, spiritual, cultural category or paradigm, and "modernity" (and "pre- or post-modernity") as the discrete period in history in which this paradigm circulated.

[11] See W.A. Visser't Hooft, "Pluralism – Temptation or Opportunity?", *The Ecumenical Review*, 18, 1966, pp.129-49. For an early Orthodox response, see Metropolitan George Khodre, "Christianity in a Pluralistic World – The Economy of the Holy Spirit", in *The Ecumenical Review*, 23, 1971, pp.118-28.

[12] From Nancey Murphy's three-fold approach to the subject (philosophy of language, epistemology, philosophy of science) I will concentrate only on the last one (*Anglo-American Postmodernity: Philosophical Perspectives on Science, Religion and Ethics*, Boulder CO, Westview, 1997). Cf. also Rodney L. Petersen ed., *Christianity and Civil Society*, Boston, Boston Theological Institute, 1995; and Jacob Neusner ed., *Religion and the Political Order*, Atlanta, Scholars, 1996.

[13] Darrell Fasching, "Judaism, Christianity, Islam: Religion, Ethics, and Politics in the (Post)modern World", in Neusner ed., *Religion and the Political Order*, pp.291-99. Also *idem., The Ethical Challenge of Auschwitz and Hiroshima: Apocalypse or Utopia?* Albany NY, State Univ. of New York Press, 1993.

[14] According to Stanley Grenz (*A Primer on Postmodernism*, Grand Rapids MI, Eerdmans, 1996, esp. pp.161-74) the hallmark of postmodernity is "centreless pluralism".

[15] Cf. E. Clapsis, "The Orthodox Church in a Pluralistic World", *Orthodoxy in Conversation: Orthodox Ecumenical Engagements*, WCC Publications/Holy Cross Orthodox Press, Geneva/Brookline MA, 2000, pp.127-50.

[16] Jürgen Habermas, "Die Moderne – Ein unvollendetes Projekt," in W. Welsch ed., *Wege aus der Moderne: Schlüsseltexte der postmodernen Diskussion*, Weinheim, Wiley, 1988, pp.177-92; Jean-François Lyotard, "An Interview", in *Theory, Culture and Society*, 5, 1989, pp.277-309, esp. p.277; *idem, The Postmodern Condition*, Minneapolis MN, Minnesota UP, 1984; Hayden White, *Metahistory: The Historical Imagination in 19th Century Europe*, Baltimore, Johns Hopkins UP, 1973; I. Petrou, "Παράδοση και πολιτισμική προσαρμογή στη δεύτερη νεωτερικότητα" *Σύναξη*, 75, 2000, pp.25-35; W. Welsch, *Unsere postmoderne Moderne*, Weinheim, VCH Acta humaniora, 1988, σελ, 7.

[17] Post-modernity's responses and reactions to the modern project of the Enlightenment to ground knowledge or "reason" as a timeless, universal construct, immune from the corrosive forces of history, has very seldom gone to the extreme. The enduring dream of modernity should not be minimized or dismissed out of hand, and the many achievements it has realized, such as a concern for universal human rights, and justice and equality, all deserve commendation and praise from the Church.

[18] Cf. my recent book, *Postmodernity and the Church: The Challenge of Orthodoxy*, Athens, Akritas, 2002.

[19] The first positive assessment of modernism within Orthodoxy I was exposed to was in (Archbishop) Demetrios Trakatellis' paper at the third conference of Orthodox theological schools in Boston ("The Gospel in a Secular Context", *Greek Orthodox Theological Review*, 38, 1993, pp.45-55). For a detailed analysis see also Stanley S. Harakas, *Wholeness of Faith and Life: Orthodox Christian Ethics*, Brookline MA, Holy Cross Orthodox Press, 1999.

[20] Peter Berger, *The Sacred Canopy: Elements of a Sociological Theory of Religion*, New York, Doubleday, 1967, pp.156ff.; also pp.106ff.

[21] F.J. Verstraelen et al. eds, *Missiology: An Ecumenical Introduction*, Grand Rapids MI, Eerdmans, 1995; also K. Raiser, *Ecumenism in Transition: A Paradigm Shift in the Ecumenical Movement*, WCC, 1991 (trans. with modifications from the German original *Ökumene im Übergang*, München, C. Kaiser, 1989, pp.54ff.

[22] What follows comes from my *Postmodernity and the Church*, pp.38ff.

[23] Cf. Kostas Delikostantis, *Human Rights: A Western Ideology or an Ecumenical Ethos?*, Thessaloniki, 1995 (in Greek).

[24] Cf. my article "Beyond Christian Universalism: The Church's Witness in a Multicultural Society", in *Επιστημονική Επετηρίδα Θεολογογικής Σχολής. Τιμητικό αψιέρωμα στον Ομότιμο Καθηγητή Αλέξανδρο Γουσίδη*, n.s. Τμήμα Θεολογίας, 9, 1999, pp.309-20.

[25] I. Bria ed., *Go Forth in Peace*, WCC Publications, 1986, p.3.

[26] G. Florovsky, "Antinomies of Christian History: Empire and Desert", in *Christianity and Culture*: *The Collected Works of Georges Florovsky*, vol. II, Belmont CA, Nordland, 1974, pp.67-100.

[27] Cf. my "Orthodox Christianity", in J. Neusner ed., *God's Rule: The Politics of World Religions,* Washington DC, Georgetown UP, 2003 (under publication). Also "Σχέσεις Εκκλησίας-Πολιτείας: Η θεολογία της κοινωνικής ενσωμάτωσης (Σχόλιο στο Ρωμ. 13,1)", in *Επίκαιρα Αγιογραφικά Θέματα. Αγία Γραφή και Ευχαριστία*, BB 15, Thessaloniki, Pournars, 2000, pp.75-82.

[28] Cf. *Common Witness: A Joint Document of the Working Group of the Roman Catholic Church and the WCC*. WCC Mission Series, 1982; the document *Common Witness and Proselytism*; also I. Bria ed., *Martyria-Mission*, WCC, 1980. Even *Mission and Evangelism – An Ecumenical Affirmation*. WCC Mission Series, 1982, 1985 (2nd ed.), is an attempt correctly to interpret the classical missionary terminology. Cf. also the most recent agreed statement of the Dorfweil/Germany consultation of CEC with the European Baptist Federation and the European Lausanne Committee for World Evangelization (12-13 June 1995) with the title: "Aspects of Mission and Evangelization in Europe Today". We must confess, however, that the traditional terminology (mission, conversion, evangelism or evangelization, christianization) still has an imperative validity and is retained as the *sine qua non* of the Christian identity of those Christian communities which belong to the "evangelical" stream of the Christian faith. A comprehensive presentation of the present state of the debate is J. Matthey, "Milestones in Ecumenical Missionary Thinking from the 1970s to the 1990s", in *International Review of Mission*, 88, 1999, pp.291-304.

[29] D.J. Bosch, *Transforming Mission: Paradigm Shifts in Theology of Mission*, New York, Orbis 1991, has described through the "Paradigm shift theory" the development of Christian understanding of mission down to the most recent ecumenical era.

[30] "Mission and Proselytism. An Orthodox Understanding", in *Eucharist and Witness*, pp.29ff.

[31] Martin Goodman, in his book *Mission and Conversion: Proselytizing in the Religious History of the Roman Empire*, Oxford, Clarendon, 1994, has discerned four different uses of the word "mission" in modern scholarship of the history of religions, and consequently four different understandings of what has come to be labelled as "Christian mission": (1) *The informative mission*. The missionaries of this type felt "that they had a general message which they wished to impart to others. Such disseminators of information may have had no clear idea of the reaction they desired from their auditors... [The aim of this attitude] was to tell people something, rather than to change their behaviour or status" (p.3). (2) *The educational mission*. "Some missionaries did intend to change recipients of their message by making them more moral or contented... Such a mission to educate is easily distinguished from a desire to win converts" (*ibid.*). (3) *The apologetic mission*. "Some missionaries requested recognition by others of the power of a particular divinity without expecting their audience to devote themselves to his or her worship. Such a mission was essentially apologetic. Its aim was to protect the cult and beliefs of the missionary" (p.4). Finally, (4) *The proselytizing mission*. According to Goodman, "information, education, and apologetic might or might not coexist within any one religious system, but all three

can individually be distinguished from what may best be described a proselytizing... [the aim of which was] to encourage outsiders not only to change their way of life but also to be incorporated within their group" (*ibid.*).

[32] *Ibid.*, p.7.

[33] Cf. the characteristic work of W.A. Visser't Hooft, *No Other Name: The Choice between Syncretism and Christian Universalism*, London, SCM Press, 1963. More in Bosch, *Transforming Mission*.

[34] It was the conviction that the "decisive hour of Christian mission" had come that impelled John R. Mott to call the world mission conference of 1910, with the primary purpose of pooling resources and developing a common strategy for the "world's conquest" for Christ. The task of "taking the gospel to all the regions of the world" was seen to be of paramount importance. On the recent history of Christian mission see J. Verkuyl, *Contemporary Missiology: An Introduction*, Engl. trans. Grand Rapids MI, Eerdmans, 1978.

[35] Raiser, *Ecumenism in Transition*, p.34.

[36] *Ibid.*, pp.79ff.

[37] This development is a radical reinterpretation of Christology through pneumatology (cf. Zizioulas, *Being as Communion*, through the rediscovery of the forgotten trinitarian theology of the undivided Church (cf. A.I.C. Heron ed., *The Forgotten Trinity*, London, 1991).

[38] For an Orthodox contribution to the debate see (Archbishop of Albania) Anastasios Yannoulatos, *Various Christian Approaches to the Other Religions (A Historical Outline)*, Athens, 1971.

[39] *Guidelines on Dialogue with People of Living Faiths and Ideologies*, WCC, 1990 (4th printing). Cf. Stanley J. Samartha ed., *Faith in the Midst of Faiths: Reflections on Dialogue in Community*, WCC, 1977.

[40] Bria ed., *Go Forth in Peace*, p.3.

[41] Cf. my "Eucharistic and Therapeutic Spirituality", in *Greek Orthodox Theological Review*, 1997, pp.1-23.

[42] Of course, the process started with the voluntary incorporation of Christianity within the Roman empire in the 4th century CE, but the eschatological vision survived, though obscured, thanks to the theological reflection of some great ecclesiastical figures such as Maximus the Confessor.

[43] P.L. Berger and T. Luckmann, *The Social Construction of Reality: A Treatise in the Sociology of Knowledge*, New York, Doubleday, 1966; C. Geertz, *The Interpretation of Cultures: Selected Essays*, New York, Basic Books, 1973, pp.126-41. One of the most imaginative insights of modern cultural anthropologists is their conviction that *ritual*, and the *liturgical life* in general, is a form of communication, a "performative" kind of speech, instrumental in creating the essential categories of human thought (E. Durkheim, *The Elementary Forms of the Religious Life*, trans. J. W. Swain, New York, Free Press, 1965 reprint, p.22). They communicate the fundamental beliefs and values of a community, outlining in this way its "world view" and its "ethos". The rituals do not only transmit culture, but they also "create a reality which would be nothing without them. It is not too much to say that ritual is more to society than words are to thought. For it is very possible to know something and then find words for it. But it is impossible to have social relations without symbolic acts" (M. Douglas, *Purity and Danger: An Analysis of the Concepts of Pollution and Taboo*, London, Routledge & Kegan Paul, 1966, p.62).

[44] Petros Vassiliadis, "Sanctus and the Book of Revelation. Some Anthropological and Theological Insights on the Communal and Historical Dimension of Christian Liturgy", in L. Padovese ed., *Atti del VII Simposio di Efeso su S. Giovanni Apostolo*, Rome, 1999, pp.143-56.

[45] What follows comes from J. Meyendorff, "Does Christian Tradition Have a Future?", *St Vladimir's Theological Quarterly*, 26, 1982, pp.140ff.

[46] It is quite characteristic that in the Byzantine liturgies of both St Basil and St Chrysostom, just before the *epiclesis*, the faithful "remember" not only the past events of the divine economy ("those things which have come to pass for us: the cross, the tomb, the resurrection on the third day, the ascension into heaven, the sitting at the right hand"), but in addition future eschatological realities (Christ's "second and glorious coming").

Christian Mission in a Pluralistic World

CHRISTOPHER DURAISINGH

I want to begin by paying a public tribute to the theological heritage of the Orthodox churches, particularly for their significant role in shaping my understanding of the nature of the mission of the Church over the past ten years.

Almost a hundred years ago the well-known journal *Christian Century* began publication. It shared the optimism of Western Christian leaders like John R. Mott at the Edinburgh world mission conference in 1910 that the whole world would be evangelized in their generation. But note what has happened by the end of the century. There has been an unprecedented revival and growth in all major non-Christian religions of the world. Most of them have become world religions and "missionary", with very well-established international communication machinery. Religious and cultural pluralization is a fact of life in every country in the West. Temples and mosques mark the landscape of the USA. Not too far from here, just at the outskirts of Ashland, Massachusetts, stands a large and beautiful Hindu temple, with people in worship most of the day. As Diana Eck, both through her major research study on pluralism and in her recent book, *The New Religious America*,[1] demonstrates in no uncertain terms, "the United States is the most religiously diverse nation in the world". The subtitle of the book is provocative: "How a 'Christian Country' Has Become the World's Most Religiously Diverse Nation".

The Church has addressed the problem of pluralism for centuries. However, in recent times, the plurality of cultures, identities, values and norms has led to competitive violence unheard of in history; forms of diversity have been conflictual. The dizzying speed of ever increasing diversity and consequent conflict and fragmentation in almost every corner of the earth are staggering. There is no reversal to this process. The fact of plural identities in a globalized world has come to shape much of the writings of current social theory as well as fiction. Words such as "heterogeneity", "diversity", "difference", "pluralism", "hybridity", "melange" and "flux" mark much creative literature. Today, more than ever before, the world cries out for credible signposts to show that human community is still possible in the midst of all that divides us. Behind it all lies a deeper crisis in understanding, and the need to deal with difference, with the other. We have come to understand that it is no longer enough to talk about diversity, without recognizing the challenge of difference; it is not enough to speak about the fact of plurality, without facing the challenges of pluralistic pictures of the world, values and norms. Whatever else the significance of many recent events may be, including those of 11 September 2001, they certainly serve as a window on how we handle difference, respond to the "other" and negotiate plurality at times of crisis.

Three dominant approaches to pluralism in our times

One may identify at least three distinct approaches to pluralism. I will briefly refer to them by name and move on to my main concern in this presentation – to develop a missionary response to a pluralistic world.

In a powerful and perceptive book, *The One and the Many*,[2] the well-known church historian Martin Marty describes two ways in which people negotiate pluralism in our times. He describes two distinctly different approaches: one is totalist and the other tribalist. Both conceive identity in essentialist terms, that is, as fixed and substance-like. Both assume that difference must be absolute. One seeks to annihilate identities that are different from itself through assimilation, dissolving difference into a greater whole; the other, the politics of identity, seeks to annihilate different and plural identities by eliminating or silencing them. Such essentializing attitudes to identity can very often lead to a universalizing of the particular. That leads to the positing of new and more insidious forms of absolutisms.

As an alternative to the totalistic and tribalistic approaches to pluralism stands a third: the liberal way of dealing with difference. Much of North American discourse in multiculturalism betrays such a liberal approach. It acknowledges that cultures and identities are diverse. But simple acceptance of diversity, as in the case of liberal pluralism, does not take seriously the asymmetric power relation between diverse identities. As Homi Bhabha puts it well,

> Although there is always an entertainment and encouragement of cultural diversity, there is always a corresponding containment of it. A transparent norm is constituted, a norm given by the host society... which says that "these cultures are fine, but we must be able to locate them within our own grid". This is what I mean by a *creation* of cultural diversity and *containment of cultural* difference.[3]

It is therefore important to seek an alternative to the dominant liberal attitude to pluralism.

My submission is that it is an aspect of the mission of the Church to point to this fourth and alternative way of dealing with difference in God's plural world. How may we be faithful to God's design of enriching human communities through healthy diversity and cultivating a pasture of permanent openness to the other, and to the plurality of cultures and traditions, however strange and unsettling they might be? That is the central question before us.

Biblical vision of an alternative response to pluralism

Already in the Old Testament we see pointers to such an option. In contrast to both the totalist and tribalist vision of the human, the biblical witness portrays humans as being constituted only in interactive relationships, as an act of grace and as gift of the others. In the Book of Genesis, the story of Babel is immediately followed by the story of the call of Abraham. In Abraham, a people is called, its identity is affirmed, and yet such an identity is inseparable from God's purpose for "all the families of the earth". In the identity of this one people, all peoples will be blessed. Philip Potter points to the fact that even the word "blessed" (in Hebrew *barak*) means to share one's strength, one's being with another, to be with the other.[4] In other words, herein is the identification of God's action as affirmation of the identity and purpose of a particular people and yet as locating it inseparably with the whole of the human community. The identity of an individual or a people is constituted only in relation to and for the sake of others. Tribalist exclusivism and the totalist assimilation are both rejected. In their place an interactive and dialogical relationship is established as the foundation of peoples and nations. The call of Abraham is a call to refuse to let one's identity be absolutized and one's borders closed. It is a call to witness to the divine purpose of constituting identity and difference for the sake of the mutual flourishing of all. An individual or a people, in an Abrahamic alternative, is both an act of divine grace and gift of others.

Since the 1970s, the voices that call the churches to take seriously the heterogeneity and plurality that mark peoples around the world, and the continuing asymmetrical power relations among churches, have grown clearer and louder, particularly from those who have been marginalized. Most of the major conferences of the World Council of Churches and its assemblies have heard them. World mission conferences in San Antonio in 1989 and in Salvador, Bahia, in 1996 are no exception. In 1991, the Canberra assembly of the WCC defined the mission of the Church, stating, "The reconciliation brought about by the cross is the basis of the mission of the Church. A reconciled and renewed creation is the goal of the mission of the Church. The vision of God uniting all things in Christ is the driving force of its life and sharing."[5] The gospel and cultures study process of the WCC provided space for many to express the uniqueness of their identities, plurality and fluidity even within a single cultural process. It stressed the impossibility of any one cultural expression of the Christian story being the norm for everyone else. At the same time, sharing the rich experiences of the gospel across diverse cultures led to the call for the active promotion of cross-contextual dialogue, challenge and mutual enrichment.

What are some of the lessons from the ecumenical learning and mutual sharing and critique for our understanding of mission in a pluralistic world?

Cross-cultural experience has taught us that underlying the dominant ways of dealing with pluralism are three factors. It is these three factors that lead peoples and groups to manage plurality, either by assimilating difference or eliminating it. These are three aspects of an attitude, a habit of thought, if you will, that lie behind the totalist, tribalist as well as the liberal ways of constructing the other that I pointed to above. They are:

– a "centring", an essentializing of one's self, one's nation, market, values, norms, etc. in such a way that they are taken to be the universal and true; the rest are conceived often in oppositional terms;
– an erecting and maintaining of borders to exclude the other; and relationships are primarily external;
– a silencing or even eliminating the voice of the other; a desire for dominating power that turns the other into "serviceable" to oneself or one's group.

I submit that an adequate understanding of the practice of mission and ministry today involves a de-centring of selves, a courageous border crossing and empowering multiple, even contesting, voices within a shared communion. Mission as reconciliation is an embracing of the other in the place of exclusion – a new relationship with God, with each other and with creation that is free of domination and fragmentation in the perspective of the reign of God. It is my belief that the life and witness the Christian communities provide us insights into such a threefold mission that is demanded of us today.

Let me develop each of these three aspects of the mission of the Church briefly.

1. Mission as a critique of a culture of autonomous identities and as a proclamation of catholic personhood in Christ

First, an authentic way of dealing with pluralism calls for a de-centring of individual and collective identities that have been constructed as autonomous and self-sufficient. Look for a moment at the story of the Pentecost. The story is set against the disciples' question whether the kingdom of Israel will be restored and their identity would be affirmed. However, Jesus' response rather highlights that when the Spirit does come upon them, they would disperse. Their collective existence will be de-centred and they will go to the ends of the earth. Their identities from now on are to be defined in terms of their plural locations and the diverse peoples among whom they will go to witness. A centripetal quest is responded to with a promise of centrifugal dispersal. There is no central place, no single language and no single authoritative seat of power, not even Jerusalem. Later on, the disciples come to learn that baptism itself is a sign of the alternative identity of a new and inclusive humanity, which replaces exclusivist ways of defining oneself. In this process there is a decentring of identities, whether they be defined either purely in terms of *polis*, that is, the nation- or city-state to which one belongs, or in terms of blood, that is, one's ethnic and blood relationships.

Further, the Pentecost story is a powerful paradigm of negotiating diversity. It is the day when in and through the operation of the Holy Spirit the quest for integration and uniqueness leads to the affirmation of diversity in communion and harmony. The narrative in Acts 2 takes care to hold the terms "each" and "all" in creative tension. Each hears in his or her native tongue and thus monologic traditions are overturned; vernacularization takes place. All cultures and languages are affirmed and yet none becomes the norm. Pentecost both destigmatizes each culture and relativizes all cultures at one and the same time, and thereby brings about a communion of diversity. All are included and yet each is decentralized. The Spirit does not bring about a homogenized, safe and secure uniformity but a differentiated and costly unity of all people: Jews, Arabs and people from many nations. There is no central place or one sacred language, nor a single seat of power, even Jerusalem. At the end of Acts 2 we are given a powerful description of a community of relational selves, socially formed, and sharing everything they had with each other.

I am increasingly convinced that one of the major missiological tasks today is to offer a radical critique of modern cultures which tend to conceive of human or one's particular group as a bounded and autonomous entity. The oldest desire or goal of Western logic has been to locate a single, stable, permanent and universal centre, which provides the unity and tames and rules over multiplicity. It is the same logic that operated in the colonial conquests, and today continues in the neo-colonial dynamics of globalization. In the process it does violence to that which is different from itself. This has been the case when a religion, a nation or a culture is made into a centre. When Christianity as a religion is envisioned as a centred religion, then, in its missionary enterprise, the alien religious traditions are adjudicated as false and the people of other faiths are turned into objects of the conversion project. Bert Hoedemaker suggests how the modern ecumenical movement as represented by the WCC is a manifestation of such a centripetal process of centring on a homogenous overarching principle of unity.[6] He also points out how other cultures and religious traditions, due to the influence of modernity upon them, have tamed plurality and stifled the popular and the particular by constructing overarching and centralized principles of national cultures and religions. The very notion of Hindutva in India is an ideological centring in order to manage and control other religious traditions in India such as Islam and Christianity.

It is urgent that we examine how in our respective contexts and cultures, through centring on an overarching principle, we ourselves have allowed plurality to be stifled and genuine otherness to be denigrated in the name of unity, sameness and truth.

Part of the reason that the Salvador world mission conference was seen as a problem and a failure by many in the Northern churches is, in my judgment, due to the fact that it did not deliver a single and unified definition of either the gospel or culture. Many could not tolerate the polysymbolic and polycentric nature of the conference. Central to the dynamic of the conference was a celebration of the plurality of cultural identities and the voicing of diverse experiences and stories of encountering Christ by people in diverse contexts. Identities cannot be artificially limited. Neither can the witnesses to the identity-shaping and freeing power of the gospel in diverse cultures. The very attempt to finalize the findings of the conference in centralized section reports ended up quite contrary in spirit and method to a locally based and rich preparatory process, as well as to the way in which diverse stories were shared during the gathering.

I often wonder what missionary practice would look like if we resisted the temptation to ensure the victory of "oneness" over multiplicity, identity over difference, or the pure over the hybrid. Many recent feminist theorists have powerfully established that there is an unmistakable correlation between domination and a kind of disembodied, abstract and transcendent form of knowledge, applicable everywhere and to everyone.[7] As the post-modern thinker J.-F. Lyotard makes clear, the rationality of consensus is only a few steps from the desire for one system, one truth, – in sum, one rationality – to dominate human civilization. In its extreme, the will to one truth has yielded the totalitarian Reign of Terror.[8]

Therefore, it is this mind-set that needs to be decentred if we are serious about healthy ways of dealing with plurality. I submit that this is an urgent missionary task that the Church is called to undertake in the power of the Spirit of the Pentecost.

Many non-Western cultures are collective cultures in which nurturing relationships and loyalty to others are supreme social values. Individuals in these cultures are not egocentric, self-contained or non-porous. As an African proverb puts it, "We participate, therefore I am." Contrast this to the Cartesian dictum: *Cogito ergo sum*, or a possible modern equivalent, "I possess, therefore I am."

Such a decentred approach to the other, in the words of Miraslov Volf, is to "create space in us to receive the other... The Spirit of God breaks through the self-enclosed worlds we inhabit." The Spirit also opens up for us "the road towards becoming... a 'catholic personality'... A catholic personality is a personality enriched by otherness, a personality which is what it is only because multiple others have been reflected in it in a particular way."[9] The Spirit of Christ brings about a catholic cultural identity in the place of either an assimilative globalization or competitive politics of identity.

2. Mission as courageous border crossing

The second aspect of the Church's missionary presence in a plural world has to do with borders that one group, community or race constructs over against others in order to negotiate plurality. More often than not, the construction of plural identities is also often controlled by binary thought forms. Monological or egocentric identities, as we saw above, are constructed oppositionally. The identity of an individual or community is defined by differentiating it from what it is not. Each is seen as sharply atomized, this from that, you from me, God from the world, and so on. This differentiation quickly turns into sharp distinctions, and then distinction turns into opposition and confrontation. Further, in order to preserve one's identity, borders are erected and maintained as non-porous. The logical consequence is that differences can no longer be tolerated.

The Acts of the Apostles portrays Peter similarly bounded by borders of race and religion; his attitude to the Gentile Cornelius is shaped by his sense of pollution of those who were different from him and his community. Yet, as the power of Pentecost operates, Peter is given the strength to cross borders and discover that God has no favourites among God's people. How then can we learn to cross borders that we have hitherto kept as not permeable? No cultural or religious borders are impermeable. Certainly, in these days the coordinates of all our borders are continuously defined and redefined in terms of our interaction with each other. As Richard Bernstein argues convincingly, "There is no horizon which is ontologically closed... There are always the linguistic and imaginative resources within any horizon that can enable us to extend our horizon."[11]

In other words, we can come to understand what initially strikes us as alien and strange if we have the willingness to cross boundaries set by us, and seek to understand the other. Behind our cultural, linguistic and even national borders there is a significant connectedness of our diverse identities and histories in these post-modern times. Many identities are hybrid, hyphenated and in constant flux. They are continuously defined and redefined in terms of our interaction with other identities. The factor behind many a nationalist conflict and ethnic cleansing in our times is the inability of a people to move beyond their own background or cultural boundaries. We need to remind ourselves that it was the ideology of the incommensurability of races and cultural horizons that motivated the demonic destruction initiated by the Third Reich. Hence, rupturing the spatial and temporal boundaries of our histories and crossing borders are an urgent imperative for our communities of faith in a conflictual and plural world.

Such a border crossing is similar to what John S. Dunne refers to as the phenomenon of "passing over and coming back". Describing this new interfaith relationship as "the spiritual adventure of our time", Dunne says,

> Passing over is a shifting of standpoint, a going over to the standpoint of another culture, another way of life, another religion. It is followed by an equal and opposite process we might call "coming back", coming back with new insight to one's own culture, one's own way of life, one's own religion.[12]

Here there is no fusion of borders that would mean our individual or group identities are lost. Nor is it a border diffusion or dissolution. But it is a crossing over and a returning so that the coordinates of one's identities may now be redrawn in a much richer way due to the gift from the other. In a dialogical context across difference, it is important that one does not bypass the elements of "strangeness" or possible contestation. Nor can one subsume difference under an already familiar category to oneself.

Such a border crossing is costly, for it first demands of us a rejection of oppositional thinking and the binary habits of thought to which we are so used. It is risky, for it calls us to be willing to be liminal, and to beat the threshold. All threshold existence is threatening; but it is only when we step across it that we may discover the creatively new.

In Isaiah 19:23-24 the prophet envisions such a border crossing. The vision speaks of an impossible possibility. Three former enemies now cross borders and walk back and forth to each other over a highway built by God. For Israel, this was costly. It had to give up its privileged position and learn to be on a par with Egypt and Assyria. It had to give up its special name as "my [God's] people" with others who have been hitherto called the Gentiles. But the Prophet speaks of the coming together of these different peoples as though it is God's dream and purpose for humanity. The mission of the Church today, I submit, is to build such a highway over which people of diverse cultures, religions and races can cross borders for both integration as well as the enrichment of their particular identities. It will, indeed, demand from the Church a critical examination and renouncing of its theologies that exclude, and of its missionary practices that maintain impermeable boundaries with others.

Let me now turn to a third aspect of mission in a pluralistic world.

3. Mission towards multi-voiced and polyphonic communities across difference

If we look back at the story of the early Church after the Pentecost experience, it appears that the Spirit did not leave the believers with border crossings alone. Certainly, such crossings brought out newer dimensions of integration or wholeness, and helped redraw the coordinates of ecclesial identities. However, the Spirit demanded more. The Spirit led the disciples to the formation of a community where differences could be articulated and contestation was possible. Particularly, those whose voices were not heard were empowered to speak. The concerns of the marginalized, for example, the Greek widows, became a factor in the structural alteration of the community and its ministries. The stories of those who had been silenced until then could now be heard. The experience of the "Gentiles" became a decisive factor in determining the future of theology and mission.

The first council in Jerusalem is a case in point. This story of Pentecost is set in a conflictual context. The powerful "Judaizers" have their say. Yet, at the centre of the story is the place given to the stories of those who are outside the Jewish community, that is, the Gentiles. Truth is shared not in propositional terms; it is rather shared as stories. James Cone points to the power of story-telling in empowerment and community building. He says,

> Indeed, when I understand truth as story, I am more likely to be open to other people's truth stories. As I listen to other stories, I am invited to move out of the subjectivity of my own story into another realm of thinking and acting. The same is true for others when I tell my story... Indeed it is only when we refuse

to listen to another story that our own story becomes ideological, that is a closed system, incapable of hearing the truth.[13]

Cone's warning that community itself is at stake and domination of one group by another is the result when we are closed in within our own stories and turn them into the only valid truth needs to be heeded. He says,

> When people can no longer listen to other people's stories, they become enclosed within their own social context, treating their distorted visions of reality as the whole truth. And then they feel that they must destroy other stories, which bear witness that life can be lived in another way.[14]

Thus the Pentecost paradigm places before us an authentic way of dealing with difference and negotiating plurality; it is by ensuring the intentional creation of a community, a space, in which the "other" who has been silenced for a long time can now be heard on his or her own terms. It is a space where monologue is given room to dialogue and tri-alogue for the co-construction of the self and others within a shared communion. It is a space that safeguards differences and yet builds up common sharing. This implies that we have many different voices in and through which we speak. We think and hear others and in and through this we relate to the world. As Mikhail Bakhtin, the Russian thinker, puts it, "We are 'the voices that inhabit us'."[15] Every relationship is mutual and multi-voiced, genuinely promoting verbal or cultural exchange, so that all those involved in the relationship are changed or enriched. Our many voices of heteroglossia offer us a richness of thinking, knowing and experiencing ourselves and everything that is around us. It is through the multi-voicedness that we are constituted as social selves. The absence of multi-voicedness leads a community to dominant modes of discourse; its definitions of truth will remain static and exclusive.

I use the term "multi-voiced" and not more familiar terms such as "multicultural" or "multi-vocal" . This is primarily to indicate that the space and the community we are envisioning here do not simply include the presence of more or less representatives of diverse groups. Rather, the space and community foster a setting where a plurality of voices is heard, and in which their diversities and contestation are expressed, and their participation matters in making decisions. Voicing implies exercising power. Therefore, in a multi-voiced community, power sharing is critical. Such a community is possible only when we are willing to give up our dominant roles and inherited structures of power and privilege. Much will be demanded of those who commit themselves for such dialogical and multi-voiced spaces in the midst of a predominantly monological world.

Mission towards a multi-voiced community, witnessing to truth as stories, will necessarily involve a radical vulnerability demonstrated by Jesus. It calls for a genuine "incarnate presence" before the other, and within the cultures and religious heritage of the people around us. Witness from within is the only proper mode of evangelism worthy of a God who does not control history from without, but rather enters into our history, suffers with it and transforms it by participating in it, fully and really. As the well-known Asian theologian, C.S. Song, puts it,

> Christian mission in essence should be a love affair of the Church with other human beings with whom God has already fallen in love... It is Christian believers building with them a community in the power of God's love. If this is what Christian mission is, then Christian mission is God's mission.[16]

The practice of mission often tends to forget this central affirmation. Mission, in essence, is an expression of God's pain, and God's love, demonstrated in Jesus Christ to all those human beings with whom God is already in love. Mission in the mode of vulnerable love is necessarily dialogical. It is a genuine listening and responding to stories of God's love as told by others, however strange these stories may sound.

One thing is certain: only when the pain-love of the crucified Christ is in us, shall we be authentic witnesses to the power of the risen Christ, which is the power of pain-love that gives life to all and voice to the voiceless. It is through the solidarity of love to the end that reconciliation of God in Jesus Christ, and the drawing of all of creation into God's embrace, is accomplished in all its plurality, thus witnessing to the multicoloured wisdom and glory of the triune God.

NOTES

[1] Diana Eck, *The New Religious America*, New York, HarperCollins, 2001.
[2] Martin Marty, *The One and the Many: America's Struggle for the Common Good*, Cambridge MA, Harvard UP, 1997.
[3] Homi Bhabha, "The Third Space", in Jonathan Rutherford ed., *Identity: Community, Culture, Difference*, London, Lawrence & Wishart, 1990, p.208.
[4] Philip Potter, *Cultures in Dialogue*, WCC, 1985, p.71.
[5] Michael Kinnamon ed., *Signs of the Spirit: Official Report of the Seventh Assembly of the WCC*, WCC, 1991, p.100.
[6] Bert Hoedemaker, "Religion beyond Modernity: A Missiological Perspective", in Philip L. Wickeri, J. K. Wickeri and Damayanthi M.A. Niles eds., *Plurality, Power and Mission*, London, Council for World Mission, 2000, pp.172f.
[7] For example, see L. Code, *What Can She Know? Feminist Theory and Construction of Knowledge*, Ithaca NY, Cornell UP, 1991; Patricia Collins, *Black Feminist Thought*, revised ed., London, Routledge, 2000; Linda Alcoff and Elizabeth Potter eds, *Feminist Epistemologies*, London, Routledge, 1993; and C.A. McKinnon, *Toward a Feminist Theory of the State*, Cambridge MA, Harvard UP, 1989.

[8] Ofelia Schutte, "Cultural Alterity: Cross-cultural Communication and Feminist Theory in North-South Contexts", in Uma Narayan and Sandra Harding eds, *Decentering the Center: Philosophy for a Multicultural, Postcolonial and Feminist World,* Bloomington IN, Indiana UP, 2000, p. 50.

[9] Miraslov Volf, *Exclusion and Embrace*, Nashville TN, Abingdon, 1996, p.51.

[10] Richard Bernstein, "The Hermeneutics of Cross-Cultural Understanding", in Anindita N. Balslev ed., *Cross-Cultural Conversation*, Atlanta, Scholars, 1996, p.35.

[11] John S. Dunne, *The Way of All the Earth: Experiments in Truth and Religion*, New York, Macmillan, 1972, p.ix.

[12] James Cone, *God of the Oppressed*, New York, Seabury, 1975, pp.102-104.

[13] *Ibid.*, p.103.

[14] Gary S. Morson and Caryl Emerson, *Mikhail Bakhtin: Creation of a Prosaics*, Stanford CA, Stanford UP, 1990, p.213.

[15] C.S. Song, *Tell Us Our Names*, Maryknoll NY, Orbis, 1984, p.108.

A Listeners' Report

VALERIE KARRAS, DEENABANDHU MANCHALA
AND ANTON C. VRAME

1. Introduction

1.1 Hierarchs, clergy, scholars and theologians, students and interested members of the community convened at Holy Cross Greek Orthodox School of Theology in Brookline, Massachusetts, 3-5 October 2002, to discuss the topic "The Orthodox Churches in a Pluralistic World". The conference was subtitled "An Ecumenical Conversation" and the speakers represented the diversity of Christian traditions. The conference was co-sponsored by the World Council of Churches and was held in cooperation with the Boston Theological Institute and the Initiatives in Religion and Public Life of Harvard Divinity School. The conversation was enriching and edifying. We thank Holy Cross and the conference sponsors for the opportunity to engage in a conversation on these issues in an atmosphere of mutual respect.

1.2 The issue was placed before the conference plainly: Dr Konrad Raiser stated "all religions have to come to terms with the reality of religious plurality". In his keynote address, His Eminence Archbishop Demetrios of America defined the challenge posed to Orthodoxy in positive terms: "The pluralistic world is not an obstacle to Orthodoxy; it is rather an opportunity. In a pluralistic global society, the Orthodox Church is challenged to match her incarnational Christology with an equally incarnational ecclesiology." His Eminence proposed the pledge of St Paul to the first-century Corinthian church as a paradigm for meeting the contemporary challenges of globalization and pluralism: "I have become all things to all people, that I might by all means save some" (1 Cor. 9:22). The challenge of pluralism is to come to terms with the challenge of relatedness between and among communities and people of different religions and cultural traditions.

1.3 The participants offered analyses and insights into the issues of globalization and pluralism, including such areas as human rights and violence, the rise of nationalism and ethnic conflict, social activism and mission, and the need for reconciliation and forgiveness.

2. Globalization and pluralism

2.1 Globalization is the transcendence of territorial boundaries and the compression of time and space through the rise of information technologies, transnational financial corporations, networks and markets, international movements seeking universal human rights and a sustainable environment, and the emergence of non-territorial, flexible organizations and networks. This reality has challenged the assumptions of modernity about privatized religion and secular public space.

2.2 Religious communities have entered the public sphere with both positive and negative messages in response to this globalization. The events of 11 September 2001 are a dramatic example of a negative response. On the other hand, religion has unexpectedly emerged as the only significant moral force against an unchecked global economism since the fall of communism. The Church has to discern how to be a public actor, agent of change and conscience-keeper without becoming a political actor.

2.3 Pluralism is the reality in which all religions now find themselves. No religious community can assume a religiously homogeneous society, but must learn to function in a "religious market-place". As Diana Eck pointed out, pluralism "is not just another word for diversity" or a "mere tolerance" of the other, but an "engagement, not the abdication, of differences and particularities". In fact, within Orthodox parishes in America, there is a parish pluralism, with communities comprised of members from many ethnic backgrounds and – through inter-Christian marriage – various Christian traditions.

2.4 According to Emmanuel Clapsis, "Particular, local cultures and communities are challenged by the new globalizing cultural realities to redefine their identities in light of the presence of... multiple others... All particular cultures and identities in a globalized [and pluralistic] world are involved in a highly complex and dialectical process of reconfiguring themselves in conversation with... multiple others, as ideas and cultural forms invade their living space."

Theologically, the Orthodox churches have been relatively silent on these realities. At times, many Orthodox churches have exhibited ambivalent behaviour in response to their new pluralistic environment, due to their socio-political history. However, as Elizabeth Prodromou has articulated, the possibilities of constructive engagement over static ambivalence is dependent upon "the willingness of Orthodox churches to remain faithful to the trinitarian concept of pluralism at the centre of the Orthodox theological imagination". The translation of the holy scriptures into multiple languages and the diversity of liturgical expressions are examples of the Church's concern for "the particular and specific cultural elements of local" communities, meeting the needs of socio-cultural and ethnic pluralism (Archbishop Demetrios).

3. Human rights and violence

3.1 The concept of human rights is a modern Enlightenment concept rooted in Western cultural and religious traditions of the Middle Ages. The ancient Greek concept of the city *(polis)* affirmed a contrary concept of what we today call "human rights". The Orthodox concept of person-hood transformed the ancient Greek political event into the eucharistic body of the Christian Church.

3.2 The Ecumenical Decade to Overcome Violence has caused us to reflect on the links between religion and violence. In the Judaeo-Christian tradition, violence is notably absent in the creation story, yet present in the journey of the Hebrew people. Orthodoxy provides a nonviolent alternative to Western Christianity's atonement theology based on Christ as sacrificial scapegoat by an incarnational soteriology in which Christ shares our mortal human nature, restoring it through his death on the cross and his resurrection. Violence is clearly a part of our sinful, fallen condition. While disagreements may exist as to whether it is permissible, much less necessary, to limit violence through violent means, such means can never be viewed as a "good". There is no just-war theology in the Orthodox tradition.

3.3 While love of one's homeland is a positive value, nationalism or ethnophyletism is destructive when it rejects pluralism, that is, "when it fails to acknowledge, or deliberately ignores the distinctiveness of others" (Tsetsis). Phyletism may be characterized as the idolization of national loyalty, which is not authentic to Orthodox tradition, but rather reflects the manipulation of the Church by the state. While the Orthodox churches condemned phyletism in 1872, "nationalism remains one of the central problems of the Church", in the words of Ecumenical Patriarch Bartholomew. Ethnic violence and ethnic cleansing caused by excessive nationalism must be condemned by all people of faith. Violence against one nation in order to "save" another nation sets us against Christ by applying the same logic used to crucify Christ. The Church's rejection of ethnophyletism, as Metropolitan John of Korce noted, is based on Ortho-dox theological anthropology, which sees the image of God in all persons, and on an incarnational soteriology, which proclaims that Christ died for all.

4. Reconciliation

4.1 Globalization and pluralism make forgiveness and reconciliation not a private affair but a public statement of far-reaching political importance. If forgiveness is real and the possibilities of reconciliation manifold, how do people and communities of faith model this reality in a civil society?

4.2 Orthodox theology requires an eschatological orientation. The Church is not to be identified as the kingdom of God, but prepares the way for the kingdom, which will culminate in the *eschaton* (Vassiliadis). "An eschatological vision of reality and the world offers a way out of the impasse" of the negative impact of globalization and pluralism (Chryssavgis). It offers a prophetic critique of our present status and offers a vision of God's intent for humanity and the cosmos. Our unrealized eschatology must be matched by a realized eschatology, with implications for our presence and conduct in the public arena. The dynamism of the *ecclesia* depends on its ability to hold together its present "being" and its "vocation" in a creative tension.

4.3 Thus, theology does not absolve the Orthodox churches from working as an agent of reconciliation and forgiveness. *Orthodoxia* requires *orthopraxia*. We pray, "Your kingdom come. Your will be done." The Standing Conference of Canonical Orthodox Bishops affirmed (20 September 2002), "As we pray, so we believe. As we pray, so we act." Evidence of Orthodox churches and Orthodox Christians acting as they pray and believe is growing on a global scale in the area of missions and evangelism, service to the poor and to victims of violence, and work to challenge structures of injustice and oppression. Nevertheless, we must strengthen our prophetic voice and our ecclesial response in solidarity with the oppressed, victims and the economically disadvantaged as a necessary consequence of our recognition of all persons bearing the image of God.

Contributors List

Rev. Dr **John Chryssavgis** has taught theology in Australia as well as the United States and is well-known for his numerous publications on the history and spirituality of the early monastic tradition.

Rev. Fr **Emmanuel Clapsis** is dean of the Holy Cross Greek Orthodox School of Theology, Brookline MA, USA.

Archbishop **Demetrios** is Primate of the Greek Orthodox Archdiocese of America.

Rev. Dr **Christopher Duraisingh** is Otis Charles professor of applied theology at Episcopal Divinity School, Cambridge MA, USA.

Prof. **Diana C. Eck** is professor of comparative religion and Indian Studies at Harvard University, Cambridge MA, USA.

Prof. **Richard Falk** is visiting distinguished professor at Princeton University, Princeton NJ, USA.

Dr **Thomas FitzGerald** is professor of church history and historical theology at Holy Cross Greek Orthodox School of Theology, Brookline MA, USA. He is also the executive secretary of the Ecumenical Commission of the Standing Conference of Canonical Orthodox Bishops in America.

Dr **Stanley Samuel Harakas** taught Orthodox Christian ethics at Holy Cross Greek Orthodox School of Theology, Brookline MA, USA, for thirty years. He is Archbishop Iakovos professor of Orthodox theology, emeritus, having retired in 1995.

Metropolitan **John** is the hierarch of the Metropolis of Korça, Albania.

Dr **Valerie A. Karras**, a specialist in Greek patristics and Byzantine church history, is currently a researcher at the Thesaurus Linguae Graecae at the University of California-Irvine, USA.

Prof. **Paschalis M. Kitromilides** is professor of political science at the University of Athens, Greece, and director of the Institute for Neohellenic Research, National Hellenic Research Foundation.

Rev. **Kwame Joseph Labi** is programme executive in the WCC team on Urban and Rural Mission.

Prof. **David Little** is T.J. Dermot Dunphy professor of the practice in religion, ethnicity, and international conflict at Harvard Divinity School, Harvard MA, USA, and director of Initiatives in Religion and Public Life, also at Harvard. He is an associate at the Weatherhead Center for International Affairs of the same University.

Rev. Dr **Deenabandhu Manchala** is programme executive in the WCC team on Faith and Order.

Dr **Rodney L. Petersen** is executive director of the Boston Theological Institute, Newton Center, MA, USA, a consortium of Orthodox, Roman Catholic and Protestant seminaries, schools of theology, and university divinity schools.

Dr **Elizabeth H. Prodromou** is associate director of the Center for the Study of Culture and Religion in World Affairs at Boston University, MA, where she is also assistant professor in the department of international relations.

Rev. Dr **Konrad Raiser** was general secretary of the World Council of Churches from 1993 to 2003.

Fr **Nicholas C. Triantafilou** is president of Hellenic College and Holy Cross Greek Orthodox School of Theology, Brookline MA, USA.

Dr **Georges Tsetsis**, Grand Protopresbyter of the Ecumenical Patriarchate, was permanent representative of his church to the World Council of Churches from 1985 to 1999.

Dr **Petros Vassiliadis** is professor of New Testament at the theological faculty of the University of Salonika, Greece.

Dr **Anton C. Vrame** is director of the Patriarch Athenagoras Orthodox Institute at the Graduate Theological Union, Berkeley CA, USA.

Prof. **Christos Yannaras** is professor of philosophy at Pantion University, Athens, Greece.